The Lake of Knives and the Lake of Fire

Studies in the topography of passage in ancient Egyptian religious literature

Eltayeb Sayed Abbas

BAR International Series 2144
2010

Published in 2016 by
BAR Publishing, Oxford

BAR International Series 2144

The Lake of Knives and the Lake of Fire

ISBN 978 1 4073 0685 8

BAR Publishing is the trading name of British Archaeological Reports (Oxford) Ltd. British Archaeological Reports was first incorporated in 1974 to publish the BAR Series, International and British. In 1992 Hadrian Books Ltd became part of the BAR group. This volume was originally published by Archaeopress in conjunction with British Archaeological Reports (Oxford) Ltd / Hadrian Books Ltd, the Series principal publisher, in 2010. This present volume is published by BAR Publishing, 2016.

Printed in England

BAR
PUBLISHING

BAR titles are available from:

BAR Publishing
122 Banbury Rd, Oxford, OX2 7BP, UK
EMAIL info@barpublishing.com
PHONE +44 (0)1865 310431
FAX +44 (0)1865 316916
www.barpublishing.com

Abstract

This research is an investigation into the safe passage of the deceased over water as exemplified in the Lake of Knives and the Lake of Fire. The journey of the deceased from death to resurrection is envisaged as taking place in a boat crossing dangerous places and ordeals. This journey was parallel to the sun god Re's passage over the waters of the sky, and in which he is threatened by the powers of chaos. The rites of passage focus on the safe passage of Re through chaos, and assert resurrection, rebirth and life after death for the deceased. The passage is re-enacted in mythical images and in ritual actions, and focuses on the safe journey of the deceased through the ordeals of the Netherworld.

This research is divided into seven chapters. Chapter One deals with the symbolism of water, knives and fire. Water is dealt with as the discharge which comes from the body of Osiris and offered to him in ritual. The second section deals with the symbolism of knives and fire. It is concluded that water mediates the passage of the deceased when it is offered to him in ritual. Water can also cause violent death. Fire and knives are used as destructive tools in rituals.

Chapter Two explores the cartographical descriptions and cosmographical locations of the two lakes, using textual and pictorial evidence. It is concluded that the lake of Knives is envisaged as extending from the east to the west of the sky. The description of the Lake of Fire varies from one context to another. The two lakes have no specific locations, but they wind through the sky.

Chapter Three is a discussion on the theme of passage over water in Ancient Egypt. The ferryman spells and the Island of Fire are taken as two examples for the passage of the deceased over water. It is concluded that the ritual aspects of the ferryman spells and the Island of Fire are not very different from the ritual aspects of the Lake of Knives and the Lake of Fire.

Chapter Four is an extension of the discussion of the theme of passage over water, and deals with crossing the lake as a ritual enacted for the deceased at the day of funeral. It is tentatively concluded that the aim of the deceased's crossing over the lake is to mediate his passage to become an *ꜣḫ*. The crossing was accompanied by recitation of ritual texts. Crossing over the Lake of Knives and the Lake of Fire was also accompanied by recitations of ritual texts.

Chapter Five deals with the Lake of Fire in the Book of the Two Ways. The journey of the deceased is constructed until he reaches the Lake of Fire. It is concluded that the Lake of Fire is a place, which the deceased visits to be reborn in the morning and starts a new journey towards the abode of Osiris on the upper waterway.

Chapter Six investigates the rites of passage concerning the crossing over the two lakes. It deals also with the handling of symbols within the rituals performed for the deceased. It is concluded that the Lake of Knives and the Lake of Fire are two metaphorical places that do not exist in rituals. They do not have fixed physical locations, but they exist in myth. Crossing over the two lakes is dangerous, but is also necessary for the deceased to continue his journey and to enter into a different status, status of being an *ꜣḫ*.

Chapter Seven draws answers for the questions of the aim of the deceased's crossing over the two lakes. It is concluded that the aim of the deceased's journey over the two lakes differs from one context to another. It is also explicit that there is no single specific explanation for the rites of passage over the two lakes, and they draw on different metaphors.

Acknowledgements

I would like to express my deepest thanks to Professor Christopher Eyre, for his valuable advice, encouragement, patience, and his continuous supervision at every stage of this research.

I am grateful to Professor Kenneth Kitchen, Dr. Roland Enmarch and Dr. Glenn Godenho for their valuable comments and insightful advice. I also would like to thank my friends and colleagues in School of Archaeology, Classics and Egyptology at the University of Liverpool for their continuous help and encouragement.

I also would like to thank Mr. Tony Taylor, Mrs. Sue Highfield, Mr. Bill and Mrs. Penny Smith for their support during my stay in England.

My eternal thanks go to my parents, my wife, my daughter Hana and my son Omar, who have been supportive over the last years. Without their aid this work would have been impossible. I dedicate this study to them.

List of Abbreviations

ÄA	Ägyptologische Abhandlungen, Wiesbaden
ÄAT	Ägypten und Altes Testament, Wiesbaden
ACE	Australian Centre for Egyptology, Sydney/Warminster/ Oxford
ADAIK	Abhandlungen des Deutschen Archäologischen Instituts Kairo, Glückstadt/Hamburg/ New York
AEL	Lichtheim, M., *Ancient Egyptian Literature*, 3 vols, Berkeley and Los Angeles, 1973-1980.
ÄF	Ägyptologische Forschungen, Glückstadt/Hamburg/ New York
ÄS	Ägyptische Sammlung
ASAÉ	*Annales du Service des Antiquités de l'Égypte*, Cairo
ASAW	Abhandlungen der Sächsischen Akademie der Wissenschaften zu Lepizig, Berlin
ASE	Archaeological Survey of Egypt, London
AV	Archäologische Veröffentlichungen, Deutsches Archäologisches Instituts, Abteilung Kairo, Mainz am Rhein
BAe	Bibliotheca Aegyptiaca, Brussels
BAR	British Archaeological Reports International Series, Oxford
BD	Book of the Dead
BdÉ	Bibliothèque d'Étude, Institut Français d'Archéologie Orientale, Cairo
BIFAO	*Bulletin de l'Institut Français d'Archéologie Orientale*, Cairo
BiOr	*Bibliotheca Orientalis*, Leiden
CdÉ	*Chronique d'Égypte*, Brussels
CDME	Faulkner, R. O., *A Concise Dictionary of Middle Egyptian*, Oxford, 1962.
Ch.	Chapter
CNI	Carsten Niebuhr Institute of Near Eastern Studies Publications, Copenhagen
Col(s)	Column(s)
CT	Coffin Text
CT	De Buck, A., *The Ancient Egyptian Coffin Texts*, 7 vols, Chicago, 1935-1961.
DAIK	Deutsches Archäologisches Instituts, Abteilung Kairo, Mainz
DAWW	Denkschrift der kaiserlichen Akademie der Wissenscahften in Wien (from 1950), later DÖAW
DE	*Discussions in Egyptology*, Oxford
DESN	Discussions in Egyptology Special Number, Oxford
DÖAW	Denkschrifte der österreichischen Akademie der Wissenschaften, Vienna
EES	The Egyptian Exploration Society, London
Essays te Velde	Van Dijk, J. (ed.), *Essays on Ancient Egypt in Honour of Hermann te Velde,* Groningen, 1997.
Essays van Voss	J. H. Kamstra, H. Milde, and K. Wagtendonk (eds), *Funerary Symbols and Religion: Essays dedicated to Professor M.S.H.G. Heerma van Voss on the Occasion of his Retirement from the Chair of the History of Ancient Religions at the University of Amsterdam*, Kampen, 1988.
EU	Egyptologische Uitgaven, Leiden

Fig(s).	Figure(s)
Fs Assmann	Meyer, S. (ed.), *Egypt-Temple of the Whole World: Studies in Honour of Jan Assmann*, Leiden, 2003.
Fs Derchain	U. Verhoeven and E. Graefe (eds), *Religion und Philosophie im alten Ägypten. Festgabe für Philippe Derchain zu seinem 65. Geburtstag am 24. Juli 1991*, OLA 39, Leuven, 1991.
Fs Hornung	Brodbeck, A. (ed.), *Ein ägyptisches Glasperlenspiel, Ägyptologische Beiträge für Erik Hornung aus seinem Schülerkreis,* Berlin, 1998.
Fs Shore	C. J. Eyre, A. Leahy and L. Leahy (eds), *The Unbroken Reed: Studies in the Culture and Heritage of Ancient Egypt in Honour of A.F. Shore,* EES Occasional Publications 11, London, 1994.
Fs Stadelmann	H. Guksch and D. Polz (eds), *Stationen. Beiträge zur Kulturgeschichte Ägyptens: Rainer Stadelmann gewidmet*, Mainz am Rhein, 1998.
GM	Göttinger Miszellen: Beiträge zur ägyptologischen Diskussion, Göttingen
GOF	Göttinger Orientforschungen, Göttingen
Göttinger Totenbuch-studien	Westendorf, W. (ed.), *Göttinger Totenbuchstudien: Beiträge zum 17. Kapitel*, GOF IV/ 3, 1975.
HÄB	Hildesheimer Ägyptologische Beiträge, Hildesheim
Hommages Fayza Haikal	N. Grimal, A. Kamel and C. May-Sheikholeslami (eds), *Hommages à Fayza Haikal,* BdÉ 138, Cairo, 2003.
Hommages Lecalnt	C. Berger, G. Clere and N. Grimal (eds), *Hommages à Jean Leclant*, 4 vols, BdÉ 106, Cairo, 1994.
JARCE	*Journal of the American Research Center in Egypt*, New York
JAOS	*Journal of the American Oriental Society*, Baltimore/ Boston/ New Haven
JEA	*Journal of Egyptian Archaeology*, London
JEOL	*Jaarbericht van het Vooraziatisch Genootschap (Gezelschap) „Ex Orient Lux"*, Leiden
JESHO	*Journal of the Economic and Social History of the Orient*, Leiden
JNES	*Journal of Near Eastern Studies*, Chicago
JSSEA	*Journal of the Society for the Study of Egyptian Antiquities*, Toronto
KRI	Kitchen, K. A., *Ramesside Inscriptions. Historical and Biographical*, 8 vols, Oxford, 1960-1990.
LÄ	W. Helck, E. Otto and W. Westendorf (eds), *Lexikon der Ägyptologie*, 7 vols, Wiesbaden, 1972-1992.
LD	Lepsius, R., *Denkmäler aus Ägypten und Äethiopien*. Abteilung 1-6 in 12 Bands, Berlin, 1849-1859.
L'acqua nell'antico Egitto	A. Amenta, M. M. Luiselli and M. N. Sordi (eds), *L'acqua nell'antico Egitto, Vita, rigenerazione, incatesimo, medicamento*, Rome, 2005.
LingAeg	*Lingua Aegyptia: Journal of Egyptian Language Studies*, Göttingen
MÄS	Müncher Ägyptologische Studien, Berlin/Munich/Mainz am Rhein
MÄSB	Mitteilungen aus der Ägyptischen Sammlung, Staatliche Museen Zu Berlin, Berlin
MDAIK	*Mitteilungen des Deutschen Archäologischen Instituts, Abteilung Kairo*, Mainz
MIFAO	Mémoires publiés par les Membres de l'Institut Français d'Archéologie Orientale du Caire, Cairo
Mysterious Lands	D. O'Connor, and S. Quirke (eds), *Mysterious Lands: Encounters with Ancient Egypt*, London, 2003.
NAWG	Nachrichten der Akademie der Wissenschaften zu Göttingen, Göttingen
n.d.	No Date
NISABA	Religious Texts Translation Series, NISABA, Leiden

OBO	Orbis Biblicus et Orientalis, Freiburg/Göttingen
OLA	Orienatalia Lovaniensia Analecta, Leuven
OMRO	Oudheidkundige Mededeelingen uit het Rijksmuseum van Oudheden te Leiden, Leiden
P	Papyrus
PdÄ	Probleme der Ägyptologie, Leiden
Pl(s)	Plate(s)
PM	B. Porter, and R. Moss (eds), *A Topographical Bibliography of Ancient Egyptian Hieroglyphic Texts, Reliefs, and Paintings*, Oxford, 1960-1981.
PMMA	Publications of the Metropolitan Museum of Art, Egyptian Expedition, New York
PT	Pyramid Text
Pyr	Sethe, K., *Die altägyptischen Pyramidentexte*, 3 vols, Lepizig, 1908-1922; reprint, Hildesheim 1960.
RÄRG	Bonnet, H., *Reallexikon der ägyptischen Religionsgeschichte*, Berlin, 1999.
RdÉ	*Revue d'Égyptologie*, Paris
Rec Trav	*Recueil de Travaux relatifs à la philology et à l'archéologie égyptiennes et assyyriennes*, Paris, 1870-1923.
SAGA	Studien zur Archäologie und Geschichte Altägyptens, Heidelberg
SAK	*Studien zur altägyptischen Kultur*, Hamburg
SAOC	Studies in Ancient Oriental Civilisation, Chicago
SAT	Studien zum Altägyptischen Totenbuch, Wiesbaden
STG	Assmann, J., *Sonnenhymnen in thebanischen Gräbern*, Theben 1, Mainz am Rhein, 1983.
Studies Lichtheim	Israelit-Groll, S. (ed.), *Studies in Egyptology presented to Miriam Lichtheim*, 2 vols, Jerusalem, 1990.
Studies Quaegebeur	W. Clarysse, A. Shoors and H. Willems (eds), *Egyptian Religion: The Last Thousand Years, Studies dedicated to the Memory of Quaegebeur*, 2 vols, OLA 84 and 85, Leuven, 1998.
Studies Redford	G. N. Knoppers and A. Hirsch (eds), *Egypt, Israel, and the Ancient Mediterranean World: Studies in Honor of Donald B. Redford*, Ledien and Boston, 2004.
Studies Stricker	DuQuesne, T. (ed.), *Hermes Aegyptiacus: Egyptological studies for BH Stricker on his 85th birthday*, DESN 2, Oxford, 1995.
Studies Wente	M. Teeter, and J. A. Larson (eds), *Gold of Praise: Studies on Ancient Egypt in Honour of Edward F. Wente*, SAOC 58, Chicago, 1999.
TbT	Totenbuchtexte, Basel
Theben	Theben, Mainz
Totenbuch-Forschungen	B. Backes, M. Munro and S. Stöhr (eds), *Totenbuch-Forschungen: Gesammelte Beiträge des 2. Internationalen Totenbuch-Symposiums 2005*, SAT 11, Wiesbaden, 2006.
TT	Theban Tomb
TTS	Theban Tomb Series, London
Urk I	Sethe, K., *Urkunden des Alten Reichs*, Leipzig, 1903.
Urk IV	Sethe, K., *Urkunden des Neuen Reichs, historische-biographische Urkunden*, Heft 1-16, Leipzig, 1906-1909, continued by Helck, W., Heft 17-22, Berlin, 1955-1958.

VA	*Varia Aegyptiaca*, San Antonio
Valley of the Sun Kings	Wilkinson, R. (ed.), *Valley of the Sun Kings. New Explorations in the Tombs of the Pharaohs*, Arizona, 1995.
WAW	Writings from the Ancient World, Society of Biblical Literature, Atlanta
Wb	A. Erman and H. Grapow (eds), *Wörterbuch der ägyptischen Sprache*, 7 vols and 5 Belegstellen, Leipzig and Berlin, 1926-1963.
YES	Yale Egyptological Studies, New Haven
ZÄS	*Zeitschrift für ägyptische Sprache und Altertumskunde*, Berlin

Table of Contents

Introduction

The River Nile was not only the centerpiece of the ancient Egyptian life, but also of their religious imagery, practices, and beliefs in the Afterlife. As an image of the river, and the cosmic water it came from, the Sacred Lakes of temples served as a focal point for religious rituals and cult activities for the gods. Dug deep into the ground, Sacred Lakes symbolise the primeval ocean Nun, and draw on the sub-soil water rather than the Nile flood.[1] On these lakes, boats sail on the water surface during religious rituals, carrying images of the gods in annual festivals, and in the Osirian secret rituals and drama. These festivals were accompanied by the performance of different rituals and recitations of religious texts, the aim of which is to mediate the passage of the gods over water.

The god's journey over the Sacred Lake was parallel to the journey of the sun god Re over the celestial waters of the sky. Thus, Re crosses the sky in his day barque (*mꜥnḏt*), and crosses the night sky in his night barque (*msktt*), equipped with recitation of religious texts. In his journey to resuscitate the body of Osiris in the hereafter, the deceased faces ordeals. He makes a journey in a boat and sails over the paths and caverns of the netherworld, meeting demons and guardians equipped with fire and knives ready to catch the unprepared. This journey includes crossing over different lakes.

Examples of these lakes are the *ḫns* Lake (*ḫns š*) and the Lakes of Destroyer (*šw ḥtmj*), which occur in CT spell 164.[2] The deceased crosses over these lakes in order to reach the place where he can cure the body of Osiris. The Lake of the Jackal (*š s3bj*) and the Lake of the Netherworld (*š dw3tj*) are also two places in the hereafter where the deceased purifies himself, as occurs in PT spell 512 and CT spell 35.[3] The deceased visits these lakes to be purified like the blessed ones. The Lakes of the Netherworld occur also in PT spell 557 with the Lakes of the Goose, and they are connected with the purification of the king and his ascent to the sky.[4] In CT spell 255 Isis nurses (*3ṯ*) the deceased in the Lake of the Jackal.[5]

As places of passage, the Lake of Meaat (*š Mꜥ3t*) and the Lake of Natron (*š ḥsmn*) occur in Book of the Dead Chapter 17. The vignettes of this chapter, as for instance on the walls of the private Theban Tomb 265 in Deir el-Medina, show the god *W3ḏ-wr* placing his two hands on two basins designating the Lake of *Mꜥ3t* and the Lake of Natron. The texts describe the two lakes as ponds where the deceased purifies himself, and locate them in Herakleopolis.[6]

The Lake of the Sky occurs in CT spell 175, which is a spell for ascending to the sky (*r3 r prt r pt*) and Horus is said to preside over it. In this spell the deceased says that he is the one whom Heket created, and he is the one who gathered the bones of Osiris. He will go up to the sky to reach the pools of the Field of Offerings of Re and he will have his meal there.[7]

In the Book of the Two Ways the Lake of Criminals (*š ḫbntjw*) is a place of passage, and the deceased wishes not to fall a victim to its guardian, who cuts and kills those who sail over it. It occurs in CT spell 1099, and it is a place where the deceased is frightened that his head can be chopped off on the slaughter block of Whose-Face-is-Behind, the Sharp One.[8] The Lake of Criminals shares with the Lake of Fire the aspects of being a place of torture for the sinners. It is also a place where the deceased is pictured as a bull and is taken to the slaughter block to be sacrificed.[9] It is a dangerous place of passage, but also a place that every deceased should sail over in his way to the netherworld.[10]

The Lake of Knives and the Lake of Fire are two places of passage over which every deceased should sail to reach Osiris and to participate in the treatment of his body. The journey of the deceased was parallel to journey of the sun god Re across the sky. As the sun god Re faces the primeval enemy Apep in his journey over the waters of the sky, the deceased who is in a state like Re faces the same ordeals in his passage over the two lakes in the hereafter. The Book of Overthrowing Apep[11] is read to mediate the passage of Re over the Sandbank of Apep, and the deceased manages to cross over the Lake of Knives and the Lake of Fire with the aid of rituals which mediates his passage over them.

The Lake of Knives and the Lake of Fire were briefly investigated in 1966 by Altenmüller.[12] He argued that the Lake of Knives *mr/š nḫ3(wj)* is a variant and another mythological equivalent of the Lake of Fire, where the fire ideogram replaced the knife in New Kingdom texts. Both fire and knife are destructive tools. He argues that here:

---

[1] Geßler-Löhr, *Die Heiligen Seen*, 187-8, 207-11, 217-8; Hugonot, *Jardin*, 158-9.

[2] *CT* III, 3a-d (spell 164).

[3] PT spell 512= *Pyr.* §1164c and *CT* I, 129b (spell 35).

[4] PT spell 557=*Pyr.* § 1530c-d. In this spell the king ascends to the sky and the Lord of the Lakes of the Netherworld meets him and witnesses his purification in the Lakes of the Goose.

[5] *CT* III, 360d (spell 255).

[6] Saleh, *Das Totenbuch in den thebanischen Beamtengräbern*, 14 and 21. In CT spell 335 a gloss locates the two lakes in Herakleopolis and describes them as places where the deceased purifies himself: *CT* IV, 216a-217c (spell 335). The same vignettes occur in the Book of the Dead Chapter 17: Naville, *TB*, Kapitel 17, pl. XXVIII.

[7] *CT* III, 61a-62e (spell 175).

[8] *CT* VII, 390a-391a (spell 1099).

[9] See below, 91-3, for the Lake of Fire as a place of punishment for sinners.

[10] For CT spell 1099 in the Book of the Two Ways, see Backes, *Das altägyptische Zweiwegebuch*, 94, 378.

[11] The Book of Overthrowing Apep dates to the 4th century B.C, and was published by Faulkner, *The Papyrus Bremner-Rhind*, 1-93; the translation also by Faulkner, *JEA* 24 (1938), 41-53.

[12] Altenmüller, *ZÄS* 92 (1966), 86-95.

.....Da nun „Messersee" und „Flammensee" im alten Sinne „Seen der Vernichtung" sind, dürfte der Ägypter in der wechselnden Schreibung mit dem Ideogrammen von Messer und Flamme beim Namen des gleichen Sees keinen inneren Widerspruch finden. Beide Schreibungen könnten Varianten sein, die der bildliche durch die Ideogramme determinierten Funktion des Sees auch metaphorisch entsprechen. Das Flammenzeichen würde dabei nur das Zeichen des Messers als Waffe der Vernichtung vertreten.[13]

Altenmüller's argument includes the following points:
A- The Lake of Knives and the Lake of Fire are cosmic regions
(Both lakes represent the critical stage in the journey of the sun god Re).
B- The Lake of Knives and the Lake of Fire are mythical regions
(The two lakes are primordial places of creation in Hermopolis).
C- The Lake of Knives and the Lake of Fire are earthly locations
(The two lakes are located in the cultic district of Hermopolis).

Hermsen argues that the Lake of Fire is a place where the sun god Re is born. It comes at the end of Re's night journey on the lower land way in the Book of the Two Ways.[14] It is also the starting point in the deceased's journey towards the abode of Osiris on the upper waterway.

In his study on CT spells 1029-1130, Backes argues that the Lake of Fire is a body of water, which separates the upper waterway from the lower land way in the Book of the Two Ways. Furthermore, *š mꜣꜥ* (the true lake), which occurs in CT spell 1054 refers to the Lake of Fire as Re's birthplace.[15] The deceased will be able to cross over the Lake of Fire because he is the heir of the sun god Re.[16]

This study addresses the roles of the Lake of Knives and the Lake of Fire as places of passage over water. It deals also with the rites of passage concerning the crossing over the two lakes and how these rites mediate the passage of the deceased over them. Evidence discussed here includes Pyramid Texts, Coffin Texts and Book of the Dead, enhanced with relevant passages from different literary texts when necessary.

Chapter One is divided into two sections: the first section deals with the symbolism of water. Water is dealt with as the discharge which comes from the body of Osiris, and is offered to him in rituals. This section deals also with how the water of the Lake of Knives and the Lake of Fire can be identified with the water which comes from the body of Osiris, and how the crossing over the two lakes can be related to the purification ritual. Furthermore, this section deals with how having water on the two banks of the Lake of Knives and raising the discharge of Osiris in the Lake of Fire, mediates the passage of the deceased over the two lakes and enables him to escape death. The end of this section deals with water as a healing element as represented in the stelae of Horus. The second section of this chapter deals with the symbolism of knives and fire. The positive and negative aspects of fire and knives are dealt with here. This is done by presenting the role of fire and knives in the creation myth and in the Book of Overthrowing Apep. This is followed by a discussion on the roles of fire and knives in the Books of the Underworld as depicted on the walls of the royal tombs in the Valley of the Kings. The role of fire and knives in driving off demons and bad spirits in nightmares is also dealt with in this section. The final section in this chapter deals with barriers and buildings surrounded by fire and knives, and how the guardians of places of passage were equipped with both of them.

Chapter Two is divided into two sections: section one deals with the cartographical descriptions of the Lake of Knives and the Lake of Fire. Pictorial and textual evidence is presented here to build an image of the two lakes. Unfortunately there is no specific description for the Lake of Knives in Egyptian representations, nor is there a direct textual reference identifying its shape, so I am using the methodology of Krauss[17] on the Winding Waterway to reach the cartographical description of the Lake of Knives. This is done by investigating the different forms of the word with which the Lake of Knives is written and looking at the different determinatives which accompanied the toponym. Textual evidence is also dealt with to reach the cartographical description of the Lake of Knives. This is followed by a description for the Lake of Fire as found in the vignettes of the Book of the Dead, the plans of the Book of the Two Ways on the floor of el-Bersha coffins, the Mythological Papyri, the Books of the Underworld, and the 21st Dynasty coffins.

Section two deals with the cosmographical locations of the two lakes. This is done by a detailed study of how the orientation of a ritualist and the placing and orientation of ritual texts on pyramid walls, coffin sides and tombs walls can be used to show how the ancient Egyptians envisaged the locations of the two lakes. In order to reach the exact orientation of a ritualist, it was necessary to investigate how to construct a ritual from a single specific text. This is followed by a study of

[13] Altenmüller, *ZÄS* 92 (1966), 93; *LÄ* IV, 113-4.
[14] Hermsen, *Die Zwei Wege des Jenseits*, 170-2: in *Studies Stricker*, 73-86. El-Weshahy conducted a study on the pictorial representations of the Lake of Fire, but she did not add anything of value: El-Weshahy, in: J.-C. Goyon and C. Cardin (eds), *Proceedings of the Ninth International Congress of Egyptologists* I, 641-52.
[15] See below, 77.
[16] Backes, *Das altägyptische Zweiwegebuch*, 323-4.

[17] Krauss, *Astronomische Konzepte*, 14-27.

each ritual in which the two lakes occur, in order to reach the exact orientation of a ritualist.

Chapter Three focuses on the deceased's safe passage over the Winding Waterway, as represented in the ferryman spells, and the Island of Fire as places of passage over water. The ritual aspects of the ferryman spells and the Island of Fire are presented to show how they are related to the ritual aspects of the Lake of Knives and the Lake of Fire.

Chapter Four presents the crossing of the lake as a ritual enacted for the deceased at the day of his funeral. Pictorial and textual evidence is presented to show how the crossing of the lake in Old Kingdom private tombs, in Old and Middle Kingdom texts, and in New Kingdom private tombs can be related to the deceased's crossing over the Lake of Knives and the Lake of Fire.

Chapter Five deals with the Lake of Fire as a place of passage in the Book of the Two Ways, which is briefly investigated in order to construct the journey of the deceased until he reaches the Lake of Fire. The texts under discussion here are CT spells 1072-1054, which occur in sections III and IV in Lesko's edition of the Book of the Two Ways. The focus will be on the spells occurring in the two long versions A and B, with a comparison with those occurring on the short version C when necessary. This is followed by a comparison between the topography of the lower land way in the Book of the Two Ways, and the Fifth Hour of the Book of the Amduat.

Chapter Six investigates the rites concerning the deceased's passage over the two lakes. This is done by a detailed study of each ritual text, its performance, the occasion of performance, and by whom the ritual might be performed. This chapter starts with a brief introduction on the rites of passage as represented in Van Gennep's and Victor Turner's studies, and which are taken as a frame for the study of the rites of passage over the Lake of Knives and the Lake of Fire. Symbols and their handling within a ritual are also presented here, to see how a performance of a ritual can constitute the smallest units of activity in ritual.

Chapter Seven puts into context the overall argument on the Lake of Knives and the Lake of Fire in Egyptian religious texts.

Chapter One

The Symbolism of Water, Fire and Knives

1.1. The Symbolism of Water:

Water as the Discharge of Osiris

Osiris functioned as the central figure of Egyptian funerary belief by the virtue of his dying and reviving as well as his position as judge and ruler of the netherworld. These aspects of Osiris are dealt with in detail by Plutarch in his treatise on Isis and Osiris of the early second century A.D., in which he described how the Ancient Egyptians equated Osiris with the River Nile and the Nile god Hapy.[18] The Ancient Egyptians called the libation water 'the discharge of Osiris',[19] which comes from the body of Osiris, and is offered to the deceased in his mortuary cult.[20]

The Papyrus of Nesmin (BM 10209)

The clearest text dealing with the offering of libation water is found in the Papyrus of Nesmin in the British Museum (BM 10209), in which the designation of water as the discharge of Osiris is made explicit.[21] The papyrus dates to the Graeco-Roman Period, when the mortuary cult at Thebes was the responsibility of the cult association of the Water Pouring Priests, the Choachytes, who were located at Medinet Habu.[22] The title of the text in this papyrus states that it was taken from a scroll used in the Festival of the Valley,[23] in which the god Amun crossed to the West Bank to offer libations to his ancestors in the 18th Dynasty temple of Medinet Habu.[24] All the dead buried on the West Bank were included in these offerings.[25] The tenth spell stresses the fact that water symbolises the discharge of Osiris.

skr-wsjr mn n=k ḳbḥwjptn	O Sokar-Osiris, take for yourself this libation,
ḳbḥw=k ḫr ḥr	Your libation from Horus,
m rn=k pfj n ḳbḥw	In that your name of Libation.
mn n=k rḏw prj jm=k	Take for yourself the discharge that has come out from you,
rdj n=k ḥr ḏr bw nb	Which Horus gives you in every place,
mḥj.n=k jm	Where you were drowned (in water).[26]

The spell does not concern the presentation of libation offering, but it is a purification spell. The liturgical context of this spell is the tomb cult chamber, where the offerings are brought to the deceased and where his mortuary cult takes place. The act of bringing offerings to the tomb is accompanied by the recitation of this spell, and the offering of libation is abbreviated and reduced to a simple allusion to libation.[27] The spell stresses the fact that the purification water comes from the body of Osiris. Water identified as the discharge of Osiris has a long history dating from the Old Kingdom Pyramid Texts.

Pyramid Texts Evidence

In many Pyramid Texts spells, the deceased is offered a libation of cool water (*ḳbḥw*) or fresh water (*rnpjt*). PT spell 436 reads:

ḏd mdw mw=k n=k	Recitation: Your water belongs to you,
bꜥḥ=k n=k	Your water flow belongs to you,
rḏw pr m nṯr	The discharge[28] that comes from the god,
ḥwꜣꜣt prt m wsjr	The decay that comes from Osiris.
jꜥj ꜥwj=k	Wash your hands!
wbꜣ msḏrwj=k	Open up your ears!
sꜣḫj sḫm pn n bꜣ=f	Transfigured is this Mighty One for his *ba*.
jꜥj ṯw jꜥj sw kꜣ=k	Wash yourself! and your *Ka* washes itself.
ḥms kꜣ=k wnm=f t ḥnꜥ=k	May your *Ka* sit down and eat bread with you,
n nwr n ḏt ḏt	Without trembling forever and ever.[29]

The same theme occurs in PT spell 32 and reads:

ḳbḥw=k jpn wsjr	This is your cool water (libation water), Osiris,
ḳbḥw=k jpn hꜣ N	This is your cool water, O N.
prj.w ḫr sꜣ=k	Which has come forth with your son,
prj.w ḫr ḥr	Which has come forth with Horus.
jw.n(=j) jn.n(=j) n=k jrt-ḥr	(I) have come and I have brought to you the Eye of Horus,
ḳb jb=k ḫr=s	That your heart may be calm by means of it.

[18] Griffiths, *Plutarch's De Iside et Osiride*, 172-4.
[19] Assmann, *Totenliturgien* II, 91.
[20] Assmann, *Death and Salvation*, 355; in: *Hommages Fayza Haikal*, 6.
[21] Haikal, *Two Hieratic Funerary Papyri*.
[22] Assmann, *Totenliturgien* II, 91; Bommas, in: *L'acqua nell'antico Egitto*, 262.
[23] Assmann, in: *Hommages Fayza Haikal*, 13-4; *Totenliturgien* III, 499.
[24] Assmann, *Death and Salvation*, 356.
[25] Assmann, *Totenliturgien* II, 93.

[26] Haikal, *Two Hieratic Funerary Papyri* I, 41, lines 5.1-5.2; II, 21: Assmann, *Totenliturgien* III, 532.
[27] Assmann, *Totenliturgien* III, 534; *Death and Salvation*, 355.
[28] On the word *rḏw* and its identification with Osiris, see Kettel, in: *Hommages Leclant* III, 315-30; Zandee, *Death as an Enemy*, 11 and 57; Beinlich, *Osirisreliquien*, 304.
[29] PT spell 436=*Pyr.* § 788a-789c.

jn.n(=j) n=k sj ḥr kbwj=k	(I) have brought it to you under your sandals.
mn n=k rḏw prj jm=k	Take to yourself the discharge (outflow) that has come out from you.
n wrḏ jb=k ḥr=s	May your heart not be weary with it.[30]

In the texts cited above, the stress is not on the act of providing the deceased with drinking water which assuage his thirst in the manner of funerary offerings, but to supply him with the life giving force water which comes from the body of Osiris.[31]

Pyramid Texts spell 32 can be divided into three sections: The first tells that this water is from Horus, son of Osiris. Water connects the son and his dead father.[32] The second describes the water as the 'Eye of Horus', which makes the heart of the deceased radiant. The Eye of Horus is the cultic expression of every item to be offered. It also shows that when an item is offered and described as the Eye of Horus, that simply means, in Assmann's words, that 'it will restore something that has been destroyed or used up, put together something that has fallen apart, or replace something that has been lost. It is the symbol of reversibility.'[33] The third section explains that this water is the discharge of Osiris, which comes out from his body. Water flows out from the deceased Osiris and then comes back to him by means of offering the libation. So, the water here symbolises life force, the medium by which life returns to the deceased.[34]

The purpose of the funeral libation in this spell is to revitalize the deceased, and to make him youth (*rnp*) again. The fresh water is the Nile efflux (*rḏw*),[35] which represents both the seepage of surface water that marks the beginning of the flood and the life force of Osiris as personification of the Nile. The water offered to Osiris is compared with the fluid which comes forth from Horus and the efflux which has gone out from the body of Osiris at the moment of death and returned to him by means of offering libation.[36] In PT spell 460, the libation offered to the deceased is the water flow that comes from his body.

mw=k ḳbḥ=k bꜥḥ wr	Your water, your cool water is the great water flow,
prj jm=k	Which has come out from you.[37]

In another Pyramid Text spell, the water offered to the deceased is described as:

mn n=k rḏw prj jm=k	Take to yourself the discharge that has come out from you.
rdj.n ḥr ḥmꜥ n=k nṯrw ḏr	Horus has caused that all the gods gather for you,
bw nb šm.n=k jm	(In) every place from where you have gone.
mn n=k rḏw prj m=k	Take the discharge that has come out from you.
rdj.n ḥr jp n=k msw=f ḏr	Horus has caused that all his sons account for you,
bw mḥ.n=k jm	(In) the place where you were drowned.
jp kw ḥr rnpj.tw	Horus inspects you, you being young,
m rn=k pw n mw rnpj	In this your name of fresh water.[38]

The spell places the deceased in relation with the gods, and alludes to the myth of Osiris in which he was drowned in the Nile by his brother Seth. Horus, as son of Osiris, gathered the gods and his sons to search for the body of his father in every place where he might have gone from.[39] The libation water is called the fresh water, which has come from the body of Osiris. The text ends here with giving this name to the deceased, as Osiris from whose corpse the Nile flows.[40] Even the word for the year in Egypt was *rnp.t*[41] 'the Fresh One'. The fresh water is the Nile efflux (*rḏw*) which designates both the water flow and the life force of the god Osiris. These libations are the actual fluids that have issued from the corpse of Osiris.

In all the Pyramid Texts cited above, it is not the water which comes from the body of the deceased that will revive him, but it is the water of the divine body of Osiris, the *rḏw* which comes from the decaying body of the god. This water reaches the deceased in the form of libation.[42]

Coffin Texts Evidence

Many Coffin Texts spells show the deceased being offered water that comes from Osiris.

ḳbḥw=k pw nn wsjr N pn	Here is your cold water O this Osiris N;
prj.w ḥr jt=k	Which has come forth from

[30] PT spell 32=*Pyr.* § 22a-23a, see also PT spell 33=*Pyr.* § 24a-25c, and PT spell 357=*Pyr.* § 589a reads 'Your name of the fresh water' (*rn=k n mw rnpw*).
[31] Delia, *JARCE* 29 (1992), 183.
[32] Assmann, *Death and Salvation*, 357.
[33] Assmann, *Death and Salvation*, 357; in: *Hommages Fayza Haikal*, 8.
[34] Blackman, *ZÄS* 50 (1912), 69-75; Zandee, *JEOL* 24 (1976), 3; Winkler, *GM* 211 (2006), 129. Willems describes libation offering as a life giving force that enables the deceased to travel to the sky: Willems, *Heqata*, 118.
[35] Kettel noted the physical appearance of the Nile inundation and compared it with the nature of *rḏw*. He argues that when the Nile flood comes, it carries decomposing plants with special colour and an odour of rotting. *rḏw* as rotting bodily fluids has the same physical resemblance of the Nile during the inundation, green-brownish and carries strong smell: Kettel, in: *Hommages Leclant* III, 323.
[36] Winkler, *GM* 211 (2006), 129.
[37] PT spell 460=*Pyr.* § 868b; Allen, *The Ancient Egyptian Pyramid Texts*, 120.
[38] PT spell 423=*Pyr.* § 766a-767a; Allen, *Inflection of the Verb*, 493; *The Ancient Egyptian Pyramid Texts*, 101.
[39] Assmann, *Death and Salvation*, 357-8.
[40] Assmann, *Totenliturgien* II, 95.
[41] *Wb* II, 429-432.5
[42] Blackman, *ZÄS* 50 (1912), 71.

	your father,
prj.w ẖr gb	Which has come forth from Geb,
prj.w ẖr ḥr	Which has come forth from Horus,
prj.w ẖr wsjr	Which has come forth from Osiris,
ḳbḥ jb=k ẖr=s	May your heart be cool by means of it.
jwj.n=j jn.n=j n=k jrt ḥr	I have come, and I have brought to you the Eye of Horus,
ḳbḥ jb=k ẖr=s s<ḳ> <jm>=s	That your heart may be cool by means of it, and be refreshed by it.[43]
mn n=k rḏw prj jm=k	Take the discharge which has come out from you.
n wrḏ jb=k ẖr=s	Your heart is not weary by means of it.
mꜣ.t(j) mꜣ.t(j) rnp.t(j)rn.pt(j)	You being new, you being new, you being young, you being young,
m rn=k pw n jmj ḳbḥ	In this your name of 'He-who-is-in-the-libation'.
sḫr.n ḥr ḫftjw=k m bꜣḥ=k	Horus has overthrown your enemies in your presence.
mj prj.t (sic) *n=k ḫrw*	Come! The invocation comes out for you,
prt-ḫrw n jmꜣḫj N jḳr	Invocation offerings for the Revered One N, the Excellent.[44]

The fresh water will revive the heart of the deceased, fresh and cool, because it comes forth from the body of Osiris himself.[45] When the deceased drinks the vital fluid of Osiris, he partakes of the god's immortality.[46] Horus as the son of Osiris defends his father and overthrows his enemies for him. The offering of libation mediates the passage of the deceased Osiris.

Breasted's and Griffiths' Studies on the Inundation and Osiris

In his study on *The Development of Religion and Thought in Ancient Egypt*, Breasted argued that the libation spells might refer to the identification of Osiris with the Inundation or the Nile.[47] The evidence he used came mainly from the Pyramid Texts. According to Griffiths,[48] Breasted's argument was much influenced by that of Sir James Frazer's *Adonis, Attis and Osiris* published in 1906. According to this interpretation, Osiris was essentially a spirit of vegetation and inundation, a grain god who was killed every year during the harvest time, and buried with the seeds and came to new birth in the spring.

The evidence used in this argument included *Pyr.* 788a-b, which Griffiths translated 'Thou hast thy water. Thou hast thine overflow (*bꜥḥ*). Thou hast thine exudation which came forth from Osiris.'[49] Griffiths argued that the word *bꜥḥ* here means overflow and there is no reason why it should be explained as the Nile inundation, as Breasted wished to do. According to Griffiths, water used for libation was of course the Nile water, but this does not necessarily mean that this water refers to the inundation and as a result to the identification of Osiris with the Nile inundation. Griffiths maintained 'the spread of the Nile flood is described as contemporaneous with the emission of Osiris' exudation, so that the two are associated though not identified.'[50]

Breasted used *Pyr.* 848a-b to argue that Osiris was identified with the Nile. He translated the text as 'The canals are filled; the streams overflow by the purification that comes forth from Osiris.'[51] However Griffiths translated the same spell 'Recitation. The canals are filled, the streams overflow, when the purification comes forth from Osiris.'[52]

Griffiths rejected Breasted's translation and argued that *m* is a conjunction and not a preposition, and the purification occurring here may in this case simply imply a bathing of the body. Griffiths argued that here:

> Contemporaneity of actions does not necessarily involve identity of the persons or things addressed or mentioned as actors. Yet this seems to be the way in which Breasted approaches the passages where he finds proof of the identity of Osiris and the Nile or its inundation. These words by no way support the identity he posits.[53]

Griffiths continued his argument that Breasted's treatment of spell 317 is likewise open to question. It is a spell, according to Breasted, which identifies the dead king Wenis with Osiris. Griffiths' objection is that the name of Osiris does not occur within the spell, and it is the content of the spell that made Breasted suggested the identification of Osiris with the Nile. Breasted translated the spell in support of his interpretation of Osiris as the Nile inundation as 'Unis comes from hither up-stream when the flood inundates…Unis comes to his pools that are in the region of the flood at the great inundation, to the place of peace, with green fields, that is in the horizon. Unis makes the verdure to flourish in the two regions of the

---

43 Amendments were done in this way according to the restoration suggested by de Buck, *CT* VII, 104, n. 8 and 9 (spell 895).
44 *CT* VII, 104k-105g (spell 895).
45 Assmann, *Totenliturgien* II, 342.
46 Delia, *JARCE* 29 (1992), 183; Kettle, in: *Hommages Leclant* III, 318-20; Assmann, *Death and Salvation*, 357-8; *Totenliturgien* II, 96-7; in: *Hommages Fayza Haikal*, 19.
47 Breasted, *The Development of Religion*, 19.
48 Griffiths, *The Origins of Osiris*, 151.
49 Griffiths, *The Origins of Osiris*, 151.
50 Griffiths, *The Origins of Osiris*, 152.
51 Breasted, *The Development of Religion*, 19.
52 PT spell 455=*Pyr.* § 848a-b.
53 Griffiths, *The Origins of Osiris*, 152.

horizon.'[54] According to Griffiths, these passages cited by Breasted do refer to Osiris, but their allusion to the Nile or to the water do not imply their identity with the god. Griffiths here rejected any identification between Osiris and the inundation or even with the Nile.

Griffiths' argument seems convincing and his criticism of Breasted is justified. Griffiths translates *bꜥḥ* as overflow, and not inundation. He supports his argument by the fact the *Wörterbuch* translates *bꜥḥ* as *Wasserfülle*, or *Überschwemmung*.[55] Griffiths pointed out that the first meaning suffices here.[56] *Pyr*. 848 a-b cited above can be translated as follows:

ḏd mdw	Recitation:
mḥj mrw jꜣḫj.w itrw	The canals have filled, the rivers have flooded,
m rf ꜥbw prj m wsjr	With the purification that comes out from Osiris.[57]

In this spell the libation water comes from Osiris. It is also Osiris who causes the canals to be filled, and the rivers to flood, but at the same time he is not the inundation god. Griffiths argued that in the spells used by Breasted there is no direct reference to Osiris, but the reference is made to the dead king. However this can in no way be used as evidence to suggest that the spell does not refer to Osiris, from whom the water flows, where the dead king is in a state like Osiris in the Pyramid Texts.[58]

Breasted and Griffiths' comments reflect their own cultural background rather than the ancient Egyptian viewpoint. Griffiths is correct about what he said of the metaphor, but at the same time this metaphor is not fixed and changes from one context to another. It is not right to give a simple single category to the water that comes from the body of Osiris. Osiris is not the god of the inundation, but the inundation is related to him, as he is not the god of vegetation, but vegetation is related to him.[59] The king is not Osiris, but associated with him in the Pyramid Texts, and the resurrection of the King's body by libation water is the resurrection of the earth or the land of Egypt by the water flow that comes forth from the body of Osiris.[60] *bꜥḥ* can be envisaged as a running water, and on the contrary, the water of the inundation can be envisaged as standing water. When Osiris dies, his body loses its water which runs out of his body, and when the body is resurrected the water is poured on his body; it comes in or returns to his body.

Elephantine and the Leg of Osiris as Source of the Inundation

In the Pyramid Texts the word *rḏw* refers to the Nile water as the water flow that comes from the body of Osiris.[61] According to the myth, Egypt was conceived as a body, and the forty two nomes of Egypt were identified with the parts of this body of Osiris.[62] The Egyptians thought that the Nile sprang from Elephantine near the first cataract, because the leg of Osiris was thought to be buried there.[63] This myth was widely spread in Egypt during the Late and Graeco-Roman Periods. The parts of the body of Osiris were united during the secret rituals of Osiris. With this annual celebration of the reuniting and the revivification of the body of Osiris during the Osirian fesitiavls, the land of Egypt and the whole cosmos were reunited and drank water from the Nile and the body of Osiris. The water of the River Nile was as an elixir of life that comes forth from the body of Osiris. When he dies, his body becomes dry, and the water which is offered to him by means of ritual, restores his life as well as all the dead who were identified with him.[64]

Most of the evidence which recounts that Elephantine was the source of the water which flows out from the body of Osiris comes from later periods, although we have some evidence dating to the Middle and New Kingdoms, referring to Elephantine as the key source of offering water. CT spell 67 reads:

rs rs N pn	Wake, wake O this N!
rs wsjr rs jnpw tp mnj=f	Wake Osiris! Wake Anubis, who is on his mooring post (=controls the place of landing).
ḏrwt=k ꜣst ḥnꜥ nbt-ḥwt	Your kites are Isis and Nephthys.
ḳbḥw=k jpn jt=j	This, your cold water, O my father,
prjw m ꜣbw	Has come out from Elephantine.
t ḥḏ=k jnpw	Your white bread is Anubis.
ḥnfw=k wsjr	Your *ḥnfw* bread is Osiris.
ḥbbnt=k nwt <=k>-nw	Your *ḥbbnt* bread *is Nutek-nu*.[65]

In Chapter 173 of the Book of the Dead, Horus presents the libation which comes from Elephantine to his father Osiris.

ḏd mdw	Recitation:

[54] PT spell 317= *Pyr*. § 507a-509a. The translation cited here is that of Breasted.
[55] *Wb* I, 448.
[56] Griffiths, *The Origins of Osiris*, 151, n. 4.
[57] Allen, *The Ancient Egyptian Pyramid Texts*, 110.
[58] For more discussion on Osiris and the Nile inundation, see Griffiths, *ZÄS* 123 (1996), 111-5.
[59] Spieser argues that the inundation of the Nile is compared in mythological terms with the reunion of the parts of the dismembered body of Osiris. As the Nile flood unites the nomes of Egypt, the libation as the Nile inundation, unites the members of the body of Osiris: Spieser, *CdÉ* 72 (1997), 217. Goyon argues that the division of the parts of the body of Osiris between the nomes of Egypt is a manifestation of the divine in the whole land of Egypt: Goyon, in: *Essays van Voss*, 34. Winkler also argues that *rḏw* is the flood of Egypt: Winkler, *GM* 211 (2006), 130.
[60] For more detail on this topic, see Smith, *Traversing Eternity*, 6-8.
[61] Kettel, in: *Hommages Leclant* II, 323: *Wb* II, 469, 5-9.
[62] Beinlich, *Osirisreliquien*, 304-6.
[63] Blackman, *JEA* 5 (1918), 118.
[64] Assmann, *Totenliturgien* II, 93 and 361.
[65] *CT* I, 282a-282h (spell 67). Elephantine as the source of the inundation occurs also in PT spell 459=*Pyr*. §. 864, which reads: *pr mw=k m ꜣbw* (your water has come from Elephantine).

h3 wsjr jnk s3=k ḥr jj.n=j	O Osiris! I am your son Horus, I have come.
jnj.n=j n=k ḳbḥw m 3bw	I have brought to you cold water from Elephantine,
ḳbḥ jb=k ẖr=f	That your heart may be fresh by it.[66]

In both texts, the water comes from Elephantine, but there is no mention of the leg of Osiris. In a text dating to the Ptolemaic Period, a direct reference to the water that comes from the leg of Osiris is made explicit.

> I purify your majesty with the water 'repeater of life', which emerges from your leg, from the source cave from which the Nile inundation springs forth, coming to your flesh, so that your majesty is new.[67]

In the second hour of the night in the *Stundenwachen*, Anubis presents libation offerings to Osiris who is lying on his bed and says:[68]

> Take your cool water, which is in this land,
> Which brings forth all living things, all the things that this land gives.
> It is the begetter of all living things.
> All things come from it.
> You may have enjoyment of them, that you may live on them.
> It may go well with you by means of them.
> You may breath the air that is in them.
> It has begotten you and you emerge, living on all the things that you desire.[69]

When Osiris dies, his body loses it water, and at the same time, the Nile inundates and its water, presented as the libation, flows and covers the whole land giving all means of life.[70] In this way, Egypt, as Assmann argues, 'constituted the body from which Nile inundation gushed forth like a bodily humor that brought life. We see thus the correspondence of microcosm and macrocosm underlay the designation of water as the discharge of Osiris.'[71]

To make that more clear, the human body as a whole consists of parts. The parts may exist without the whole, but the whole cannot exist without the parts. The water or the fluid that issued from the body of Osiris is one of the most important parts of his body, as recorded on the lists of the Graeco-Roman temples with names of the different parts of the dismembered body of Osiris.[72] For the god to live again, he needs his body to be assembled. So, the water efflux (*rḏw*), or the water flow (*bꜥḥ*) as vital parts of the body of Osiris, symbolise the totality of the body of the god. The water which has come out of his body will return to him by means of libation. When the body dies, it loses its water. The body serves here as a container for the water which needs to be placed back in the body to be a whole and sound. The water offered will make the parts a whole, the unsound sound, and will cause the decomposition to stop.[73]

[66] Naville *TB*, Kapitel 173, pl. CXCV, line 30.
[67] Mariette, *Dendérah* I, pl. X; the translation uses Assmann, *Totenliturgien* III, 541.
[68] Junker, *Stundenwachen*, 78.
[69] The translation is that of Assmann, *Death and Salvation*, 361-2; see also Assmann, *Totenliturgien* III, 541-2.
[70] Winkler argues that 'the libation is perceived as the microcosmic ritual counterpart of the macrocosmic revivification process, the inundation, a natural event that was ritualized in the resurrection ritual. The connection between the libation and the annual flooding is found in a comparison between the drought of the land and the dehydration of the body': Winkler, *GM* 211 (2006), 132.
[71] Assmann, *Death and Salvation*, 361.

Thus in many representations of libation offerings, the water which comes from the libation vessels carry symbols of life. For instance, in the libation offerings scenes on the walls of the New Kingdom temples, the king is represented being purified by Thoth and Horus from a libation vessel. The water is depicted as a chain consisting of hieroglyphs for life. For example, on the walls of the temple of Amada, King Amenhotep II is represented standing while Horus and Thoth pour water on him (fig. 1).

Fig.1. King Amenhotep II being purified by Horus and Thoth (after Gauthier, *Le Temple d'Amada* I, pl. XXIV).

The water offered to the gods is also the source of life for all living things.[74] In a hymn to Isis in her temple at Philae on the north wall of room X, the king stands reciting a hymn before Isis, while he is offering her water. He says:

nts stj ḥꜥpj	She is the one who pours out Hapy,
jrj ꜥnḫ ḥr nb	Which (i.e. Hapy) makes all people live,
sḫpr w3ḏw3ḏ[75]	And green plants grow,
rdjt ḥtpw-nṯr n nṯrw	She who (i.e. Isis) provides offerings to the gods,
prt-m-ḫrw (n) 3ḫw	And invocation offerings for the *3ḫw*,
ḥr ntj nts nb(t) pt	Because she is the Lady of Heaven.

[72] Beinlich, *Osirisreliquien*, 218.
[73] Winkler, *GM* 211 (2006), 131.
[74] Colin, in: *L'acqua nell'antico Egitto*, 285.
[75] *Wb* I, 270. 6-7.

ṯ3j=s m nb dw3t	Her man is the Lord of the Netherworld.
s3=s m nb t3	Her son is the Lord of the Land.
ṯ3j=s m wʿb	Her man is the Pure One,
rnpj=f m snmwt r tr=f	Who refreshes himself at Biggeh at his time.[76]

Isis, as the wife of Osiris and mother of Horus, pours water to her husband, which already comes from him. Osiris is the source of water and the one who refreshes himself by the water which has come out from him. The same theme of purification is also found in New Kingdom private tombs. In the tomb of User at Thebes (TT 21), two men are represented pouring water from two water vases. The deceased sits on a large vessel at the bottom of which two *ʿnḫ* signs are depicted (fig. 2).[77]

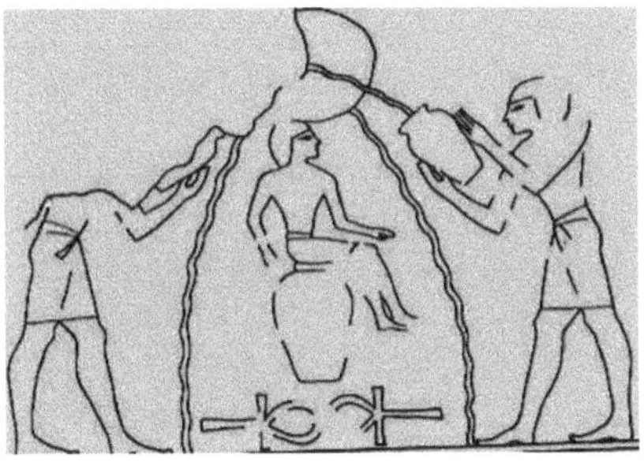

Fig. 2. The purification scene in the tomb of User (TT 21) (after Davies, *Five Theban Tombs*, pl. 21.)

The Primeval Water

The primeval ocean Nun was the place where the first act of creation took place. In one of the Coffin Texts spells, Nun is the self-created god who formed himself in the Abyss.

jnk nw wʿ jwtj-sn.nw=f	I am Nu the Sole One, who has no equal.
ḫpr.n=j jm sp wr n mḥt=j	I came into being in the Great Occasion of my flood,
ḫpr.n=j	I came into being.
jnk p3j ḫpr=f ḏbnn jmj swḥt=f	I am he who flew up, whose manifestation is (that of) *ḏbbn*who is in his egg.
jnk š3ʿ m nw	I am the one who began from the Abyss.
mk ḥḥw prj n=j	See! *ḥḥw* is the one who came out to me.
mk wḏ3=j	See! I am hale.[78]

The deceased also proclaims that he is Re in the primeval ocean Nun:

jnk rʿ prj m nw.w	I am Re who has come out of Nun.[79]

The primeval water was also the place where the humans are born new. One of the texts reads:

> We live again anew, after we enter the primeval water, and it has renewed us into one who is young for the first time. The old man is shed, a new one is made.[80]

The Nile also flowed from the primeval ocean Nun, the water that surrounded the earth, the sky and the underworld. The morning sun bathes in the primeval water drawing strength for a new day and a new ascent to the sky.[81] This water was poured out for the deceased so as to give him life, to connect him with the gods, and to mediate his passage to ascend to the sky. In one of the purification texts we read:

> Pharaoh is Horus in the primeval water.
> Death has no power over him.
> The gods are satisfied with the pharaoh's purity.[82]

This creative water was envisaged in the offering libation as the creative power that comes from Nun. In the ritual of Amenophis I, which is preserved on the walls of the temple of Medinet Habu, King Ramesses III is shown offering libation water to Amun Re. The water offered to the god is said to come from Nun.

> I brought to you your libation, which you have lifted up under the Great <Seat>, your libation which comes from Elephantine, that your heart may be refreshed with it in your name of What-goes-forth-from-*ḳbḥw*. The heart of Amun Re, Lord of the Thrones of the Two Lands, is satisfied with what comes forth from Nun.[83]

The Discharge of Osiris in the Lake of Knives and Lake of Fire

The Lake of Knives, as a place of passage, is mentioned together with the primeval water and the creation mound. According to the Hermopolitan myth, the sun god Re was born on the Island of Fire which was in the midst of the Lake of Knives. The text reads:

swḥt n mw nḫḫ n t3	Egg of the water, fluid of the land,
mʿj n ḫmnyw	And fruit of the Ogdoad,
wr m pt sr m dw3t	Great One in heaven, prince

[76] Žabkar, *JEA* 69 (1983), 133-4, pl. XVI.
[77] Davies, *Five Theban Tombs*, pl. 21.
[78] *CT* VI, 343j-344a (spell 714).
[79] Lapp, *Papyrus of Nu*, pl. 60, line 13.
[80] Gardiner, *HPBM, Papyrus Chester Beatty* IV, recto, 11, 8-9 (the translation is that of Assmann, *Death and Salvation*, 184).
[81] Assmann, in: *Hommages Fayza Haikal*, 16; *Death and Salvation*, 362-3.
[82] Schott, *Die Reinigung Pharaohs in einem memphitischen Tempel*, 55 (quoted from Assmann, *Death and Salvation*, 363).
[83] Nelson, *JNES* 8 (1949), 216.

	in the underworld.
jmj sšj ḫntj mr nḫ3wj	He who is in the nest, before the Lake of Knives.
pr.n=j ḥnʿ=k m mw	I came out with you from the water.
bsj=j ḥnʿ=k m sšy=k	I flowed out with you from your nest.
jnk mnw n gbtjw	I am Min of Coptos
jnk mnw nb t3 gbtjw	I am Min, Lord of the land of Coptos.[84]

The Lake of Knives was the place from which the egg of the sun god in a nest hatched revealing the sun god.[85] On the walls of Hibis temple, the same theme occurs:

st=k ḏr-ʿ m k3jt nt wnw	Your ancient throne is on the mound of Hermopolis.
s3ḫ=k t3 m mr dswy	You reach land from the Lake of Knives.
ḫʿ=k m nt m swḥt jmnt	You appear from the water surface[86] as the hidden egg.
jmnt m-ḫt=k	Amunet is behind you,
hnj.n=k ḥr 3ḥt	When you have alighted on the *3ḥt* cow.[87]

In the Hermopolitan creation myth, Amun as a cackler is the god who laid the cosmic egg from which he emerged.[88] He is said to come out from the primeval water and reached the land from the Lake of Knives.[89] As argued above, the primeval water is the source of life and the place from which the whole of living substances emerge. So the Lake of Knives, the water flow of Osiris, and the primeval ocean Nun all have the aspects of being places where the deceased is born new. This is expressed by the wish of the deceased to drink water on the two sides of the Lake of Knives. An offering text in TT 127 reads:

nmj=k njwt d3j=k ḥrt	May you cross the city and traverse the sky.
swr=k mw ḥr gswj mr nḫ3wj	May you drink water on the two banks of the Lake of Knives.[90]

The deceased Osiris on his bier was symbolically equated with the sun god in his barque, and by sailing over the Lake of Knives and drinking from its water he mediates his passage over it. In all the texts in which the Lake of Knives appears, it is connected with the navigation of the solar barque, particularly in the New Kingdom hymns. In these texts, the barque is threatened by the Sandbank of Apep, which can provide an allusion to Osiris who is on his bed and threatened by Seth. The sun crosses the Lake of Knives safely, and Osiris escapes death by the libation offered to him while he is on his bier. So the deceased will face the same fate of the sun god in his barque, and that of Osiris on his bed. It is not surprising to find this idea of navigation alluding to the mummification of the deceased. This navigation across the sky, which is also full of water, and the safe passage over the Lake of Knives might simply refer to the deceased being purified by water. In a composite text, put together from variant texts in a number of tombs, the journey of the sun god Re over the Lake of Knives is described as:

jnḏ ḥr=k rʿ m wbn=k	Hail to you Re, at your rising.[91]
jtmw m ḥtp=k nfr	Atum, at your beautiful setting,
ḫʿ=k psḏ=k ḥr psḏ mwt=k	You appear and shine on the back of your mother,
ḫʿ.tj m nswt psḏt	Appearing as the king of the Ennead.
jrj nwt njnj n-ḥr=k	Nut greets you with *njnj*.
ḥtp tw m3ʿt r trwy	Maat embraces you at the two times.[92]
nmj=k ḥrt ib=k 3w	You cross the sky, with your heart joyful.
mr nḫ3wj ḫprw m ḥtpw	The Lake of Knives has become in peace.[93]
mr nsrsr bʿḥj m ḥtpw variant	The Lake of Fire is inundated with offerings.[94]
sbj ḫrw ʿwj=fj k3sw	The enemy is felled and his arms are cut off.
ḥsk.n dmt ṯswt=f	The knife has cut his spine.
wnn rʿ m m3ʿw nfr	Re is in fair wind.
msktt sk.n.s pḥ sj	The *Msktt* Barque, it has destroyed the one who attacked it.
st3w tw rsjw mḥtjw	The southerners and northerners tow you,
imntjw j3btjw ḥr dw3=k	And the easterners and westerners worship you.

[84] Leitz, *Magical and Medical Papyri*, section K, VI, 10-VII, I.
[85] Roeder, *Hermopolis*, 169.
[86] *nt* is the water upper surface, and not *nwnt* the female counterpart of Nun: Klotz, *Adoration of the Ram*, 103.
[87] Cruz-Uribe, *Hibis Temple* I, 135.
[88] Klotz, *Adoration of the Ram*, 103.
[89] *nt*-water might also refer to the celestial cow upon which Re sets at night, and through which his body is reborn in the morning: Klotz, *Adoration of the Ram*, 103. The sun god Re also regenerates himself in water when he enters in the body of the goddess Nut to be born young and new the next day: Beinlich, *Das Buch von Fayum* I, 314-8.
[90] Assmann, *Totenliturgien* II, 373.

[91] On the stela of Nakhtmin, it reads: *jnḏ ḥr=k rʿ nb m3ʿt* 'Hail to you Re Lord of Maat': Assmann, *Liturgische Lieder*, 267.
[92] The hymn not only stresses the worship of the sun god in all his different forms during the whole day, but it also puts emphasis on his worship during his rising and setting in the horizon, day and night. These two *Ersheinungphasen* play important roles in the cult of the sun in Theban private tombs. The role of the hymn in the cult of the sun god is obvious from its title which stresses worshipping the sun god Re in his rising and setting: Assmann, *Liturgische Lieder*, 268. The sunrise and sunset were, as Stewart argues, the chief occasions to worship and adore the sun god Re: Stewart, *JEA* 46 (1960), 84.
[93] In TT 41, the text reads *mr nḫ3wj bʿḥw m ršwt=k* 'the Lake of Knives inundates with your joy', Assmann, *STG*, text 51, p. 66, line 9.
[94] This variant occurs on a door leaf Louvre C 66: Assmann, *Liturgische Lieder*, 267.

In this text, the barque crosses the Lake of Knives in joy, and on a variant, the Lake of Fire is said to be inundated with offerings. To be inundated with offerings (*bꜥḥj m ḥtpw*) might refer to the fact that the Lake of Fire is filled with the discharge (*rḏw*) of Osiris. The lake of Fire has its connection with the discharge (*rḏw*) of Osiris. In the Book of the Dead of Nu, Chapter 63B has the title of 'Spell for Not Being Burnt in Water'.

r n tm wbd m mw	Spell for not being burnt in water.
ḏd mdw jn N mꜣꜥ-ḫrw	Recitation by N the justified;
jnk mꜥwḥ pwj ꜥpr	I am this equipped oar,
ḫnnw rꜥ jm=f ḫnn jꜣjwt	With which Re is rowed when the Old Ones row.
wṯs rḏw wsjr r š ꜣsbjw	The discharge of Osiris is raised up in the Lake of Fire,
jwtj ꜥwg n=f	Which is not dried out for him.
ḥfd.n=j m jꜣḫw	I have climbed in the sunshine.[95]

This chapter, with chapter 63A, belongs to a group of texts entitled as spells for having power over water and not being scorched by fire. The deceased will not be burnt by the fire of the Lake of Fire because he will raise up the discharge of Osiris. The safe passage of the deceased over the Lake of Fire is secured by pouring libations. On some of the New Kingdom papyri, the deceased is represented pouring libation water on the doors of the Lake of Fire (fig. 3).

Fig. 3. The deceased pours libation on the two sides of the Lake of Fire
(after Piankoff, *Mythological Papyri*, pl. 8).

The early versions of BD 63B is CT spell 359,[96] and belongs to a large collection of Coffin Texts spells entitled as 'having power over water in the necropolis'.[97] CT spell 359 reads:

jnk mꜥwḥ pw n rꜥ	I am this oar of Re,
ḫnnw n=f jꜣw.t jm=f	With which the Old Ones are transported for him.
n ꜥḥm=j n nwḫ=j	I am not burnt; I am not scorched.
jnk bꜣbj sꜣ tp n wsjr	I am Babi, the first son of Osiris,
jꜥb n=f nṯr nb	Who assembles for him every god,
m-ḫnw šnw n jrt=f m jwnw	Within the circuit of his eye in Heliopolis.
jnk sꜣ n wsjr	I am the son of Osiris,
jnk jwꜥw n wsjr	I am the heir of Osiris,
kf wr wrḏ ḏs=f	Who comforts the Great One who is weary himself.
jw kf.n wr wrḏ ḏs=f	(I) have comforted the Great One who is weary himself.
jw sḫm.n=j jm=f	I have power through him.
jw nḥm.n=j sḫm kj jm=f	I have taken away the power of the other one (Seth) through him.[98]

The spell states that the barque of the sun god Re transports a group of beings called the Old Ones. These beings might represent the primeval gods who ascend on the barque of the sun god Re before the sun rise. They might also represent the two Old Women mentioned in CT spell 362, and who quench their thirst with the *rḏw* that comes out from the body of Osiris.[99] They might also represent a group of beings dwelling in the horizon, or they might also represent the souls of regeneration who ascend to the solar barque before the sun rise.[100]

The deceased in this spell identifies himself with the oar of Re with which the gods are transported. He envisages himself as an implement which sets the solar course.[101] The deceased then says that he is Babi, the first son of Osiris, who assembles the gods in the barque for Re in Heliopolis. He is not scorched by the heat of the sun because he is Babi, the god of fire. He may also have been associated with inundation and, by extension, with water.[102] The Eye of Horus might represent the solar barque of the sun god Re on which the god ascends before the sun rise.

The cosmic situations described in this text are not particular to one specific place or moment, but they describe a range of such situations. These situations are described by Willems as *Kosmische Gesamtsituation*.[103] It does not present clear data on the journey of the sun god, but what is more explicit is the theme of a speaker, probably the deceased, who claims a prominent position in the solar barque. According to

[95] Lapp, *Papyrus of Nu*, pl. 35, line 1-2.
[96] Willems, *Heqata*, 338.
[97] These spells were studied by Zandee, *JEOL* 24 (1976), 1-47.

[98] *CT* V, 12Cc-14b (spell 359).
[99] According to Willems, this might be the reason that CT spell 359 consistently writes the Old Ones as *Ꜣw.t* with *t* ending, signifying these two Old Women are to be interpreted here: Willems, *Heqata*, 339; Zandee has also argued that these Old Ones might be identical with the two Old Women mentioned in CT spell 44: Zandee, *JEOL* 24 (1976), 23-4.
[100] Hornung, *Totenbuch*, 452.
[101] Willems, *Heqata*, 340
[102] Bidoli, *Fangenetze*, 57-59; Zandee, *JEOL* 24 (1976), 22-3, Willems, *Heqata*, 340. Babi is also son of Re, god of protection, and has power over water: Leitz, *Lexikon der ägyptischen Götter* II, 737.
[103] Willems, *Heqata*, 339.

the later version of this spell (BD 63A),[104] the deceased does so in an address to Osiris, the Bull of the West whom he approaches.

In the final section of the spell, the speaker assumes that he is the son and heir of Osiris, which should refer to Horus as the son of Osiris. He asserts that he accomplishes his filial duty to his father Osiris, where he eases his pain and protects him against Seth, described here as 'the other one'. The deceased claims that he takes part in the treatment of Osiris' corpse, and thus he participates in the embalming of his father. An interesting parallel noted by Zandee,[105] in his comment on this spell, is CT spell 451, which has the double aim of enabling the deceased to enter into the presence of Osiris and to have power over water.[106] As Willems argues:

> It is almost as if the mummification of Osiris, who manifests in the inundation, is a precondition for the availability of water for the deceased's personal benefit.[107]

So the deceased's wish to drink water on the two banks of the Lake of Knives, raising up the discharge of Osiris in the Lake of Fire, and having power over water are all themes which might refer to his wish to have a safe passage over water. Drinking water or having power over water might also refer to the healing power of the water.

The patient's wish to drink the healing water is found in the well-known crocodile stelae known as Cippi of Horus. These stelae are distinguished by a central representation of Horus the child standing on top of two or more crocodiles, and holding in his hands scorpions, serpents, lions and gazelles. The head of the god Bes hovers above the head of Horus (fig. 4).[108]

Fig. 4. Horus on Crocodile, Stela Louvre E 20008 (after Gasse, *Stèles d'Horus sur les crocodiles*, 37).

The stelae had protective and healing purposes, which is made explicit in the image of Horus as the patient who suffers from a disease, and who tramples over the helpless Seth in the image of a crocodile. The scenes and spells inscribed on these stelae are derived from the myth of the defeat of Seth, who had wounded Horus with an army of scorpions before attacking him in the form of a crocodile, and also the defeat of Apep, the serpent of chaos who threatened the boat of the sun god Re.[109] Through identification of the scorpion, serpents, and crocodiles with the demons, the spells guarantee their defeat, and with the identification of the fate of the patient with that of the victorious god, the spell guarantees a cure. As healing media, Horus stelae were sometimes set up in public areas as public shrines, perhaps before a temple to serve the general community.[110]

The stelae were sometimes carried by priests playing the role of healers. They were immersed in a bowl full of water, or water might have been poured over them and then drunk by the patients, which might also explain the reason that some of them were provided with a basin to collect the water.[111] For instance, the healing shrines at Karnak are distinguished by the remains of basins and jars. The patient might also have rubbed their bodies with these stelae, or have kissed them, which might also explain the worn surface of many of Horus stelae.[112]

Water poured over the stelae was collected and drunk by the patient who had been bitten by a snake or a scorpion. The poison runs in the body of the patient like fire, and the water when drunk would extinguish the burning of the patient. Water will ease the pain of the patient as it will extinguish the heat of fire when the *rḏw* of Osiris is raised by the deceased in the Lake of Fire.

To conclude, water played important roles in Egyptian myth and ritual. In Egyptian myth, water was the first element from which life came into being. In water lies the power of creation. This creative image of water was envisaged in the annual Nile flood which covered the whole land brining all life substances to the land of Egypt. Nun was the place where the dead reappear to a new life.[113] In ritual, water was the elixir of life, which is poured to the deceased during ritual so he can be refreshed by means of it. The water offered to the deceased comes from the body of Osiris, and it returns to his body during libation offering. Water was also the

[104] Naville, *TB*, pl. LXXIII, line 2.

[105] Zandee, *JEOL* 24 (1976), 23-24; Zandee, *Death as an Enemy*, 67.

[106] Zandee, *JEOL* 24 (1976), 23.

[107] Willems, *Heqata*, 340.

[108] For more detail on the iconography of these stelae in Louvre Museum, see Gasse, *Stèles d'Horus sur les crocodiles*, 17-22.

[109] Ritner, in: Allen et al., *Religion and Philosophy in Ancient Egypt*, 105.

[110] The most striking example is a shrine housing the statue of Horus and the healing inscriptions were carved on its walls: Ritner, in: Allen et al., *Religion and Philosophy in Ancient Egypt*, 106.

[111] Gasse, *Les stèles d'Horus sur les crocodiles*, 22.

[112] These stelae were small in size, and they were the property of the healers who carried them to cure their patients: Gasse, *Stèles d'Horus sur les crocodiles*, 22-3.

[113] Bickel, in: *L'acqua nell'antico Egitto*, 191.

means by which the deceased mediates his passage and becomes an *ꜣḫ*.

As water was the power of life, it also caused violent death. The negative aspects of water are made clear in many texts dating to different periods. The High Nile can cause damage to the whole land. This theme occurs in one of the Pyramid Texts where the king is described as the High Nile who strikes his enemies.

jw nḏ.n sw N m-ꜥ jrj.wnn [r=f]	N has saved himself from those who do this [against him],
nḥmw šbw=f m-ꜥ=f sk sw wn	Who would take his food from him when it is Present
nḥmw msjt=f m-ꜥ=f sk sj wntj	Who would take his supper from him when it is present,
nḥm ṯꜣw m [fnḏ=f]	Who would take the air from [his nose],
sꜥḥꜥ hr=f n ꜥnḫ	Who would bring his days of life to a standstill.
nḫt N r=sn ḫꜥj wḏbw=f	N is stronger than them, risen on his shores.
j.ḫr jbw=sn n ḏbꜣw=f	Their hearts fall to his fingers.
bskw=sn n jrw pt	Their innards are for those who belong to the sky.
dšrw=sn n jrw tꜣ	Their blood for those who belong to the earth.
jwꜥw=sn n šwꜣt	Their heirs are for poverty.
prw=sn n znznt	Their house to conflagration.
ꜥrrwt=sn n ḥꜥpj wr	Their courts for the High Nile.[114]

Pyramid Text spell 254 is a cannibal hymn, where Unas is envisaged as a bull of the sky who defeats his enemies.[115] He is pictured here as the one who butchers his enemies. The last passage in the spell refers to the destruction caused to the enemies of the king where their houses are burnt and their courts are struck by the High Nile. The power of the High Nile is envisaged here as a destructive weapons against the enemies of the king.

The high flood of the Nile can cause damage to the temples of the gods. In a hieratic inscription in the hypostyle hall of Luxor Temple, which dates to third year of the reign of king Osorkon III, the high flood which enters the temple is described as:

> Nun came up, filling this land entirely,
> He rose above the two riverbanks like in the first occasion.
> The land became as powerful as the sea,
> No man-made dam could withstand its attack,
> Everybody was like ducks.
> He raged over his city,
> Standing high in the (temple) like the sky,
> All the temples of Thebes were like marshes.[116]

[114] PT spell 254= *Pyr.* § 290c-292d.
[115] Eyre, *Cannibal Hymn*, 167.

The whole land of Egypt was covered with water, even the temples of the gods. This image shows how aggressive the high flood can be and the damage it can cause to the land.

1.2. The Symbolism of Fire and Knives

Fire and Knives of Birth

According to the Egyptian vision of cosmos, the act of creation was repeated every day in the appearance of the sun in the eastern horizon. This act was preceded by the conflict with Apep the primeval enemy of the sun god Re. The sun god Re overcame his enemy by the aid of fire which burnt and destroyed Apep. In the Book of Overthrowing Apep, the fire of the sun god Re is described:

sḏt jm=k nsrt=s jm=k	Fire is in you (Apep), its flame is in you.
sḏt jm=tn ḫftjw nw(sic) *ꜥnḫ wḏꜣ snb*	Fire is in you, O enemies of the pharaoh, l.p.h,
ꜥm=s tn	And it devours you.
ṯsj tw jr=k rꜥ	Raise yourself Re!
sswn ḫftjw=k	Destroy your enemies!
rdj sḏt m ꜥꜣpp	And fire is set in Apep.[117]

Fire is envisaged here as a cosmic force which burns and destroys the enemy of Re.[118] This might also refer to the uraeus at the forehead of the sun god Re, which burns his enemies as occurs in CT spell 284.

nbt nswt	Lady of the Flames,
wrt jmjt wpt jtn jꜣḫw	The Great One who is between the horns of the sun disk of light,
psḫt m rꜣ=s	Who bites with her mouth,
wꜥḥt m sd=s	And looses with her tail.[119]

The theme of punishment by fire was developed in the Book of the Amduat, where the enemies are cooked by the fire of Re. On the lower register of the Twelfth Hour of the Book of the Amduat, the eye of Re is described as:

ntsn ḫsf ꜥꜣpp	They are those who drive off Apep,
m jꜣbt pt m-ḫt mswt nṯr	In the eastern sky after the birth of the god.
irrt=sn pw jrjt stsw n jtn ꜥꜣ	What they have done is to elevate the great sun disk,
m ꜣḫt jꜣbtt nt pt rꜥ-nb	In the eastern horizon of the sky every day.

[116] Jansen-Winkeln, *Inschriften der Spätzeit* II, 298, lines 1-6; the translation is that of Bickel, in: *L'acqua nell'antico Egitto*, 197.
[117] Faulkner, *Papyrus Bremner-Rhind*, 44, line 22, 14-5; *JEA* 23 (1937), 167.
[118] Goebs, *GM* 194 (2003), 31.
[119] *CT* IV, 34d-g (spell 284).

jn ns m jrt=f	It is 'He who burns with his eye',
psswḫftjw rꜥ m nhpw	Who boils the enemies of Re at sunrise.[120]

The eastern horizon as Re's birthplace is envisaged to be surrounded by fire. According to the Hermopolitan creation myth the sun god Re is said to be born on the Island of Fire. This island was on a hill in the midst of the Lake of Knives.[121]

The image of the fire surrounding the birthplace of sun god Re is also found in the Lake of Fire. In the Book of the Two Ways, the deceased makes a journey on the two ways to reach the Lake of Fire where he is born. The deceased who is associated with the sun god Re sails over the Lake of Fire to reach the birthplace of the sun god Re, and starts a new journey on the upper waterway to reach Osiris. The image is well illustrated on a coffin from the 21th Dynasty. On this Coffin, the sun disk is shown flanking the Lake of Fire (fig. 5).

Fig. 5. The sun disk flanks the Lake of Fire (after Niwinski, *Deir El-Bahri Coffins*, fig. 135).

Fire and knives play important roles in the myth of overcoming Apep. The Book of Apep is a magical protection of the sun god Re in his daily journey across the sky. It also includes a description of the process of creation of the sun, and a description of the conflict of Re with the powers of chaos and Apep. A spell in the Book of Overthrowing Apep reads:

ndr sp2 mnḥj	Seize! Scize! O butcher.
sḫr ḫftj nw rꜥ m ds=k	Fell the enemy of Re with your knife!
ndr sp 2 mnḥj	Seize! Seize! O butcher.
sḫr ḫftj nw <pr-ꜥ3> m ds=k	Fell the enemy of <Pharaoh> with your knife.
tpw=tn nn sbjw	These are your heads, O rebels,
ḏ3ḏ3t=k pfj nn ꜥ3pp	This is that head of yours, O Apep,
m šꜥd. n ꜥḥ3-ꜥ m ds=f	Which the warrior has cut up with his knife.
spd spdt	Be sharp! O *Sothis,*
nsrt 3sbjt ḥrj tk3	Flame of *Asbjt*, who has authority over fire,
sḫr=tn sbj m ds=tn	You will fell the rebel with your knives,
bḫn=tn wntj m ds=tn	And you will cut off *Wntj* with your knife,
šꜥd=tn ḥr ḏw=tn	You are cut off because of your evil,[122]
bḫn=tn ḥr jrjt.n=tn	You are cut up because of what you have done,
mtrw n jm=tn	There is a testimony against you,
jrtj=tn ḥr ḏw=tn	You are dealt with because of your evil.
m3ꜥ-ḫrw rꜥ r=tn	Re is triumphant over you,
ḥr bḫn=f tn	And Horus cuts you up.[123]

The spell, which is a protection to both the sun god Re and the Pharaoh, relates that Apep will be seized and cut up with the knife of the sun god Re. The image is that the enemy's head will be chopped off with a knife and then fire will be set to his body. Here both knife and fire are used as symbolic agents of destruction. All these actions will be done to Apep because of the evil he has done to the sun god Re.[124] The end of the spell relates that Horus as the son of Re will cut up Apep, and Re will be triumphant over his enemy. The next spell in the Book of Overthrowing Apep also deals with setting fire to Apep, and reads:

r3 n rdjt sḏt jm ꜥ3pp	A spell for setting fire in Apep.
ḏd mdw	Recitation:
sḏt jm=k ꜥ3pp ḫftj pfj n rꜥ	Fire is in you, O Apep, that enemy of Re,
sḫm jrt ḥr m b3 m šwt n ꜥ3pp	The Eye of Horus shall have power over the soul and shades of Apep.
wnm 3ḫt jrt ḥr m ḫftj pfj n rꜥ	The flame of the Eye of Horus shall devour that enemy of Re.
wnm 3ḫt jrt ḥr ḫftjw nb	The flame of the Eye of Horus shall eat all the enemies,
nw <pr-ꜥ3>ꜥnḫ wḏ3 snb m mt m ꜥnḫ	Of <Pharaoh> l.p.h, dead or alive.[125]

After being cut into pieces, the body of Apep is burnt by fire. The Eye of Horus has power over the shade and the soul of Apep, which might refer to the fact that by destroying these two elements, which constitute the essential elements of personality,[126] Apep will not be able to survive. At the end of the spell, the Eye of

[120] Hornung, *Amduat* I, 203; *Amduat* II, 191-2; *The Egyptian Amduat*, 375.

[121] See below, 50-1.

[122] The suffix *tn* should refer to the evil one and *Wntj* and not to *Sothis* and *Asbjt*: Faulkner, *JEA* 23 (1937), 176.

[123] Faulkner, *Papyrus Bremner-Rhind*, 45, line 22, 21-23; *JEA* 23 (1937), 168.

[124] According to Neith cosmogony in the temple of Esna, Neith was the mother of both Re and Apep, and both of them came out from the same umbilical cord: Quack, *SAK* 34 (2006), 378.

[125] Faulkner, *Papyrus Bremner-Rhind*, 45, lines 22, 24-23, 1; *JEA* 23 (1937), 168.

[126] Zandee, *Death as an Enemy*, 15.

Horus, symbol of protection will devour the enemies of the sun god Re and the Pharaoh.

The two spells mentioned above show the role that fire and knives have played in the myth of the creation and in the protection of the sun god Re against Apep. The image of fire and knives and the reference to total destruction occurs also in funerary literature. In CT spell 335, the deceased is frightened that he might be taken to the slaughter house of the followers of Osiris and be burnt with the fire of the Lake of Fire. The spell reads:

prt m ḥr	Going out by day.[127]
j rꜥ jmj swḥt=f wbn m jtn=f[128]	O Re who is in his egg, who rises in his disk,
psḏ m ꜣḫt=f[129]	Who shines in his horizon,
nbjw ḥr biꜣw=f	Who swims on his firmament,
jwtj snw=f m nṯrw	Who has no equal among the gods,
sḳd ḥr sṯsw šw	Who sails over the props (supports) of Shu,
dj ṯꜣw m hhj n rꜣ=f	Who gives winds by the blast of his mouth,
sḥḏ tꜣwj m ꜣḫw=f	Who illuminates the two lands with his rays,
nḥm=k wj m nṯr pw štꜣ jrw[130]	You shall save me from this god whose shape is secret,
ntj jnḥw[131]*=f m rnmwj mḫꜣt*	Whose eyebrows are the arms of the balance,
ḥr pf ḥsbt ꜥꜣw	(On) that day of the calculation of difference,[132]
m-bꜣḥ nb r-ḏr	In the presence of the Lord of All,
dj spḥw m isftjw	Who puts a lasso on the evildoers,
r ḥwt-nmt=f dn bꜣw	At his house of the slaughter-block, and who kills[133] the *bas*.
sj pw nṯr pn jnḥw=f m rnmwj mḫꜣt	Who is this god whose eyebrows are the arms of the balance?[134]
ḥr pw nb ḫm	He is Horus, Lord of Khem.[135]
nḥm=k wj m-ꜥ jrw sṯꜣw wsjr	You shall save me from these wound-inflictors of Osiris,
jmḫjw mr ḏbꜥw nw wsjr	The painful-fingered butchers of Osiris.
ḏd mdw jr jmḫjw nw wsjr	Recitation: as regards the butchers of Osiris,
ḏꜣḏꜣt tn pw nt wsjr	They are this tribunal of Osiris,
ḫsf ḫftjw wsjr N mꜣꜥ-ḫrw	Who punishes the enemies of Osiris N the justified.
nn sḫm dsw=sn jm=j	Their[136] knives will not have power over me.
nn hꜣj=j r wḫꜣt=sn	I will not go down to their cauldrons.[137]
nn ꜥḳ=j r ḫnw jꜣṯw=sn	I will not enter into their butchery,
ḥr ntt wj rḫ.kw rnw=sn	Because I know their names.
jnk wḏꜣ tp tꜣ ḫr rꜥ	I am prosperous on earth before Re,
mnj nfr wsjr	And moor Osiris beautifully.
nn ḫpr ꜥꜣbwt=sn jm=j	Their offerings will not be made from me,
n nꜣ n ḫr ꜥḫw=sn	Because of those who are in charge of their braziers,
jmjw ktwt=sn	And those who are in their cauldrons.
jw=j m sšm nb psḏt	I am in the train of the Lord of the Ennead,[138]
sš n ḫprw	And the scribe[139] of those who exist.
ꜥpj=j m biꜣk ng=j m smn	I fly up as a falcon, and cackle as a goose.
skj=j nḥḥ mj nḥb-kꜣw	I pass eternity like Nehbkaw.
j jtmw nb ḥwt-ꜥꜣt jtj psḏt	Oh Atum Lord of the Great Mansion,[140]Sovereign of the Ennead,
nḥm=k wj m nṯr pw ꜥnḫ m ḫrjt	Save me from this god who lives by slaughter,
ntj ḥr=f m ṯsm inm=f m rmṯ	Whose face is of a dog and his skin human,
ꜥnḫ m ḫrjt//////	And who lives by slaughter//////
jrj kꜣb pw n š n sḏt	He who is warden of[141] the windings of the Lake of Fire,[142]
ḫnp ḥꜣtyw wdj sṯꜣw	Who seizes hearts and causes injuries,
n mꜣꜣ.n.tw=f	While he is not seen.
ḏd mdw ir nṯr pn ntj	Recitation: as for this god,
ḥr=f m ṯsm inḥ=f m rmṯ	Whose face is of a dog and his skin human,
ꜥmꜥm rn=f	Swallower is his name.[143]

[127] This is the title of the spell as occurs in *CT* IV, 184a (spell 335).
[128] *CT* IV 292 (spll 335), B9C[b], B3C, B14, Sq1C, and M4C read *psḏ*.
[129] *CT* IV 294 (spell 335), B9C[b], B3C, Sq1C, and M7C read *wbn*.
[130] *CT* IV, 299a (spell 335).
[131] *jnḥ* 'eyebrow': *Wb* I, 99. 1-2.
[132] This translation is after Willems, *Chests of Life*, 241. T3Be reads *ḥr pw ḥskt ꜥꜣw* 'On this day of the chopping of the heads of the Great Ones'.
[133] *Wb* V, 463.7-11; *CDME*, 313.
[134] Gloss.
[135] An alternative gloss reads, 'He is Thoth', M4C, MS4C and L1N4, P. 302C. M57C adds; 'it is Nefertem, son of Sekhmet the Great'.
[136] As Faulkner points out, five versions read *sn* 'their', and seven texts of the twelve have *tn*: Faulkner, *Coffin Texts* I, 269.
[137] Variant, 'I will not fall to your knives': M4C, M54C, M57C and M1NY.
[138] Only B9C[b] has *nb psḏt*, while all other versions have *nb ḫt* or similar. Faulkner suggests that *nb psḏt* is a better reading, while the other readings may be corruption of *nb psḏt*: Faulkner, *Coffin Texts* I, 269, n. 85.
[139] Other versions put *r* in front of *sš*.
[140] *ḥwt-ꜥꜣt* is the name of the temple of Heliopolis where Horus was restored to his throne and was justified by the tribunal against Seth: Assmann, *STG*, 46, n. g. Some other version put *jmj* in front of *ḥwt-ꜥꜣt*
[141] Can also be translated as 'He is the keeper of the windings of the Lake of Fire'.
[142] Can also mean 'who goes round the Lake of Fire', or 'he is the guardian of the Lake of Fire'.
[143] *CT* IV, 293-314d (spell 335).

In this spell the deceased asks Atum to save him from the butchers of Osiris, with pain-giving fingers. They cause injuries with their knives and take the unworthy to their cauldrons.[144] The image of being cut into pieces and taken to the cauldrons resembles the same image of being cut up into pieces and setting fire to the body as occurs in the Book of Overthrowing Apep mentioned above. In both texts knives and fire are used as symbolic agents of total destruction.

The vignettes of Book of the Dead Chapter 137B shows the deceased standing before Osiris holding a fire pot with two flames emerging from it. The chapter is for lighting the lamp,[145] and forms a part of Amun Temple Liturgy.[146] The vignettes of this chapter resemble the scenes from the daily temple liturgy from the temple of Seti I at Abydos.[147] In this ritual the lamps are presented for both the deceased and the god as means by which he can get rid of Seth. The text reads:

r3 n st3 tk3 n N	Spell for lighting a lamp for N:
jj jrt ḥr ḥḏt	The bright Eye of Horus has come,
jj jrt ḥr 3ḫt	The shining Eye of Horus has come
jj.t(j) m ḥtp psḏ.t(j) mj rꜥ m 3ḫt	Coming in peace and shining like Re in the horizon,
dr=s sḫmw stš	It shall drive out the powers of Seth,
tp rdwj n jnj sj	Before the feet of the one who brought it,
swt jṯj st3=s r=f	He is the one who takes its flame against him.[148]

Here the lamp is envisaged as the Eye of Horus, which is presented to both the god and the deceased. The ritual of lighting a lamp takes place before dawn in the temple, at the moment when Re rises in the sky. The lamp being lit is compared with the sun in the horizon. The light of the lamp, which is here compared with fire, is the power that drives out darkness and also the fire that is directed to the enemy of the god and the deceased.[149]

Fire has both negative and positive forces; it is the power on which the whole world lives, and it is the flame that kills and burns Apep. In Chapter 149 of the Book of the Dead the deceased who addresses the third mound says:

j3t nt 3ḫw	The Mound of Spirits,
jwtt sḳdwt ḥr=s	Which is not sailed on,
jw=s ḫr 3ḫw	It is under spirits,
jw ns=s m 3ḫt nt bs	And its flame is from the burning fire.
j j3t twj nt 3ḫw ḥr=ṯn m-ḫrw	Oh this Mound of Spirits, whose faces are downcast,
ḏsr w3wt=ṯn swꜥb j3wt=ṯn	Your roads are cleared; your mounds are purified.
wḏḏ.t(w) jrj=tn pw jn wsjr n ḏt	It is commanded by Osiris that you do that forever,
jnk///// dšrt jmjt wpt j3ḫw	I am …..Red Crown, which is between the horns of the sun-shine,
sꜥnḫt tmw m hh n r3=s	Which causes the whole world to live with the flame of its mouth,
nḥmt rꜥ m-ꜥ ꜥ3pp	And saves Re from Apep.[150]

The passage describes a mound called the mound of spirits over which no one can travel. The mound has spirits and burning flames over it. The deceased asks the mound to do for him what Osiris has commanded to be done. The last passage may refer to the cobra at the forehead of Re which burns his enemies and saves him from Apep.[151]

In the Book of the Two Ways, the guardians of the gates are equipped with fire and knives ready to kill and burn the unworthy. In CT spell 1057 on coffin BIC, the keeper who guards the bend of the Lake of Fire is represented as a hound with long ears and holds a knife in both hands. The text reads:

mds jrj š	The Sharp One, the keeper of the Lake,
jrj ḳ3b pw pw	This is the keeper of this bend.[152]

In CT spell 1054 the Lake of Fire is called Aatiu, and is written with the determinative of a knife, [153] which also refers to the destructive nature of this lake. As a place of passage, it is envisaged as a dangerous place, where no one can escape its fire. It is also a true place of passage, which takes the deceased to an advanced stage in the netherworld. The lake's fire is envisaged as an ambivalent force. It is a place where the sinners are burnt, and it is also a true place of passage. In the Underworld Books, fire and knives play also important roles in the protection of the sun god Re in his journey across the caverns and gates of the netherworld.

Book of the Amduat
The Seventh Hour

In middle register of the Seventh Hour of the Book of the Amduat, the journey of the sun god Re comes to a critical point in its progression through the netherworld

[144] For the full comment on this spell and its role in passing the place of passage over the Lake of Fire, see below, 91-3.
[145] The vignettes of this chapter occur also on the walls of TT 218 and TT 3: Saleh, *Das Totenbuch in den Thebanischen Beamtengräbern*, 75-6. On the relation between BD 137B and the temple liturgy of Amun, see Gee, in: *Totenbuch-Forschungen*, 82-5.
[146] The liturgy occurs on Papyrus Berlin 3055, *Hieratische Papyrus aus den Königlichen Museen zu Berlin*, pl. 1, lines 2-5.
[147] Gee, in: *Totenbuch-Forschungen*, 82.
[148] Naville, *TB*, Kapitel 137B, pl. CLI, lines 1-3.
[149] Gee, in: *Totenbuch-Forschungen*, 85.
[150] Naville, *TB*, Kapitel 149, pl. CLXVIII, lines 17-21.
[151] For the mounds in the Netherworld, see Quirke, in: *Mysterious lands*, 161-81
[152] *CT* VII, 309b (spell 1057).
[153] On the Lake of Fire as place of passage in the Book of the Two Ways, see below, 77.

over the Sandbank of Apep. The middle register contains five scenes. In the first scene the sun god Re is shown standing in a shrine encircled by the protective snake Mehen. The protective deities in this Hour are Isis who stands at the prow of the barque facing Apep, Sia (*sjꜣ*), the Eldest Magician (*ḥkꜣw smsw*), Mehen (*mḥn*), Wepwawet, Horus of the Fragrance (*ḥr-ḥnkw*), Bull of Maat (*kꜣ mꜣꜥt*), The Vigilant One (*nhs*), Hu (*ḥw*) and Guide of the Barque (*ẖrp wjꜣ*). The text above the barque reads:

sḳdd nṯr pn ꜥꜣ m njwt tn	This Great God sails in this city,
m wꜣt nt ḳrrt wsjr	On the path of the cavern of Osiris.[154]

The next scene shows the enemy of the sun god Re Apep in the shape of a huge serpent, depicted stabbed with knives by two deities. At the head of Apep stands the goddess *srḳt ḥtjt* 'She who lets the throat breathe', and the inscription at the tail of Apep describes the god standing there as *ḥrj-dsw=f* 'He-who-is-above-his-knives'. The text describing Apep and his Sandbank reads:

ṯs nḥꜣ-ḥr m dwꜣt	The Sandbank of Horrible-of-Face in the netherworld,
mḥ 440 pw m ꜣwt=f	It is 440 cubits in its length,
jw=f mḥ=f sw m ḳꜣbw=f	He (Apep) fills it with his coils,
jrj.t(w) ꜥḏt=f r=f	And his slaughter is made against him,
jwtj ꜥpp nṯr pn ꜥꜣ ḥr=f	Without this Great God passing by him,
sṯnm=f wꜣt r=f r tpḥt wsjr	When he turns away from him towards the cavern of Osiris.
sḳdd nṯr pn m njwt tn	This Great God sails in this city,
m sšmw n mḥn	In the image of the Mehen serpent.[155]

Then follow four punishing goddesses, holding knives in their hands and watching over Apep. The inscriptions over them designate them as *dmḏjt* 'She-who-binds-together', *dnjt* 'She-who-cuts', *njkt* 'She-who-punishes' and *ḥtmjt* 'She-who-destroys'. The text above these goddesses read:

nṯrwt pw njkjwt ꜥꜣpp m dwꜣt	These are the goddesses who punish Apep in the netherworld,
ḫsfwt jḫt nt ḫftjw nw rꜥ	And repel the assaults of these enemies of Re.
wnn=sn m sḫr pn ḥr njkwt=sn	They are like this, under their punishing knives,
njk=sn ꜥꜣpp m dwꜣt rꜥ-nb	And they punish Apep in the netherworld daily.[156]

[154] Hornung, *The Egyptian Amduat*, 228.
[155] Hornung, *The Egyptian Amduat*, 231.
[156] Hornung, *The Egyptian Amduat*, 233.

The next scene contains four coffers, each with two human heads and a knife on its lid. Hornung argues that these coffers represent the burial places of the sun god Re in his different forms. The inscriptions on the four coffers designate them as *ḥrj sšmw jtmw* 'which contains the image of Atum', *ḥrj sšmw ḫprj* 'which contains the image of Khepri', *ḥrj sšmw rꜥ* 'which contains the image of Re' and *ḥrj sšmw wsjr* 'which contains the image of Osiris'.[157] The text which describes this section reads:

jrww pw štꜣw n dwꜣt	These are the mysterious forms of the netherworld,
ḥnw tꜣ tpw štꜣwt	The caskets of the earth, the heads of the mysteries;
wnn=sn m pḥwj ṯs pn	They are at the end of this Sandbank.
prj tpw dsw jmjw=sn	The heads and knives which are in them come out,
sḏm=sn ḥkꜣ nḥꜣ-ḥr	When they hear the enchantment of 'The Horrible of Face',
ꜥm.ḫr=sn sšmw=sn	Then they swallow their images,
m-ḫt ꜥpp nṯr pn ꜥꜣ njwt tn	After this Great God passes this city.[158]

The Seventh Hour of the Amduat represents the place of passage of the sun god Re over the Sandbank of Apep (fig. 6).

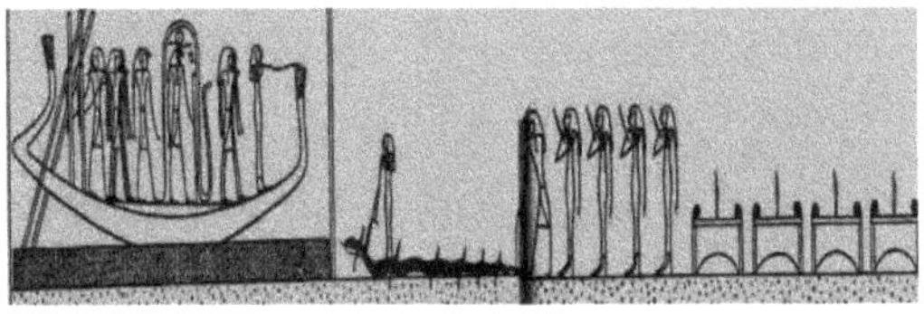

Fig. 6. The middle register in the Seventh Hour of the Book of the Amduat
(after Hornung, *The Egyptian Amduat*, 214-5).

The same theme occurs also in the Book of the Dead Chapter 39. The chapter is a spell against Apep the enemy of the sun god Re, and reads:

rꜣ n ḫsf rrk m ẖrt-nṯr	Spell for repelling Rerek in the necropolis.
ḥꜣ=k sbn jntj m ꜥꜣpp pf	Backwards! Glide away! Withdraw then! O that Apep,
js mḥj=k r š nw	Go and swim to the pool of Nun,
r bw wḏt jt=k jrj.t(w) šꜥt=k jm	To the place where your father has ordered your slaughter to be carried out.
ḥrjw r msḫnt twj nt rꜥ	Be away from that birthplace of Re,
jmjt sdꜣw=k	In which you tremble.
jnk rꜥ jmj sdꜣw.n=f	I am Re who is in the one who

[157] Hornung, *The Egyptian Amduat*, 234.
[158] Hornung, *The Egyptian Amduat*, 235.

	is trembled at (?),[159]
ḥꜣ=k sbj m dsw sšp=f	Backward rebel, at the knives of his light!
ḫr.n rꜥ mdw=k	Re has rejected your case.
pnꜥ ḥr=k jn nṯrw	Your face is overturned by the gods,
šdj.t(w) ḥꜣtj=k jn mꜣfdt	Your heart is torn out by Mafdet,
wdj.t(w) ḳꜣsw=k jn ḥddt	You are put into bonds by Hededet,
wdj.t(w) nkn=k jn mꜣꜥt	And your execution is inflicted by Maat,
sḫr=s tw jmjwtj	She overthrows you midway.
ḫr sbn ꜥꜣpp ḫftj n rꜥ	Fall down! Glide away! Apep, enemy of Re,
j. rwj ꜥd m jꜣbt pt	Leave the edge in the east of the sky,
ḫr ḫrw ḳrj nhmhm	At the thundering sound of roaring.
wn sbꜣw ꜣḫt tp-ꜥ rꜥ	The gates of the horizon open before Re,
prj=f	That he may go out.[160]

Here is a spell against Apep enemy of the sun god Re who is ordered to swim to Nun where a slaughter will be carried out against him in the birthplace of Re.[161] He is also asked to leave the eastern edge of the horizon where he will be slaughtered with knives. The eastern edge of the sky is also the place where Apep is active, and the place where the sun rises every day.[162] Mutilation of the body of Apep will be carried out by Mafdet and Maat, who might be compared with the crew of the barque of Re in the Book of the Amduat. The punishment by Mafdet occurs also in the Pyramid Texts and also in BD 149.[163] The punishment is also carried out by Hededet, who is another manifestation of the scorpion goddess Serqet. Those on the road, as Borghouts argues, might represent the guardians along the water roads over which the sun god Re sails in his boat.[164]

It is interesting to note the pun in *mds*, where the rays of the sun are described as knives that penetrate into the body of Apep. In summer, the heat of the midday sun in Egypt can beat on the backs of people like knives. It is also important to note that the Seventh Hour represents the journey of the sun god Re in its peak, where he is still in the middle of the sky. It is a striking description of the effect of the sun rays entering the body of the enemy.[165] This theme is also known in Middle Kingdom Coffin Texts. The rays of the sun in CT spell 414 are described as:

mk ḥwt prj m pt	Look, a flame has come out from the sky,
m ḫnw tpḥt sbj	Into the interior of the cavern of the rebel.[166]

The Eleventh Hour

In the Eleventh Hour of the Book of the Amduat on the lower register, Horus is depicted leaning on a staff with a sun disk on his head, and a short stick in the shape of a uraeus in his right hand. In front of Horus stands a snake goddess called *sṯj ḥḥw* 'She-who-burns-millions', and she spits her flames to the pits with the sinners in front of her. The first five pits are guarded by fire goddesses holding knives in their hands, who spit fire into the pits. In the first pit there are three sinners guarded by a goddess with the head of a lioness and called *ḥrjt ktwwt=s* 'She-who-is-above-her-kettles'. The second pit has three *ḫwt* 'corpses' of sinners, and a goddess is watching over them called *ḥrjt ḥꜣdw=s* 'She- who-is-above-her pits.' The sinners in the third pit are depicted as *bꜣ* birds and are watched over by a goddess called *nknjt* 'She-who-severs.' The fourth pit has the *šwwt* 'shadows' of the sinners, and the goddess who watches over it is called *ḥrjt nmwt=s* 'She-who-is-above-her-slaughtering blocks'. The fifth pit has the *tpw* 'heads' of the sinners and is guarded by a goddess called *ḥrjt sfw=s* 'She-who-is-above-her-knives'. The sixth and final pit has no guardian, and the sinners inside it are described as *sḫdw* 'Those-who-are- upside down' (fig. 7).[167] The text which describes the scene reads:

wḏ mdw jn ḥm n nṯr pn	Orders given by the Majesty of this god (Horus),
jrj.t(w) šꜥt ḥwjw jt=f wsjr	That a slaughter should be made (to) those who strike his father Osiris.
ḫwt ḫftjw ḥꜥw mwt	The corpses of the enemies, the limbs of the Dead,
sḫdw jnṯw šmt jrw ḥtmw	Those who are upside down, who are prevented from going, and the shapes of the annihilated.
prj=j jm=f	I have come forth from him,
ḥwj jt=j m-ḫt bꜣgj=f	And (now) my father strikes (back) after he has been weary!
njk n ḫwt=ṯn m njkjt	Punishment for your corpses by the punisher (knife)!
ḥtm n bꜣw=ṯn	Destruction for your *bꜣw*!
hbjt n šwwt=ṯn	Trampling down for your shadows!
jsḳ n tpw=ṯn	Severing for your heads!
n ḫpr=ṯn sḫd=ṯn	You have not come into being;

159 This might refer to Re who is encircled by the Mehen snake in his journey through the underworld.
160 Naville, *TB*, Kapitel 39, pl. LIII, lines 2-7. The translation uses Borghouts, *Book of the Dead [39]*, 12-3.
161 Borghouts, *Book of the Dead [39]*, 57.
162 Borghouts, *Book of the Dead [39]*, 35.
163 *Pyr* 230c which reads 'your mouth is closed by *šst* (*tmm rꜣ=k jn šst*), the mouth of *šst* is closed by Mafdet (*tmm rꜣ n šst jn mꜣfdt*), for BD Chapter 149, see below, 22-4.
164 Borghouts, *Book of the Dead [39]*, 34.
165 Borghouts, *Book of the Dead [39]*, 33.
166 *CT* V, 414d (spell 414). The rays of Re are also the power which overthrows Apep. In P. Bremner Rhind, a spell reads: Apep the enemy of Re is overthrown (*sḫr ꜥꜣpp ḫft rꜥ*) in the storm under the rays of Re (*m ẖꜣpt ḫr psḏ rꜥ*): Faulkner, *Papyrus Bremner-Rhind*, 46, line 23.9.
167 Hornung, *The Egyptian Amduat*, 344.

	You are upside down;
n sṯs=ṯn ḥr.n=ṯn m ḫ3dw=ṯn	You do not rise, since you have fallen into your pits.
n bnj=ṯn n d3=ṯn	May you do not escape, and you will not become loose.[168]
3mwt jmjt stj ḥḥw r=ṯn	The fire which is in 'She who burns millions' is against you.
w3w3t ḥrjt ktwwt=s r=ṯn	The fiery glow of 'She who is above her kettles' is against you.
nswt ḥrjt ḫ3dw=s r=ṯn	The flame of 'She who is above her pits' is against you.
bḫḫw jmj r3 n ḥrjt nmwt=s r=ṯn	The heat from the mouth of 'She who is above her slaughtering blocks' is against you.
ds jm=ṯn n ḥrt sfsw=s	The knife of 'She who is above her knives' is in you.
jrj=s ʿḏt=ṯn wdj=s šʿt=ṯn	She makes your massacre and commits your slaughter,
n m33=ṯn ʿnḫw tp t3 ḏt	And you do not see those living upon earth forever.
wnn=sn m sḫr pn m dw3t	They are like this in the netherworld.
jw wḏ.tw ʿḏt=sn rʿ nb	Their slaughter is ordered every day,
jn ḥm n ḥr dw3tj	By the Majesty of Horus of the Netherworld.[169]

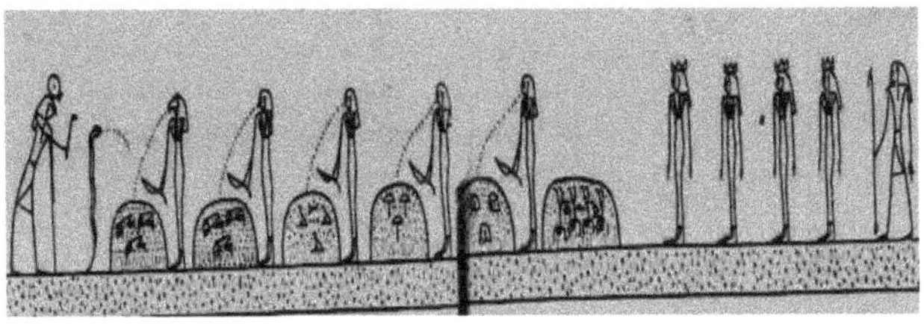

Fig. 7. The lower register in the Eleventh Hour of the Amduat (after Hornung, *The Egyptian Amduat*, 324-5).

The text is a speech by Horus of the Netherworld to the enemies of Osiris. The punishment includes the destruction of the essential parts of the body, including heads, souls and shadows. The goddesses who stand watching over the pits carry knives in their hands and spit fire in these pits. Both fire and knives are used here as tools of destruction and anyone who would fall to them will suffer punishment. This punishment will be repeated daily according to the orders of Horus of the Netherworld. The image of the slaughtering block and fire also resembles the same image, which occurs in CT spell 335 mentioned above.

[168] *CDME*, 309.

[169] Hornung, *The Egyptian Amduat*, 345-6.

Book of the Earth

On the fourth register of section D, scene 14 in the Book of Earth, both fire and knives are used as tools of punishment for the sinners (fig. 8). In the scene on the right hand side there are two arms depicted supporting a kettle in which the heads and the fleshes of the sinners are placed. Under the kettle there is a head which spits fire under the kettle to heat it. The same scene is also repeated on the left hand side. The arms under the boiler on the left side are called 'the arms of fire' and 'the arms of the slaughter place'. Beside each kettle stands a guardian holding a knife in his hand. The guardian on the right side is called 'the cutter', while the guardian on the left is called the 'the one who slaughters'. Between the two boilers there are two goddesses depicted, one called 'the one of the beard, and the other called 'the one of the heart'. Both goddesses place their hands on a heart sign bowl.[170]

Fig. 8. The fourth register in section D in the Book of the Earth (after Hornung, *Unterweltbücher*, 477).

Book of the Caverns

In the Book of Caverns, there is also a representation of a kettle in the sixth register of the fifth division. In this scene, there are two arms also supporting a kettle in which there are the *bas* and the shadows of the sinners being burnt.[171] There are two goddesses blowing in the fire and called the 'the Flaming One' and 'the Burning One'. There is a cryptographic inscription between the two arms refers to the arms as coming out from the Duat.[172] The accompanying text is an address to the two goddesses describing them as the Great Flame (*ʿ3t sḏt*), and Powerful Heat (*sḫmt rkḥ*), who heat their kettle with the bones of the enemies (fig. 9).

[170] Hornung, *Unterweltbücher*, 477. Another example for knives and fire as tools of punishment is found in the Book of the Caverns in the third register of the fifth division, where there are two arms coming out from the earth supporting a kettle in which there are sinners with heads chopped off and hands tied behind their back. Under the kettle there are two snakes heating it with flames coming from their mouths. The cobras are called the 'the One who stands, and 'the Burning One': Hornung, *Unterweltbücher*, 380.

[171] In the hypostyle hall in the temple of Edfou, the king is shown holding a stick in his hand while four figures of enemies are burnt in fire in what might be described as a kettle. Horus stands on a pedestal watching over the whole operation. The text which accompanies the scene realtes that these enemies are punished by the king for what they have done against him: Derchain, *GM* 220 (2009), 30.

[172] Hornung, *Unterweltbücher*, 384; *Höllenvorstellungen*, 24, pl. II; Verhoeven, *Grillen, Kochen, Backen*, 149.

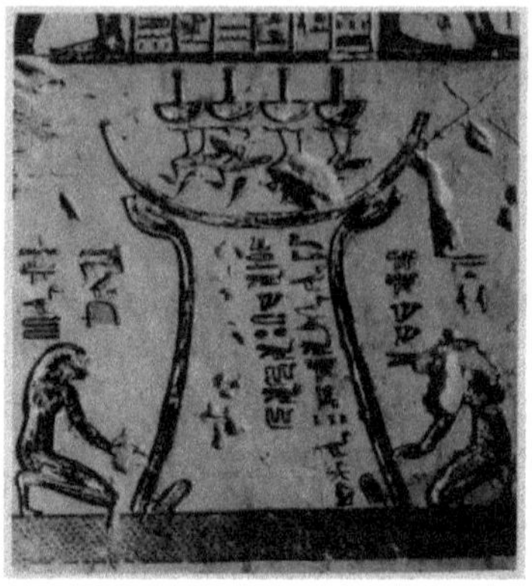

Fig. 9. The kettle with the shades and bas of the sinners (after Piankoff, *Tomb of Ramesses VI*, vol. 1, 115, fig. 19).

Book of the Gates

On the lower register of the Fourth Hour of the Book of the Gates, scene 22, four fiery pits for the punishment of the enemies of Osiris are depicted. They are painted in red and guarded by four keepers escorted by Horus, who holds a scepter and *ꜥnḫ* sign in his hands. The four guardians are called *ḥrj ḥtmw* 'those who are in charge of destruction'. The text above the scene reads:

jn ḥr n nn n nṯrw	Horus speaks to these gods:
nḏrw.n=ṯn ḫftjw jt=j	You have seized the enemies of my father,
ḫnpw.n=ṯn r ḥꜣdw=ṯn	And you have dragged[173] (them) to your pits,
ḥr nn mr jrj.n=sn r ꜥꜣ	Because of this evil which they have done against the Great One,
gmm. tw msj wj	Who has been found, and who has begotten me.[174]
ḫrt=ṯn n=ṯn m dwꜣt	Your requirement belongs to you in the Duat,
sꜣwtj ḥꜣdw bḫḫjw m wḏw rꜥ	Guard the pits[175] and the fire according to the commands of Re.
ḏwj=j n=ṯn swt js jrj m ḫrw=ṯn	I call upon you, that he is the one who deals with your affairs,
wnn nṯr pn ꜥḥꜥ ḥr tp nn n ḥꜣdw	And this god will be standing in charge of these pits.[176]

Horus speaks to the guardians of the fiery pits asking them to catch the enemies of his father Osiris, and to punish them for the evil they have done against Osiris. They watch over these pits according to the commands of Re. At the end of the passage, Horus asks the guardians of the fiery pits to keep watching their pits.[177]

The Lake of Fire was also considered as a place of punishment for the sinners, where on one of the Papyri of third Intermediate Period; the sinners are shown punished in the Lake of Fire (fig. 10).

Fig. 10. The sinners are burnt in the Lake of Fire (after Piankoff, *Mythological Papyri*, pl. 12).

1. 3. Fire and Nightmares

Fire was used as a magical protection against bad spirits and nightmares.[178] For instance, three texts dealing with nightmares are preserved in Papyrus Leiden I 348 vs. 2,[179] Ostracon Gardiner 363,[180] and Papyrus Chester Beatty III, r. 10.10-19.[181] The three spells deal with nightmares as external forces, which threaten the sleeper, and not as psychological phenomena.[182]

In Chester Beatty III Papyrus, nightmares are caused by *ḏwwt* and *ṯmsw* which were created by Seth. The spell is pronounced as interaction between the dreamer as Horus, and Isis as healer. The dreamer is the son who has just woken up, who calls upon his mother Isis for help. Isis as mother asks him not to tell his dream, to be silent, and promises to drive away the demons, and bad dreams by the aid of fire and flame. The spell reads:

> Words spoken by a man who wakes up on his place:
> (Dreamer):
> "Come to me! Come to me <my> mother Isis!
> Behold, I see something far away from me, as something that touches me."
> (Isis):
> "Here I am, <my> son Horus.
> Do not divulge that, which you saw,

---

173 *ḫnp* can also mean to catch (*Wb* III, 290. 5-17), but drag makes better sense here.

174 There is a pun here, where the one who has been found is Osiris, and as Hornung argues, this might refer to the body of Osiris when it was found in Nedit: Hornung, *Pfortenbuch* II, 120.

175 Can also mean fish trap: *Wb* III, 36. 4-6.

176 Hornung, *Pfortenbuch* I, 136-8; *Pfortenbuch* II, 119-20; Zeidler, *Pfortenbuchstudien* II, 108-9.

177 Hornung, *Pfortenbuch* II, 120. For more discussion on the punishment of the sinners by fire, see Hornung, *Höllenvorstellungen*, 25-8.

178 Szpakowska, *JARCE* 40 (2003), 120.

179 Borghouts, *The Magical Texts of P. Leiden I 348*.

180 Ritner, *JARCE* 27 (1990), 25-41.

181 Gardiner, *HPBM*.

182 Szpakowska, *JARCE* 40 (2003), 121.

(In order that) your numbness may be completed,
Your dreams retire,
And fire goes forth against that which terrifies you.
Behold, I have come that I may see you,
That I may drive out your bad things,
And that I may extirpate all the ailments."
(Dreamer):
"Hail, O you good dream, which is seen in the night and in the day.
Drive out all the ailments and bad things, which Seth, son on Nut created.
As Re is vindicated against his enemies, I am vindicated against my enemies."
This spell is to be spoken by a man who wakes up on his place, after he has first been given *pesen* bread and some fresh herbs, (which have been) marinated in beer and incense. The man's face should be rubbed with them; all the bad dreams that he has seen will be driven out. (*P. Ch.B.* III, r.10. 10-19).[183]

As typical of magical spells, this spell includes recitation and physical treatment, where the spell is recited and the man's face is rubbed with *pesen* bread and fresh herbs marinated in beer and incense.[184] The spell describes in detail the bad dreams and how the sleeper can be protected against them. At the end of the spell, the effective treatment is prescribed for the dreamer. The title of the spell states that the spell should be recited by a man 'who wakes up on his own place' (*s rs=f ḥr st=f*), [185] which refers to the sleeper while he is still on his bed, and receives the treatment with the herbs and bread. Horus as the patient refers to the myth of Isis and Horus, in which the mother Isis shields her fatherless son Horus against suffering and dangers.[186]

In P. Leiden I 348, the dreamer calls upon the protective deities like Atum and Wadjet to protect him, and the recitation of the spell goes as follows:

Book of Driving out Terrors which come in order to descend upon a man in the night:
'Put <your> face backwards, when you raise your head, together with your *ba*, your shapes, your corpses, your magic, together with your shapes, your forms.
Oh male *akhs,* female *akhs*, male dead (*mwt*), female dead. Male adversaries (*ḏ3j*), female adversaries in the sky and in the earth:
It is the Lord of All, and it is those who are, it is Atum, it is Wadjet the Lady of the Dread in the great barque,
It is the Child,
It is the Lord of Truth,
It is the Lord of Truth,
It is the figure of Atum on the upper road,
It is the consuming flame by Sia, Lord of Heaven.
The earth is on fire, the sky is on fire, the people and the gods are on fire.
You say you are hidden from it (but) 'it is come'— as its name in truth.
Beware of the flame which comes forth from the Two Horizons!'
Words to be said over the image which is in drawing, made upon a choice piece of linen, to be placed (on) the throat of a man until he is seen to be quiet.[187]

The spell includes here references to the hostile powers that cause nightmares, which comes from the earth and the sky. They fall upon the sleeper at night while he is asleep. It is also directed to all the powers of nightmares whether male or female, and asks the demons to be backwards and to turn their head or face away from the sleeper. Borghouts argues that when the demon is asked to turn his face backwards, that is because the dreamer wants to avoid falling victim to the evil eye, which might affect the sleeper.[188] In the spell for mother and child the demon's face is turned around, and is described as 'the one who came in the utter darkness, who entered creeping, and his nose is behind him and his face is turned back.'[189] Not only the face should be turned back, but also the whole manifestations of the demons are also prohibited from turning forward; his *ba*, his shape, his body, and his magical powers.[190]

The dreamer calls upon the gods to help him repulsing the demons. These gods are Osiris, Atum, Wadjet, the Child, and the Lord of Truth.[191] The vignettes which accompany this spell contain a representation of a barque on which the image of Osiris is depicted flanked by Isis on the right side and Nephthys on the left side and both goddesses adore Osiris. On the left side of the barque, Anubis is depicted holding an object in his hand which might represent a mummy.[192] Borghouts argues that although the titles of these deities are obscure, they might be identified with the deities participating in the night journey of the sun god Re in his barque.[193]

[183] The translation is that of Szpakowska, *JARCE* 40 (2003), 120; *Behind Closed Eyes*, 163.
[184] For using mortuary literature within magical, healing, and defensive spells as occurs in P. BM EA 10081, see most recently, Bommas, *ZÄS* 131 (2004), 109-112.
[185] Szpakowska, *Behind Closed Eyes*, 164.
[186] Nordh, *Aspects of Ancient Egyptian Curses and Blessings*, 57.
[187] The translation is that of Szpakowska, *Behind Closed Eyes*, 168.
[188] Borghouts, *The Magical Texts of P. Leiden I 348*, 176-8.
[189] Papyrus Berlin 3027, C 1, 9-2, 6 in Erman, *Zaubersprüche für Mutter und Kind*; Translation in Borghouts, *The Magical Texts of P. Leiden I 348*, 41, 65.
[190] Szpakowska, *Behind Closed Eyes*, 169.
[191] For an expanded argument on the protective deities upon whom the dreamer call for help, see Eschweiler, *Bildzauber im alten Ägypten*, 59-63.
[192] Eschweiler, *Bildzauber im alten Ägypten*, 67.
[193] Borghouts, *The Magical Texts of P. Leiden I 348*, 32. Borghouts noted that there is an illustration of a barque, which resembles the

Fire here is envisaged as a cosmic force that comes forth from the two horizons and will save the dreamer from the demons and bad spirits. The whole cosmos is envisaged as surrounded by fire and the bad spirits and demons who visit the sleeper in his dream will not be able to escape this fire.[194]

The source of the fire is 'Sia Lord of Heaven' who, as Borghouts argues, might be identified with the sun god Re.[195] The dreamer calls upon Wadjet, who is as a cobra is associated with fire, to protect him from the demons. The association between the snake goddess and fire is well represented in the spell under discussion. The cobra goddess is known as being ready to strike and kill with her piercing gaze, and spits fire with her fiery flame. The identification between the snake and fire is well known since the Pyramid Texts, where PT spell 273 reads:

jw k3w Wnjs ḥ3=f	The *kas* of Unas are behind him,
jw ḥmswt=f ẖr rdwj=f	And his *hemsut* are under his feet.
jw nṯrw=f tp=f jʿrwt=f m wpt=f	His gods are upon him, his Uraei are at his brow.
jw sšmwt wnjs m-ḥ3t=f	The guiding-snake of Unas is at his forehead:
ptrt b3 3ẖt n ṯbs	The spier-out of *ba* (s), the fiery snake for burning.[196]

The cobra or the snake goddess is also known to protect the bedrooms and the sleepers in a bedroom. P. Chester Beatty VIII, vs. I, 1-2, 4 reads:

> NN born of NN has conjured (*šnj*) the widow. He is a tomcat. NN born of NN has conjured the chink. He is a female falcon. NN born of NN has conjured the bolts. He is Ptah. NN born of NN has conjured the hole. He is Nehb-kau. NN born of NN has conjured the hiding-place (*jmnw*). He is the one whose name is hidden (*jmn rn*=f). NN born of NN has conjured the cross timbers. He is the Master of mysteries. NN born of NN has conjured his (own) place, his room, and his bed. He has conjured the four noble ladies (*špswt*) in whose mouth are their flame and whose fire goes behind them to chase away any male enemy (*ḫftj*), any female enemy, any male dead (*mt*), and any female dead who are in the body of NN born of NN. They will not come for him in the night, by day or at any time. They will not fall [upon] the four noble ladies [.....] their flame in their mouth [.....] rushes.[197]

Ostracon Gardiner 363 from the Ramesside Period reads:

> Oh male adversary [female adversary, male ghost, female ghost] be far from [me (?)...]. Oh dead man, dead woman, without coming (?). He will not go forth with face forward, with limbs as [sound] limbs, (since) his heart is destined for the Evening Meal of the One in the act of striking. NN born of NN has [extracted] your hearts, O dead ones. [He] has taken your hearts, O dead men and dead women. To the striker he has offered them [for] his sustenance of (his) limbs. As for you, you will not live; your limbs are [his(?)] offering cakes. You will not escape from [the four Noble Ladies (?)] from the fortress of Horus who *jmj-šnwt*. Recite over 4 [ura]ei made of pure [......] with flames in their mouths. One is placed in [each] corner [of every room/ of any bedroom] in which there is a man or a woman sleeping. (O. Gardiner 363, recto, 1-11).[198]

The spell combines both the power of the cobra and fire, which means total destruction for the demons of the nightmares. Ritner argues that the striker or the striking power is the uraeus itself.[199] The sleeper will be protected from the hostile demons by placing four clay cobras at the four corners of each bedroom.[200] The four corners designate the four cardinal points as suggested by the vignettes in Chapter 151 of the Book of the Dead. The snake will strike and spits fire against the demons that might come from any of the four cardinal points.[201]

1. 4. Barriers and Portals surrounded by Fire and Knives

The Egyptian religious literature is full of examples of buildings, barriers and gates surrounded by fire and knives. The best examples can be found in the Book of the Two Ways,[202] Coffin Text spell 336,[203] and BD 149. BD 149 names fourteen mounds which the deceased has to pass in his way to the netherworld. These mounds are given numbers and are arranged from the first to the fourteenth. The seventh mound is described:

---

nšmt barque of Osiris, and he argues that since the barque of Osiris plays a crucial role in such kind of texts, it is not surprising to find that this barque can act as a divine being. The deceased by calling upon these gods he is asking the otherworld powers to come and rescue him since he is in a state like death: Szpakowska, *Behind Closed Eyes*, 169.

194 Szpakowska, *Behind Closed Eyes*, 170.

195 *The Magical Texts of P. Leiden I 348*, 182-4.

196 PT spell 273=*Pyr.* § 396a-c; the translation is after Eyre, *Cannibal Hymn*, 7.

197 The translation is that of Borghouts, *Ancient Egyptian Magical Texts*, 10-11.

198 Gardiner and Černý, *Hieratic Ostraca*, 29. The translation is that of Ritner, *JARCE* 27 (1990), 25-6.

199 Ritner, *JARCE* 27 (1990), 36.

200 Szpakowska, *JARCE* 40 (2003), 120.

201 Ritner, in: Szpakowska (ed.), *Through a Glass Darkly*, 205-17.

202 For gates and barriers surrounded by creatures holding knives in the Book of the Two Ways, see below, 74-5.

203 For the content and description of the three portals in CT spell 336, see blow, 93-5.

ḏd mdw jn N	Recitation by N:
j jss pwj ḥrj r mꜣꜣ	Oh This Ises,[204] which is far out of sight,
jw hh=f m sḏt	Its blast is of fire,
jw ḥfꜣw jm=f rrk rn=f	(And) there is a snake[205] in it, its name is Rerek.
nj-sw mḥ 7 m ꜣw n psḏ=f	It is seven cubits in length of its back,
ꜥnḫ=f m ꜣḫw	And it lives on spirits,
ḥtm m ꜣḫw=sn	Who are equipped with their magical powers.
ḫꜣ rrk jmj jss	Get back Rerek who is in Ises!
psḥ m r=f	Who bites with his mouth,
gbꜣ[206] *m irwt=fj*	And binds with his eyes.
sḏ ḳsw=k	Your bones shall be broken.
bdš mtwt=k	Your poison shall be weak.
nn jwt=k r=j	You shall not come against me.
nn hꜣb mtwt=k jm=j	You shall not send your poison in me.
ḫr sḏr šmmt=k m tꜣ	Fall! Lie down! May your hot rage (fever) be in the ground,
sptj=kj m bꜣbꜣw	Your lips shall be in the hole.
ḫr kꜣ=f n sḏḥ ṯs pḫr	His *Ka* falls to the snake *sḏḥ*[207] and vice-versa.[208]
ḫwj.kw	I am protected,
ḥsḳ.t(w) tp=k jn mꜣfdt	And your head is chopped off by Mafdet.[209]

The seventh mound is of Ises, and it is fiery and out of human sight. There is a snake there called Rerek and eats even the equipped spirits of the dead. The mountain represents a place of passage to be crossed by the deceased before he gains entrance to further roads and portals of the netherworld. The passer directs his speech to the mountain itself, to overcome the power of the snake.[210] The connection between the snake Rerek, fire and poison is made explicit. Being bitten by a snake is like being burnt by fire, which is obvious from the pun in *šmmt* which can mean both heat and fever.[211]

The image here is of a huge snake which lies on a mountain, waiting and ready to direct his poison to anyone who passes by his locality. Rerek as a snake appears to share his characteristics with other serpents of the netherworld. These serpents dominate certain territories and localities, and share in most cases the same characteristics of Apep, the cosmic opponent of Re.[212] The tradition of the role of a serpent as a keeper or a guardian dates to the Pyramid Texts and can be traced to the Late Period.[213] The image of a mountain, which is guarded by a fiery serpent, is also known in CT spell 160, which reads:

jw=j rḫ.kw ḏw pw n bꜣḫw nt pt	I know this mountain of Bakhu of the sky,
rhn=s ḥr=f	And upon which it (the sky) rests.
wnn=f m////	It is of......
ḥt 300 m ꜣw=f	It is 300 rods in its length,
ḥt 120 m wsḫ=f	And 120 rods in its width.
wnn sbk nb bꜣḫw m jꜣbt ḏw pn	Sobek, Lord of Bakhu mountain is in the east of this mountain,
wnn ḥwt-nṯr=f m ḥsrt	And his temple is of carnelian,
wnn ḥfꜣw=f ḥr wpt ḏw pf	His serpent is at the brow of that mountain,
mḥ 30 m ꜣw=f	It is 30 cubits in its length,
mḥ 3 ḫnt m ḥꜣt=f m ds	And 3 cubits of its forepart is of flint.
jw=j rḫ.kw rn n ḥfꜣw pf	I know the name of this serpent,
tp ḏw=f	Who is upon his mountain,
jmj whm=f rn=f	He who is in his burning, is its name.[214]

The scenery here is also of a serpent which threatens the course of the boat of the sun god Re, who has to pass this locality in order to enter into the netherworld. This resembles exactly what happens on the 7th mound of the BD Chapter 149 mentioned above. In both texts, the serpent threatens the passer with its fire. It worth noting that the forepart of the snake is of flint (*ds*), which can also be translated as knife, and both refer to power of the snake which guards the mountain.

The fourth mountain in BD Chapter 149 is also guarded by a serpent, and the deceased directs his speech to it and says:

j ḥrj-tp jꜣt štꜣt	O who is upon the secret mound,
j ḏw pwj ḳꜣj ꜥꜣ	O this great and high mountain,
jmj ḫrt-nṯr	Which is in the necropolis,
ḫnnw pt ḥr=f	And upon which the sky alights,
n-sw ḥt 300 m ꜣw=f	It is of 300 rods in its length,
ḥt 150 m wsḫ=f	And 150 rods in its width,
jw ḥfꜣw ḥr=f stt dswj rn=f	There is a serpent on it 'Shooter of the Two Knives' is its name,
nj-sw mḥ 70 m sjn=f	It is 70 cubits it its circuit,
ꜥnḫ=f m ḥsḳ ꜣḫw mwt m ḫrt-nṯr	It lives by cutting up spirits of the dead in the necropolis.
ꜥḥꜥ=j m ḏrj=k	I stand at your enclosing wall.
mꜣꜥ sḳdwt mꜣ.n=j	The sailing is aright, and I

[204] A place name: *Wb* I, 133.2.
[205] Pun with flame and heat.
[206] *Wb* V, 164.4.
[207] *Wb* IV, 394.6.
[208] *CDME*, 308.
[209] Lapp, *The Papyrus of Nu*, pl. 84, lines 46-50.
[210] In the Book of the *ba* the deceased wishes to take the shape of different snakes when he goes out by day and participates in the festivals of the gods: Beinlich, *Das Buch vom Ba*, 46-7.
[211] *Wb* IV, 469. 5-7; *CDME*, 264.
[212] For a survey on the Rerek snake in CT and BD, see Borghouts, *Book of the Dead [39]*, 21-4.
[213] This already has been done by Leitz, *Orientalia* 65 (1996), 381-427.
[214] *CT* II, 375c-379a (spell 160).

w3t r=k	have seen the road to you.
jnk dmḏ n=k	I am the one who gathered (himself) for you,
jnk ṯ3j ḥbs tp=k	And I am the male who covered your head.
wḏ3=j wḏ3=k	If I am hale you are hale,
jnk wr ḥk3w	I am Great of magic.[215]

The scenery here is also of a mountain, which is located in the realm of the dead, and is guarded by a snake. The guardian of this mountain is called the Shooter of the Two Knives, and lives by cutting up the heads of the spirits and dead. The deceased who has to pass this mountain stands in the locality of this serpent. The deceased, who might be compared with one of the members of crew of the barque of the sun god Re, says that the sailing is fair, which refers also to the same situation when the Re crosses over the Lake of Knives.[216]

In the three spells cited above the guardians of the mountains have the same functions, and they can also be compared with the serpent Apep which threatens the course of the sun. Guarding a mountain, a bank or even a lake, all have the same implications as a challenge to the passer by and all are equipped with fire, knives, or with both.

To conclude, in Egyptian myth fire and knives made their first appearance with that of the universe. The sun god Re was born on the Island of Fire in the Lake of Knives. During the creation process, the sun god Re and the whole universe was threatened by the opponent Apep. In his victory over Apep, fire and knives were the means by which the sun god Re overcame his enemy.

The punishment and the mutilation of the body of Apep by fire and knives became the normal theme for the punishment of the sinners in the netherworld. Apep appears in the Books of the Underworld stabbed with knives or burnt by fire or with both. Every deceased is Re and Osiris, who will be confronted by Apep in his way to the netherworld, and fire and knives are the means by which he can punish him.

Fire and knives were also used in daily and funerary rituals. They were used to ward off the harm of the enemy of the god and the deceased. In dreams demons and nightmares are driven off by the aid of fire and knives. The guardians of the places of passages are also equipped with fire and knives; serpents spit their flames against the damned, chop off the heads of the unprepared dead, and shoot their knives against the passers. The names of the places of passage are also connected with fire and knives, and named after them; the Island of Fire, the Lake of Fire and the Lake of Knives.

---

[215] Lapp, *The Papyrus of Nu*, pl. 83, lines 25-9.

[216] For the passage of the Barque of Re over the Sandbank of the Lake of Knives, see below, 86-8.

Chapter Two

The Cartographical Descriptions and the Cosmographical Locations of the Lake of Knives and the Lake of Fire

2. 1. The Winding Waterway: Methodology for Cosmic Geography

Krauss' work on the astronomical concepts and afterlife beliefs in the Pyramid Texts is based on a textual investigation of the celestial cosmology of the Pyramid Texts, enhanced with relevant passages from the Coffin Texts and later literature, and a study of the astronomical phenomena of the night sky in Egypt.[217] Krauss' study begins with an investigation of the Winding Waterway. He argues that *mr n ẖ3* is a strip of water winding through the sky from the east to the west, and that it reflects the Ancient Egyptian observation of the ecliptic, which the sun, the moon and the visible planets follow in their motion across the sky.[218] *mr n ẖ3* can also explain the Egyptian division of the sky into two skies (*ptj*). According to Krauss, the sky to the north of the ecliptic (the Winding Waterway) was called the Field of Offering (*sḫt ḥtp*), the home of the Imperishable Stars (*jḫmw-sk*), while the area to the south of the ecliptic (the Winding Waterway) was called the Fields of Reeds (*sḫt j3rw*), and the home of the Unwearying Stars (*jḫmw-wrḏ*). The aim of the deceased's journey along the Winding Waterway is to cross from the south of the sky to its north, where he can join the Imperishable Stars in the Field of Offerings.[219]

In his argument on why the *mr n ẖ3* is a winding or a shifting waterway, Krauss does not give a clear explanation. First he argues that the Winding Waterway was written with the sign *mr* ,[220] which according to Krauss, is not straight in most cases, but it winds or shifts. He collected the different shapes of the sign  from the Pyramid Texts, and argues that *mr n ẖ3* follows a winding and turning course, which is the normal course of all the water courses in Egypt, as the geographical landscape does not allow straight courses to exist.[221]

Krauss used the textual evidence to reach the cartographical description of the Winding Waterway and to reconstruct the journey of the sun god Re over it. He concluded that the Winding Waterway runs from the south to the north of the sky, and that it has two banks; eastern and western banks. *mr n ẖ3* is a place where the sun god Re crosses the sky in his *wj3*-barque.

rꜥ j.wḏ (T) n m3-ḥ3=f mḫntj n mr n ẖ3	Re, entrust (T) to Mahaef, the ferryman of the Winding Waterway,
jnt=f mḫnt tf nt mr n ẖ3	So he may bring that ferryboat of the Winding Waterway,
ḏ33t=f nṯrw jm=s	In which he may ferry the gods,
jr pf gs n mr n ẖ3	To that (the other) side of Winding Waterway,
jr gs j3bt n pt	To the eastern side of the sky.[222]

It is a common theme in the Pyramid Texts, according to Krauss, that the journey of the sun god Re in his *wj3*-barque starts from the eastern horizon in the Winding Waterway.[223]

h3=f m wj3 mj rꜥ	He descends in *wj3*-barque like Re,
ḥr jdbw mr n ẖ3	On the banks of the Winding Waterway.[224]

The deceased crosses the Winding Waterway from the southern side of the sky to reach the northern side, the place of the Imperishable Stars.[225]

mwt nt N jst	The mother of N is Isis,
mnꜥt=f nbt-ḥwt	His nurse is Nephthys,
snḳt N sḫ3t-ḥr	And the one who suckles this N is *sḫ3t-ḥr* Cow.
njt m-ḫt=f srḳt tp-ꜥwj=f	Neith is behind him, and Serket is in front him.
ṯsj ꜥḥw=f sm3j mḫnwt=f	His ropes are tided and his ferries landed,
n s3 n jtmw ḥḳr jbj jbj ḥḳr	For the son of Atum who is hungry and thirsty, thirsty and hungry,
m pn gs rsy n mr n ẖ3	In this the southern side of the Winding Waterway.
ḏḥwtj jmj-ḏr šw nj b3t=f	Thoth in the limit of your bush's shade
(w)dj N tp ꜥnḏ ḏnḥ[=k]	Put N on your wingtip,
m pf gs mḥtj n mr n ẖ3	In that the northern side of the Winding Waterway.[226]

Krauss argues that the *jdbw* are the northern and southern sides of the Winding Waterway,[227] and that they are distinguished from each other. In *Pyr.* 1375a-1377c cited above, the southern side is referred to as *pn gs*,[228] while the northern side is referred to as *pf gs*.[229]

[217] Krauss, *Astronomische Konzepte*.

[218] Kees was the first to argue that the *mr n ẖ3* is located in the eastern horizon: Kees, *Totenglauben*, 110. Some other scholars translated *mr n ẖ3* as 'the Lake of the Lily': Breasted, *Development*, 105.

[219] Krauss, *Astronomische Konzepte*, 14-27.

[220] For the list of the different forms of *mr n ẖ3* and how it was written, see Krauss, *Astronomische Konzepte*, 23.

[221] Krauss, *Astronomische Konzepte*, 24, n. 58.

[222] PT 359=*Pyr.* § 599b-d.

[223] Krauss, *Astronomische Konzepte*, 21.

[224] PT spell 548=*Pyr.* § 1345c.

[225] Krauss, *Astronomische Konzepte*, 21.

[226] PT spell 555=*Pyr.* § 1375a-1377c.

[227] Krauss, *Astronomische Konzepte*, 24.

[228] PT spell 555=*Pyr.* § 1376c.

The bank of the Winding Waterway is also called *spt*. PT spell 304 reads:

jnḏ ḥr=k njw ḥr spt mr n ḫ3	Hail to you Ostrich at the bank of the Winding Waterway.
j.wn w3t n N sw3 N	Open a path for N that N may pass.[230]

The two banks of the Winding Waterway in the Coffin Texts, according to Krauss, must designate the northern and southern banks.[231] The northern bank is distinguished by the large number of its cities. In CT spell 1129, the northern bank of the Winding Waterway is described as:

spt mḥtjt nt mr n ḫ3	The northern bank of the Winding Waterway,
nwt=s n rḫ ṯnw	The number of its cities is not known.[232]

On the southern bank of the Winding Waterway the deceased descends into the barque of the sun god Re in his way to the northern sky, to the place of offerings.[233] When the deceased says that he is hungry and thirsty on the southern side of the Winding Waterway, and he is traveling in his boat to the northern side, that means he will have his offerings on the northern side of the Winding Waterway.[234]

Krauss's argument does not seem convincing and is not substantiated with hard evidence. It is not possible to envisage that the Winding Waterway runs from the east to the west of the sky, and at the same time from the north to the south. Furthermore, it is not possible to locate the Winding Waterway in one specific location, but it winds and shifts through the sky.

Krauss also does not give a clear explanation of why the northern side is bigger than the southern one. The only acceptable explanation is that the Winding Waterway follows the seasonal movement of the sun, and it shifts or winds according to the movement of the sun during the different seasons of the year, since the sun tends to move to the south. This interpretation is not hinted at in Krauss' argument. The diagram below shows that the Winding Waterway tends to shift or wind to the south. The curved lines represent the movement of the sun and its course during the different seasons.

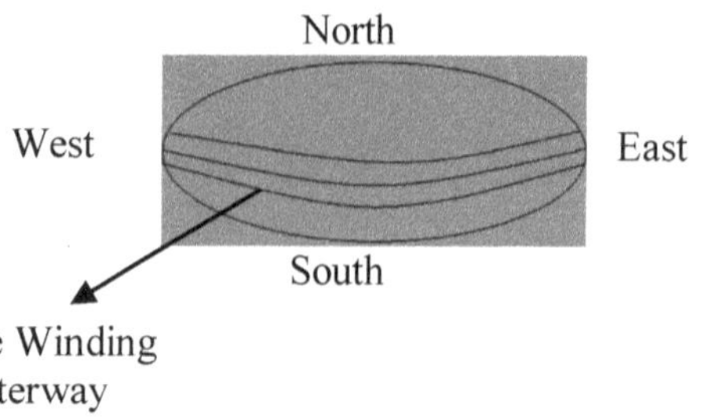

2.2. The Cartographical Description of the Lake of Knives

Pictorial Evidence

Unfortunately there is no specific description for the Lake of Knives in Egyptian representations, nor is there direct textual reference identifying its shape. For that reason, the methodology of Krauss can be applied on the Lake of Knives to find out how the Ancient Egyptian envisaged this lake. The Lake of Knives is written with different water signs. The table below shows these signs:

	*CT* VII, 23l-24f, Spell 823.[235]
	Book of the Dead, Chapters 15 A. III, and 15B.1.[236]
	Book of the Dead, Chapter 153.[237]
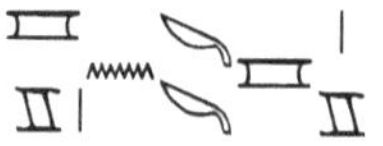	Papyrus Berlin 3027, Verso, line, 4-5.[238]
	Magical Papyrus Harris BM 10042.[239]
	Stela of Thutmosis from Memphis.[240]
	Chapel of Amenirdis I at Medinet Habu.[241]

As shown in the table above, the first sign is  , which according to Gardiner's Sign List is read *mr* and is used with words referring to lakes, rivers, and canals.[242] It is also interchangeable with some other

[229] PT spell 555=*Pyr*. § 1377a.
[230] PT spell 304=*Pyr*. § 469a-b.
[231] Krauss, *Astronomische Konzepte*, 25.
[232] *CT* VII, 458m-n (spell 1129); Lesko, *Book of the Two Ways*, 128.
[233] Krauss, *Astronomische Konzepte*, 25.
[234] Sethe had argued that the northern side of the Winding Waterway is a place where the Field of Offerings is located and a place where the deceased consumes his offerings. The same interpretation was adapted later by Barta, *Die Bedeutung der Pyramidentexte*, 88-9.

[235] *CT* VII, 23p (spell 823).
[236] Naville, *TB*, Kapitel 15 A.III, pl. XVI, line 10, and Kapitel 15B.1, pl. XVIII, line 6.
[237] Naville, *TB*, Kapitel 153, pl. CLXXVII, line 27.
[238] Erman, *Zaubersprüche für Mutter und Kind*, 52,
[239] Leitz, *Magical and Medical Papyri of the New Kingdom*, BM EA 10042 Section K, VI, 10-VII, I.
[240] Edwards, *BM Stelae* VIII, pl. XXXIX, line 16.
[241] Daressy, *Rec Trav* 23 (1901), 4-18.
[242] Gardiner, *Egyptian Grammar*, N 36.

signs used with the same words referring to the same bodies of water. For instance, in Gardiner Sign List N 37 is a sign that can replace .[243] In her study on the Temples Sacred Lakes, Geβler-Löhr argues that the Egyptians did not differentiate sharply between lakes, canals, and islands as we do nowadays. *mr* as a sign refers to running water, while *š* refers to a standing body of water and is bordered from all sides. *š* is a lake that is actually located within a temple, and it can designate both artificial and natural lakes. It might also refer to a temple harbour or temple garden.[244] It is also not explicit whether to read as *mr* or *š*.[245] It is also not clear how to differentiate between and in Egyptian Texts before the Graeco-Roman Period.[246]

On the other hand, *š* can also refer to a temple lake dug deep to tap the sub-soil water and ensure a permanent self-feeding water supply.[247] This was typical for the sacred temple lake which was dug deep in the ground symbolising the primeval ocean Nun, and draw on the sub-soil water rather than the flood of the Nile.[248] An example for this type of excavated lakes is the Sacred Lake at Karnak. [249] In such water basins dug in the flood plain, the water would rise and fall according to the seasonal movement of the Nile flood.[250]

On the stela of Amenhotep III from his funerary temple on the West Bank of Thebes, he records that he has dug a pond or a lake for his father Amun-Re as a place of recreation in the Beautiful Festival.

wḥm mnw jrj.n ḥm=f n jt=f jmn	An additional monument which his Majesty has erected for his father Amun.
jrj.t(w) n=f m3rw m ḥtp-nṯr	A Maru was made for him as a divine offering,
ḫft-ḥr n jpt-rsjt	In front of Luxor Temple,
st sḏ3 n jt=j m ḥb=f nfr	A precious place for my father at his beautiful feast.
s[ʿḥ]ʿ.n=j ḥwt-nṯr ʿ3t m [ḫn]w=s	I have erected a Great temple in its interior,
mj rʿ ḫʿʿ=f m 3ḫt	Like Re, when he appears in the horizon,
srwḏ.tj m ḥrrwt nbwt nfr	It being planted with all sorts of beautiful flowers,
<mj>nw jmj š=f r tr nb	<And> Nun who is in his lake for all time.
wr n=f jrp r mw	It is richer in wine than water.[251]

In a royal decree dating to the Old Kingdom reign of King Pepi I from Dahshour concerning the taxes collection from the Pyramid town, lakes and canals occur and they are written with two different signs.

> My Person has decreed against the assessing (*jp*) of the canals (*mrw*), lakes (or pools) (*šw*), wells (*šdwt*), runnels (*ḫnmwt*), and the sycamore trees (*nhwt*) in the Pyramid town.[252]

The lakes, the pools, and the canals in Pepi I's Decree are connected with productive areas, which were not inundated with the water of the flood. These productive areas at least had wells, and ponds used for the hand-watering of trees out of the season. They are not flood basins, but they are areas which include trees where the perennial water is available.

An interesting scene to be cited here is found in the tomb of the Two Brothers at Saqqara. The scene shows on the lower register a pool occupying the middle section with birds and papyrus. Men are shown catching birds and collecting papyrus. To the left of the scene, which concerns us here, gardeners are shown 'watering the vegetable plot on the pool of the estate'. Here the planting of the tress depends on hand-watering from a pond, and they are not inundated (fig. 11).[253]

[243] Gardiner, *Egyptian Grammar*, N 37; Geβler-Löhr, *Die Heiligen Seen*, 21.
[244] Furthermore *š* can also refer to a district within a temple or an area that is surrounded or enclosed and takes the shape of : Geβler-Löhr, *Die Heiligen Seen*, 21.
[245] Geβler-Löhr, *Die Heiligen Seen*, 21.
[246] Geβler-Löhr, *Die Heiligen Seen*, 22.
[247] Hugonot, *Jardin*, 158-9.
[248] Geβler-Löhr, *Die Heiligen Seen*, 187-8, 207-11, 217-8.
[249] The Lake Moeris in Fayum is also said to be dug by the primeval gods. A text in the Fayum Book reads 'they have dug the Lake with their own hands, and Nun came forth into him from the depth of million of millions': Beinlich, *Das Buch von Fayum*, 260; *GM* 100 (1987), 15-18.
[250] During the excavation in the forecourt of the temple of Amenhotep son of Hapu, there was a stepped basin discovered, surrounded by a platform and a staircase leading to the courtyard of the temple. Around the basin, plants and trees were discovered. The basin was dug deep in the ground to reach the water table and thus fed by what the Egyptians called the primeval ocean Nun: Eyre, *JEA* 80 (1994), 64, and note the references cited there.
[251] *Urk* IV 1651, 7-13; Beylage, *Aufbau der königlichen Stelentexte* I, 394, II, 737-9; Klug, Königliche Stelen, 397. Cabrol argues that the lake in this text was linked with the Nile by a channel and in turn was filled by its water: Cabrol, *Les voies proceesionnelles de Thèbes*, 604.
[252] Sethe, *Urk* I, 209-213; Strudwick, *Texts from the Pyramid Age*, 104; Eyre, *JEA* 80 (1994), 69; Goedicke, *Königliche Dockumente aus dem Alten Reich*, 55-77; Schenkel, *Bewässerungsrevolution*, 26.
[253] Eyre, *JEA* 80 (1994), 61.

Fig. 11. Hand-watering as shown on the lower left side in the tomb of the Two Brothers
(after Moussa and Altenmüller, *Das Grab des Nianchchnum und Chnumhotep*, fig. 8).

It is also important to note that Pepi I's Decree is an official one and the distinction between the different water sources must be made clear, which is the only interpretation that can be applied here. In religious texts this distinction does not actually exist. For that reason words designating these bodies of water might be written with different determinatives. There is an overlap with the use of these signs and there is no need to distinguish between them. This is the only interpretation given by Schenkel[254] and Geβler-Löhr.[255]

š as a term refers to standing water, and can be either artificial or natural. It is also connected with productive areas like gardens. The term also refers to lakes held in a flood basin.[256] This theme of the basins was developed in Old Kingdom offering tables such as that of the Overseer of Scribes Setju Cairo CG 1330,[257] shown as a rectangular basin surrounded by trees, with the pond stepped in different levels. The inscriptions on the steps of the basin are marked for three seasons: twenty-five cubits for the inundation; twenty-three cubits for *peret*; twenty–two cubits for *shemou*.[258] In addition, the word *nht* 'sycamore' is depicted on each corner which might indicate that the pond was meant to be surrounded by trees.[259]

In the New Kingdom representation, this effect of the rise and fall of the water is represented in a slightly different way, where on the Eighteenth Dynasty painting of the tomb of Nebamon in the British Museum, a garden with a blue pond, birds and plants is shown. The theme is developed more fully in the later Book of the Dead of Nakht, where there is a blue pond surrounded by an area of grey-brown, and a larger area of white, at the edge of which trees and vines are growing, each in its tree-pit (fig. 12).[260]

Fig. 12. The Garden of Nakht (BM 10471)
(after Hugonot, *Jardin*, 147).

In a libation basin from Abydos there are depictions of four boats on the narrow step of the basin. This might indicate that these basins might have served as substitutes for the lakes over which these boats sail.[261] The evidence which supports this hypothesis is the offering table of Ankh-Wedjes Louvre E 25368. This offering table consists of three basins with lotus flowers carved into the stepped inner sides of the basins. The decoration on the long outsides show the deceased sitting in a boat being offered ducks while sailing is in progress.[262]

The use of these offering tables with basins refers to their use in the rituals of libations, where the basins serve the source of water poured for the deceased. On the ritual level, the libation water represents the primeval ocean as well as the lake upon which the deceased performs his journeys to the netherworld.[263]

Depending on a determinative to reach the exact shape of the lake of Knives is not helpful, because as we have seen that the Lake of Knives was followed by different determinatives. For that reason it is crucial to examine the textual evidence.

Textual Evidence

In Chapter 15B.I of the New Kingdom Book of the Dead, the Lake of Knives is described as a place where the sun god Re crosses the sky in his day barque. The text reads:

mꜥnḏt m h3j hnw	The day Barque is in celebration and jubilation,
t3 m ḥb	And the land is in festival.
nṯrw m ḥsfw b3=f ḥrj-ib ṯ3wj=fj	The gods are greeting the one whose soul dwells in his two children,[264]
spr=f r jmnt nfrt m ḥtp	He arrives in peace to the Beautiful West,
ḏ3.n=f mr nḫ3wj	(After) he crossed the Lake of Knives,
r hnw=f w3w wḏ3	According to the movement of

[254] Schenkel, *Bewässerungsrevolution*, 26.
[255] Geβler-Löhr, *Die Heiligen Seen*, 23.
[256] Hugonot, *Jardin*, 17-18.
[257] Borchardt, *Catalogue Général* I, 14, pl. 5.
[258] Hugonot, *Jardin*, 191-3, Geβler-Löhr, *Die Heiligen Seen*, 71.
[259] On the functions of these offerings tables and basins, see Hölzl, in: *L'acqua nell'antico Egitto*, 314-5.
[260] Eyre, *JEA* 80 (1994), 61-2.
[261] Hölzl, in: *L'acqua nell'antico Egitto*, 313.
[262] Hölzl, in: *L'acqua nell'antico Egitto*, 313-4.
[263] For more details, see below, 62-3.
[264] Shu and Tefnut as the son and daughter of the Sun god Re, *Wb* VI, 340.

sp 2	its waves, safely (completely).[265]

The sun god also crosses the sky in his night barque. Chapter 15 A III reads:

nnj n ḥr=k	Adoration to your face;
ḥpt ṯw m3ᶜt r trwj	Maat embraces you at the two times,[266]
nmj=k ḥrt m 3w-ib	When you traverse the sky in joy.
mr nḫ3wj ḫpr m ḥtpw	The Lake of Knives has become in peace.
njk ḫr ᶜ3wj=fj ḥsk	The *Nik* Serpent is overthrown and his arms are cut off.
šsp.n sktt m3ᶜw nfr	The *msktt* Barque has received good wind.
jmj ḳrs=f ib=f nḏm	He who is in his shrine, his heart is pleased.[267]

According to Krauss, the sun god Re crosses the sky in his day barque over the Winding Waterway, starting his journey from the eastern horizon. The sun god Re also crosses the sky over the Lake of Knives in his day barque (*mᶜnḏt),* and he starts his night journey over the Lake of Knives in his night barque (*msktt).* So the Lake of Knives, as the Winding Waterway, extends from the east to the west of the sky. In the Book of the Dead Chapter 153 the deceased says that he sits in the barque of Re and crosses to the northern sky.

ḥms=j m wj3 n rᶜ	I sit in the barque of Re,
ḏ3=j mr nḫ3wj r pt mḥjt	And ferry across the Lake of Knives to the northern sky.
sḏm (=j) nṯrw	(I) hear the (words of) the gods,
irj=j irjt=sn	I do as they do,
(ᶜnḫ=j) ᶜnḫ=sn	And (I live as) they live.[268]

When the deceased ferries across the Lake of Knives to the northern sky, that simply means his starting point is the southern bank of the Lake of Knives. So the Lake of Knives also has northern and southern banks. In the New Kingdom Sun Hymns, the barque of the sun god Re crosses the Lake of Knives and it is towed by the northerners and southerners, while the easterners and westerners worship the sun god Re.[269]

In another text the deceased drinks water and consume his offerings on the two banks of the Lake of Knives. In the Book of the Dead Chapter 169 the text reads:

ḫfᶜ=k sm m 3bḏw	You shall grasp the whip in Abydos.
jw sšm.n=k šbw n wrw	You have guided the food offerings of the Great Ones,
mḥwt n ḥrjw	And the offering bowls of those who are above,
sm3w m ḥb n wsjr	And who join in the festival of Osiris,
dw3t nt w3g ḥr sšt3w	In the morning of the Wag Festival and of the mysteries.
ḫkrw=k m nbw	You shall be adorned with gold.
wt=k smtrw m p3kt	Your bandage is measured out (?) of fine linen,[270]
ḥwj ḥᶜpj ḥr šnbt=k	And the inundation shall beat on your breast.
3ḫ n=k st r ḥtj ḥr ᶜb	It is more beneficial to you more than what is carved on an offering stone.
swr(=k) ḥr gswj mr nḫ3wj	(You) shall drink on the two sides[271] of the Lake of Knives,
ḥsj ṯw nṯrw ntjw Jm	The gods who are there shall praise you.
prj=k r pt ḥnᶜ nṯrw	You shall ascend to the sky with the gods,
sᶜrjw m3ᶜt n rᶜ	Who cause Maat to ascend to Re.
sṯ3.tw=k m-b3ḥ psḏt	You shall be brought in the presence of the Ennead,
jrj.tw=k mj wᶜ jm=sn	And you shall be made as one of them.
ntk ḫ3r jt n r3w	To you belongs the Syrian goose the father of the Grey geese.[272]
wdn=k sw n ptḥ rsj jnb=f	You shall offer it to Ptah to the south of his wall.[273]

The deceased's wish to consume his offerings and drink his water on the banks of the Lake of Knives might refer to the fact that the Field of Offerings is located on one of the two banks of the Lake of Knives. It is possible to argue that the Lake of Knives is a body of water that extends from the east to the west of the sky. It is also a place which divides the sky into the southern and northern skies. The deceased's wish to cross from the southern side of the sky to its northern side over the Lake of Knives might refer to his wish to travel from the Field of Reeds to the Field of Offerings where he can consume his food and drink his water on the two banks of the Lake of Knives.

2.3. The Cartographical Description of the Lake of Fire

The Lake of Fire is depicted on the floor of some Middle Kingdom coffins from el-Bersha in what is

[265] Naville, *TB*, Kapitel 15B.I, pl. XVIII, lines 3-7.
[266] Day and night, or in his rising and setting: Assmann, *Liturgische Lieder*, 268.
[267] Naville, *TB*, Kapitel 15 A.III, pl. XVI, lines 10-11.
[268] Naville, *TB*, Kapitel 153, pl. CLXXVII, lines 27-28; Faulkner, *BD*, 121.
[269] For the sun Hymn, see above, 10.
[270] *CDME*, 229, *Wb* IV, 145, 1-27.
[271] For this form of the two sides in Egyptian language, see Badawy, *ZÄS* 103 (1976), 1-4.
[272] This passage might allude to a deceased as a bird crossing a place of passage.
[273] Naville, *TB*, Kapitel 169, pl. CXC, lines 23-27.

known as the Book of the Two Ways.[274] In this book, the Lake of Fire is represented as a stretch of water that is painted in red (fig. 13).

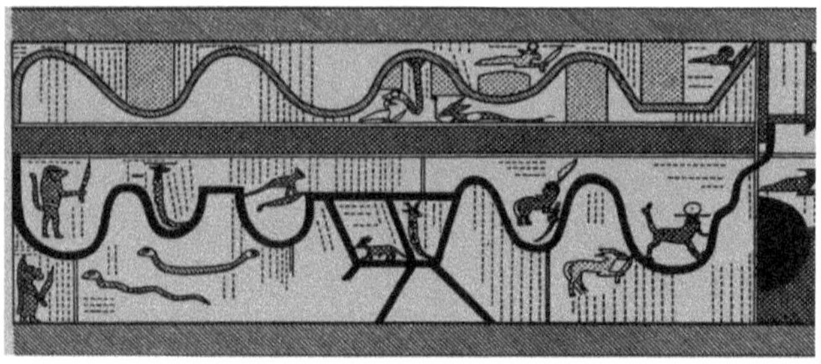

Fig 13. The Lake of Fire in the Book of the Two Ways: Coffin of Sepi
(after de Buck, *CT* VII, pl. I).

The Lake of Fire in the Book of the Dead

The Lake of Fire is found also in the Book of the Dead Chapter 126 (fig. 14). The vignettes of this chapter show four baboons sitting at the four corners of the Lake of Fire with four  *nsrt* signs on its four sides. The four baboons sitting at the bow of the barque of the sun god Re are connected with the sunrise. They act as judges in the divine tribunal and decide who may gain access to the sacred portals of the west, or who shall be thrown to the monster that guards the interior of the Lake of Fire. In CT spells 335 and 336, the deceased asks the gods who are in the divine tribunal to save him from the monster whose face is that of a dog and whose skin is that of human.[275]

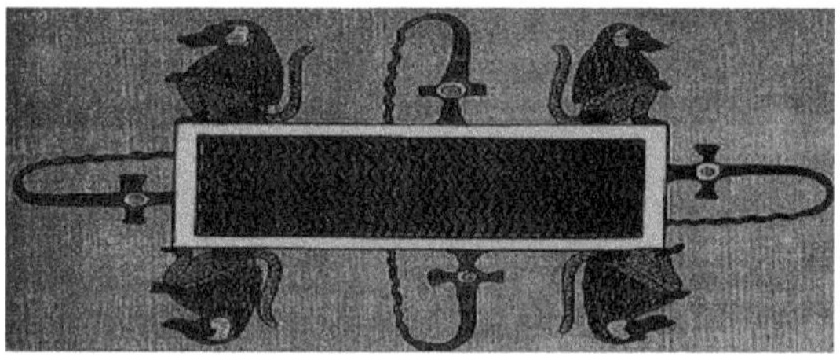

Fig. 14. The Lake of Fire in chapter 126 of the Book of the Dead
(after Faulkner, *Book of the Dead*, Ch. 126).

The Lake of Fire in the New Kingdom Mythological Papyri

In the New Kingdom mythological papyrus of *Nstj-tꜣ-nbt-tꜣwj* Cairo Museum, no. 40017, the deceased is represented offering libation on the two sides of the Lake of Fire.[276] The four baboons are also represented on the four corners with  *nsrt* sign in front of each one (fig. 15). The deceased is shown pouring water on the two sides of the Lake of Fire, which should refer to the deceased raising the discharge of Osiris in the Lake of Fire as occurs in the Book of the Dead chapter 63B.[277]

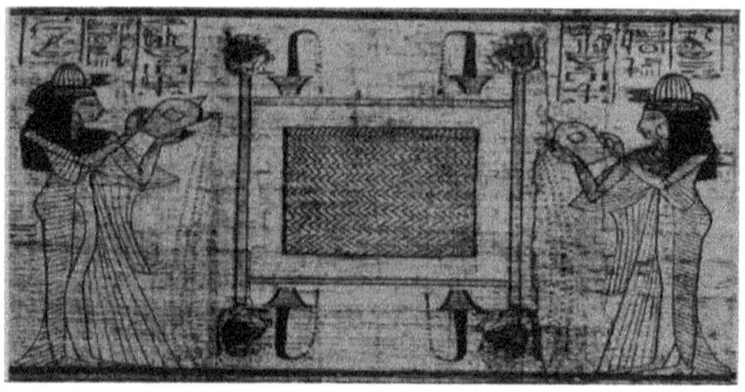

Fig. 15. The deceased pours libation on the two sides of the Lake of Fire
(after Piankoff, *Mythological Papyri*, pl. 8).

In a unique scene in the Papyrus of *bꜣk-n-mwt* Louvre no. 3279, the sinners are represented burnt in the Lake of Fire, while fire signs surrounding the four sides of the lake are depicted. Between the *nsrt* signs, *dwꜣt* (underworld) is written (fig. 16).

Fig. 16. The sinners are burnt in the Lake of Fire
(after Piankoff, *Mythological Papyri*, pl.12).

The Lake of Fire in the Book of the Amduat

In the Book of the Amduat, the Lake of Fire is represented at the lower register of the Fifth Hour. It occupies the whole lower register above the sand, and is represented as an oblong. It is half-filled with wavy lines to enable the insertion of a text. The water lines are painted bright red (fig. 17). The texts describe the Lake of Fire as a place for the sinners, and a place where the boat of the gods cannot sail. Its water is described as the 'waves of water that cannot be controlled'.

nwt jꜣkbjw nṯrw jmjw jmḥt	The water of mourning of the gods in Imhet (necropolis),
n ꜥpj.n wjꜣ ḥr=sn	No barque can traverse over them.
n sḫm.n dwꜣtjw m mw=sn	The ones who are in the underworld have no

[274] For the Lake of Fire in the Book of the Two Ways, see below, 77-8.
[275] For more detailed discussion on these two spells, see below, 91-6.
[276] The same scene occurs also on the Papyrus of Ta-shed-khonsu (Cairo Museum no. 531 and 40016), Papyrus of Nesi-pa-ka-shuty (Louvre Museum no.E17401), and the Papyrus of Pa-Neb-Kemet-Nekht (Cairo Museum no. 85): Piankoff, *Mythological Papyri*, pls. 18, 9, and 25.

[277] See above, 11.

	power over their water,
wnn m ẖrt-nṯr pn	Which is in this necropolis.
wnn mw=sn r ntjw jm=s m sḏt	Their water is fire for those who are in it.[278]

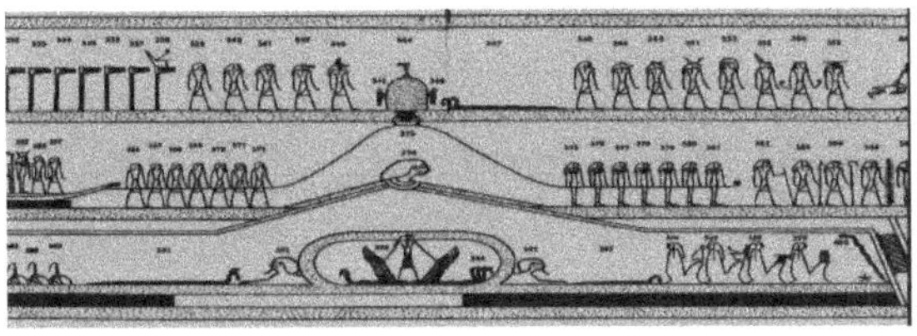

Fig. 17. The Lake of Fire in the lower register of the Fifth Hour of the Book of Amduat
(after Hornung, *The Egyptian Amduat*, 138-9).

The Lake of Fire in the Book of the Gates

In the old versions of the Book of the Gates in the tomb of Horemheb and the Osirion at Abydos, the two short sides of the Lake of Fire are oval and the lake is painted blue. The oval ends of the two sides refer to the nature of the underworld roads and waters. The bodies of water and the ways to the hereafter, according to Hornung, are usually represented as zigzags.[279] In the later versions of the Book of the Gates in the tombs of Ramesses IV and Ramesses VI, the two oval end sides are straight and the Lake itself is painted red.[280] The barley that springs from the Lake of Fire is painted green in the tomb of Seti I, while at the Osirion at Abydos the spikes are painted yellow. The barley in the Lake of Fire is nourishment for the righteous, and yellow might refer to its natural colour at harvest season. The mummified gods on top of the Lake of Fire are described as 'The gods who are in the Lake of Fire' (*nṯrw jmjw š ḫbt*).[281] These gods are depicted as wrapped mummies with their heads painted black (fig. 18). In the tomb of Seti I, the wrapping is painted in white.

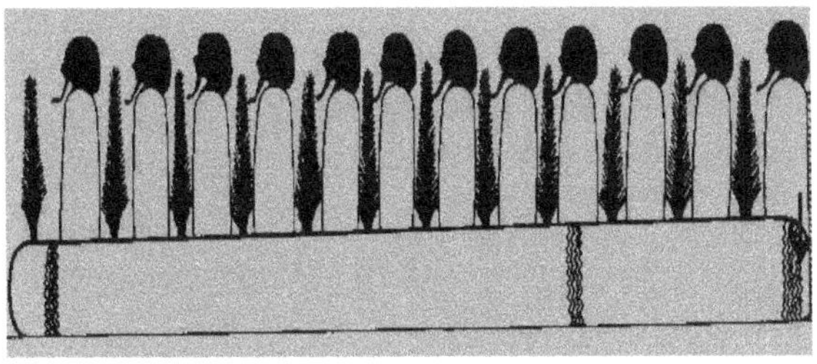

Fig. 18. The Lake of Fire at the upper register of the third Hour in the Book of the Gates
(after Hornung, *Das Buch von den Pforten* II, 80).

In the sixth Hour of the Book of the Gates, the Lake of Fire is depicted at the end of the lower register. It is represented as a cavity full of fire. Inside this cavity, a uraeus is depicted. In front of the fire cavity, there are two gods depicted in mummy form, while there are twelve kneeling gods depicted on one of the sides of the fire cavity. This cavity of fire is described as another variant of the Lake of Fire (fig. 19). The text which describes the fire cavity reads:

nṯrw jmjw ẖꜣst tꜣ	The gods who are in the fire cavity of the earth.
nbj-ḥr stj-ḥr	The Flaming-Face and the Glittering-Face (the two guardians around the fire cavity).
wnn=sn m dbnw n ẖꜣst tn	They exist in the circumference of this cavity.
wnn jꜥrt ꜥnḫt m ẖꜣst tn	The living uraeus exists in this cavity.
wnn mw n ẖꜣst tn m sḏt	The water of this cavity is fire,
jwtj hꜣj nṯrw tꜣ bꜣw tꜣ r ẖꜣst tn	Which the gods of the earth and the *bas* of the earth cannot traverse into this fire cavity,
m-ꜥ nsr n jꜥrt tn	Because of the flame of this snake.
srḳ nṯr pn ꜥꜣ ḫntj dwꜣt m mw ḏsr n ẖꜣst tn	This Great God, Foremost of the Underworld breathes from the sacred water of this fire cavity.
jn n=sn rꜥ	So says Re to them.
jhj jrf nṯrw sꜣjw ẖꜣst ḏsrt	Oh gods who guard this sacred fire cavity,
dd=tn mw n ḫntj jgrt	You give water in front of the realm of the dead.
jw mw n ẖꜣst n wsjr	The water of this fire cavity belongs to Osiris.
ḳbḥw=ṯn ḫntj dwꜣt	Your libation is in the front of the netherworld.[282]

Fig. 19. The Fire Cavity, Six Hour of the Book of the Gates
(after Hornung, *Das Buch von den Pforten* II, pl. 6).

The Lake of Fire on the 21st Dynasty Coffins

The Lake of Fire occurs on some of the 21st Dynasty coffins, although there is no reference to the lake within the texts on these coffins. Images on these coffins can be interpreted as displays of religious ideas.[283] They replace the texts, which in most cases have a long tradition dating from the Middle Kingdom

[278] Hornung, *The Egyptian Amduat*, 171.
[279] Hornung, *Das Buch von Pforten* II, 80.
[280] Hornung, *Unterweltsbücher*, 31-2.
[281] Hornung, *Das Buch von Pforten* II, 80.
[282] Hornung, *Das Buch von Pforten* I, 243-247, *Das Buch von Pforten* II, 172; Zeidler, *Pfortenbuchstudien* II, 184-186.
[283] Niwinski, in: Schoske et al., *Akten des vierten internationalen Ägyptologen Kongresses München 1985* III, 304.

Coffin Texts. During the 21st Dynasty new iconographic compositions were introduced, and were placed on coffins sides. The Late Period coffins can serve as a miniature for the tomb, at the time when richly decorated tombs were no longer built.[284] Instead of depicting hereafter scenes on the walls of the tombs,[285] they were placed instead on the inner and outer sides of the coffins and also on papyri.[286] The decorations on the sides of the coffins not only include representations of the underworld scenes as found on the royal tombs,[287] but also have vignettes of the New Kingdom Book of the Dead.[288]

For instance, on the exterior of the Cairo Coffin CG 6153,[289] the scene of the judgment of the dead is depicted with the Lake of Fire as a place of punishment for the sinners. The scene is another version of the vignettes of BD Chapter 125 (fig. 20a). In this scene the deceased is depicted presenting his heart, mouth and eyes to the judges as if he is making declarations of his innocence. Then he is accompanied by his *ba* waiting for the verdict. The rest of the scene depicts the deceased standing holding the feathers of Maat in his hands while the goddess of the West with her emblem on her head adores him. To the right of this scene, the weighting of the heart takes place, and Anubis stands beside the balance. To the right of this scene, Thoth as Lord of Maat reports the result of the weighing of the heart to Osiris who is sitting on his throne and accompanied by Isis.[290] The swallower or the devourer of the Dead is depicted between Osiris and Thoth. On the far left side of this scene, there is a depiction of the Lake of Fire. It is depicted with four baboons on the four sides, and eight braziers between them. The lake itself is surrounded by four serpents, which might spit fire into the lake (Fig. 20b).[291]

Fig. 20a. The deceased presents his eye, mouth and heart in the judgment of the dead (after Niwinski, *The Second Find of Deir El-Bahri (Coffins)*, 100, fig. 136).

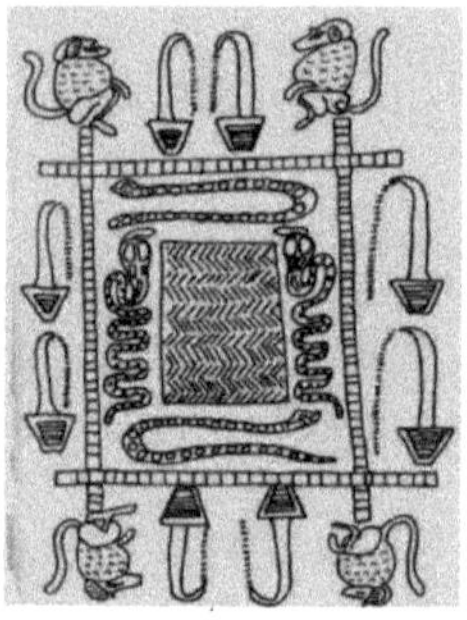

Fig. 20b. The Lake of Fire on Cairo Coffin CG 6153 (after Niwinski, *The Second Find of Deir El-Bahri (Coffins)*, 100, fig. 135).

On another Cairo coffin CG 6190, the Lake of Fire is guarded by four baboons and four fire signs on the four corners. The Lake is attended by Shu, who is depicted with a long feather on his head and holds *ˁnḫ* sign in his left hand while with the right hand he holds a snake with a long feather on its head. On the other side of the Lake of Fire, the goddess Maat stands holding *ˁnḫ* sign in her right hand and the same snake with a feather on its head (fig. 21). This scene is described by Niwinksi to belong to the vignettes of BD Chapter 126.[292]

Fig. 21. The Lake of Fire attended by Shu and Maat (after Niwinski, *The Second Find of Deir El-Bahri (Coffins)*, 88, fig. 123).

On the Cairo coffin CG 6180 there is an interesting depiction of the Lake of Fire. The scene is divided into two registers. On the upper register Osiris is depicted squatting and flanked by Isis and Nephthys. The lower register shows the Lake of Fire flanked by solar discs from the top and bottom, and four fire signs on two sides with the *ˁnḫ* sign between them. On the two sides

[284] Niwinski, *21st Dynasty Coffins from Thebes*, 15.
[285] The scene of the sky goddess Nut supporting the sky and separated from the earth god Geb by Shu, which is a well known scene in the royal tombs, is found on the Cairo coffin CG 6153: Niwinski, *The Second Find of Deir El-Bahri (Coffins)*, 98, fig. 132.
[286] Most of these coffins included also religious papyri found inside them. They contained vignettes from different chapters of the Book of the Dead: Niwinski, in: *Totenbuch-Forschungen*, 260-2; in: Uehlinger (ed.), *Images as Media*, 21.
[287] On the coffin of Pinudjem II from Cairo Museum (JE 26197), there are depictions of a solar boat being dragged along the ways of the Netherworld, and Apep is shown speared with knives. This depiction of the scene resembles the motif that is found in the Eleventh Hour of the Book of the Gates: Niwinski, *21st Daynsty Coffins from Thebes*, 115 (coffin No. 65). On the vignettes from the Book of the Dead on the Coffin of Pinudjem II and his wives, see Niwinski, in: *Totenbuch-Forschungen*, 255;
[288] Niwinski, in: *Totenbuch-Forschungen*, 245-64.
[289] Niwinski, *The Second Find of Deir El-Bahri (Coffins)*, 100.
[290] Niwinski, *The Second Find of Deir El-Bahri (Coffins)*, 101.
[291] On the association between fire and snakes, see above, 23-4.
[292] Niwinski, *The Second Find of Deir El-Bahri (Coffins)*, 86.

there are two deities attending the scene and each one holds a ribbon in an extended hand, while with their other hands they adore this ribbon. The deity on the right hand side is a female-headed vulture accompanied by the two birds perching on the symbol of the west. The deity on the left is a male deity accompanied by another bird perching on the same symbol of the west.[293] The solar disk and the two *ˁnḫ* signs might indicate that the Lake of Fire is a place from which life comes into existence (fig. 22).[294]

Fig. 22. The Lake of Fire flanked by the two solar discs and attended by two deities (after Niwinski, *The Second Find of Deir El-Bahri (Coffins)*, 67, fig. 101).

Instead of presenting the judgment of the dead ritual in texts for recitation, the ritual is illustrated.[295] The iconographic depiction of the ritual plays the same role as the texts presented for recitation. This suggestion is confirmed by the fact the scene of the judgment of the dead on this coffin is preceded by *ḏd mdw* 'recitations'. This raises the question of whether there were ritual texts recited and performed with the depiction of the ritual, and whether the representation of the ritual in captions on the sides of the coffin can replace the texts intended for recitation.

The depiction of the Lake of Fire, as occurs in the vignettes of BD Chapter 126 and as presented in the Books of the Underworld, has a bearing on the question of the ritual significance of these images as presented on the 21st Dynasty coffins. The coffin as a ritual machine[296] carries all the items that are necessary for the performance of rituals on or for the deceased. This means that the coffin should have the ritual elements necessary for the performance of funerary rituals. The ritual elements include texts, equipment, actions, and speech. All these elements are found on the Middle Kingdom coffins. The ritual performance is kept in both words (Coffin Texts), and also vignettes (the object frieze) and both form liturgies recited for the deceased in the night before burial or at the day of his funeral.[297]

As in the Middle Kingdom coffins, the 21st Dynasty coffins serve as a universe for the deceased and also reflect the rituals performed for him from the moment of his death until his burial. So, as Niwinski argues, 'every decorative element found on the coffin may be assigned to these two spheres of meaning'.[298] The 21st Dynasty coffins and their antecedent coffins of the 18th and 19th Dynasties have depictions of the funeral scenes, which are well- preserved on the walls of the tombs and also preserved in texts.[299]

Furthermore, on these coffins one can find the figures of the Sons of Horus supporting the sky. These were depicted on the Middle Kingdom coffins at the four corners of the coffin. They functioned as supporters of the sky, and they have ritual functions.[300] They play the same roles on the 21st Dynasty coffins,[301] and they became the dominant feature of the iconography during this period.[302]

Another instance is the depiction of Osiris on his bed, attended and protected by Isis and Nephthys. This depiction refers to the roles of the two goddesses as kites protecting the deceased.[303] It is a key for all the rituals performed for him in the place of embalming in the night before burial. On the Middle Kingdom coffins, these rituals are preserved in texts, while on the 21st Dynasty coffins, the rituals are kept in vignettes and captions placed on the sides of the coffin.[304]

To sum up, the appearance of the Lake of Fire on the 21st Dynasty coffins has ritual significance. To interpret one of the vignettes, it is then crucial to look at the surrounding scenes to have a clear picture of the ritual aspects of these images. The role of the Lake of Fire as a place of passage on these coffins is not different from its role on the Middle Kingdom coffins. The same can be said about the depiction of the Lake of Fire on the New Kingdom Mythological Papyri.[305] On these papyri, which include vignettes from the Book of the Dead and scenes from the Underworld Books, the rituals are kept in images. They are not mythological but ritual papyri. The depiction of the Lake of Fire on these papyri can also refer to rituals performed for the deceased, and the images depicted there were not merely representations of the

[293] Niwinski, *The Second Find of Deir El-Bahri (Coffins)*, 66.
[294] For the Lake of Fire as a birthplace of the sun god Re in the Book of the Two Ways, see below, 77.
[295] For the ritual of the judgment of the dead and how it was performed, see below, 95-7.
[296] Willems, *Chests of Life*, 148-60.
[297] For the liturgies on Middle Kingdom coffins, see Assmann, *Totenliturgien* I.

[298] Niwinski, in: *Totenbuch-Forschungen*, 261.
[299] On what Niwinski called as the white coffins, which date to the 18th Dynasty, there are depictions of burial rites, scenes of mourners, mummy transport, and offerings before the deceased: Niwinski, *21st Dynasty Coffins from Thebes*, 11.
[300] For their roles in the protection of the deceased, see below, 35.
[301] Niwinski, in: *Totenbuch-Forschungen*, 262.
[302] Niwinski, in: Uehlinger (ed.), *Images as Media*, 32.
[303] On the role of Isis and Nephthys as mourners and kites, see below, 35.
[304] Niwinski argues that these depictions will equip the deceased magically, and ensure his protection and resurrection in the hereafter: Niwinski, *21st Dynasty Coffins from Thebes*, 15.
[305] Van Walsem argues that the vignettes on the Mythological Papyri and the Late Period coffins have the same functions: Van Walsem, *The Coffin of Djedmonthuiufankh*, 353.

underworld, but they contain rituals performed for their owners. For that reason the depiction of the Lake of Fire on these papyri and also on the New Kingdom coffins might allude to different rituals performed on different occasions, which can also explain the different forms of the lake. Sometimes it is depicted with baboons and fire signs as in the vignettes of the BD 126, or as a place where the sinners are burnt in fire.

2.4. The Cosmographical Locations of the Lake of Knives and the Lake of Fire

The Egyptian Vision of Cosmos

The Pyramid, the tomb, and the coffin, all serve as a metaphor for the cosmos, which the dead inhabit and pass through. The key point of interest here is where the observable inhabited parts of the world merge with the invisible 'Otherworld', and how the Egyptians envisaged and ordered the physical world (sky, earth, and horizon) within this wider cosmos. The proper organization of the Egyptian cosmos was of great importance and it displays a fixed form during rituals connected with birth and rebirth, death and resurrection, as well as when the Egyptians created their own ritual landscape of pyramids, coffins and tombs. These ritual landscapes were envisaged or mirrored as microcosms of macrocosms.[306]

In Egyptian ritual texts the exact orientation of a performer was prescribed by the specific religious context.[307] Ritual landscapes within these ritual texts were oriented or placed in specific cosmographical locations according to the kind of ritual performed. For instance, when a priest performs a ritual in which he is worshipping the sun god Re at his rising and setting, he faces east and west respectively, and the ritual landscapes should also be placed at east or west. Not much has been written on the orientation of Egyptian ritual texts, but studies of this kind have been restricted to orientation of Egyptian architecture.[308]

When investigating the orientation of ritual texts, the first problem encountered is how one can construct a ritual from a single specific text. The placing of the text corpus on coffin sides, temple and tomb walls will be presented to reach the construction of a ritual. After reaching the construction of a ritual, the orientation of the performer of the ritual will be investigated in order to show how the ritual landscape within a ritual is oriented according to the orientation of the performer. This methodology will then be applied to the texts in which the Lake of Knives and the Lake of Fire occur, to show how the cosmographical locations of the two lakes change from one text to another, depending on the ritual performed and which direction the performer of the ritual is facing.

The Pyramid and the Pyramid Texts

It is not always explicit how a ritual can be constructed, and sometimes it is impossible to give a specific explanation to a ritual text.[309] For instance, the Pyramid Texts are not provided with vignettes, representations, or ritual directions. It is a single exception, that spell 355 in the Pyramid of Teti is entitled 'Opening of the Doors of Heaven'. The Pyramid Texts only preserve the ritual recitations.[310] Allen argues that the Pyramid Texts that address the deceased in the second person are ritual in nature. They were recited in the rites probably taking place during the funeral or after burial, and they were inscribed on the walls of the chambers of the pyramid to ensure their ongoing effect.[311]

Although the Pyramid Texts are best approached for analysis in three major groups (Offering rituals, Resurrection Ritual and Morning Ritual) it is difficult to give a precise description for the episodes and continuity of each ritual.[312] On the basis of his study of the Cannibal Hymn within the Pyramid Texts, Eyre argues that the reconstruction of a liturgy within the Pyramid Texts should be 'imaginative exercise,'[313] and needs to connect between the mythological and the ritual context of the spell. In addition, some other elements should be considered, for instance where the spell was placed on the walls of the pyramid and its sequence. In fact each pyramid should be dealt with as a unity and the ordering of the texts on the walls of the pyramids varies from one to another.[314] The Pyramid Texts are arranged in vertical columns on the interior walls of each pyramid. The arrangement and the numbering of the Pyramid Texts since their initial publication by Sethe has caused confusion in referring to the actual orders and functions of these spells on the walls of each pyramid.[315] Sethe arranged the Pyramid Texts starting with the Pyramid of Unas and then, Pepi I, Merenre, and Pepi II, in chronological order, but this arrangement does not refer to the actual order of the spells within each pyramid. This has led modern scholars of Egyptology to study the texts of each pyramid individually.[316]

---

[306] Raven, *JEA* 91 (2005), 37.

[307] Raven, *JEA* 91 (2005), 37. On the relation between ritual, man and cosmos order, see Assmann, in: Assmann, A. (ed.), *Stimme, Figur Kritik und Restitution*, 110.

[308] For the different ways the ancient Egyptians used to orient their buildings, see Isler, *JARCE* 29 (1989), 191-206; on the most recent discussion on the orientation of the pyramids at Giza, see Magdolen, in: Bárta and Krejčí (eds), *Abusir and Saqqara in Year 2000*, 491-8.

[309] Allen, in: *Hommages Leclant* I, 5-28. For the full discussion of the placing of the spell of the Cannibal Hymn, see Eyre, *Cannibal Hymn*, 41-7

[310] Eyre argues that only the offering rituals in which lists show the items to be offered can be used as evidence of a ritual direction within the Pyramid Texts: Eyre, *Cannibal Hymn*, 41.

[311] Allen, *The Ancient Egyptian Pyramid Texts*, 5.

[312] Allen, *The Ancient Egyptian Pyramid Texts*, 5-6.

[313] Eyre, *Cannibal Hymn*, 40.

[314] Leclant, in: *Textes et Langages de l'Égypte pharaonique* II, 37-52.

[315] Sethe, *Die altägyptischen Pyramidentexte*.

[316] Leclant, *Les Textes de la Pyramide de Pepy I er*; Allen, *The Ancient Egyptian Pyramid Texts*.

Many of the Pyramid Texts spells were presented in the first person to be spoken by the deceased himself and thus personalising the text to an individual.[317] The shifting from the first person to the second person within the Pyramid Texts may refer to the fact that the origin of the Pyramid Texts was a papyrus roll, read by a priest and addressed to the deceased, and this shifting of the pronouns refers to the editorial revisions and thus personalizing the text in each pyramid. In the pyramids of Unas and Pepi these editorial corrections are very clear on entire wall sections.[318]

The attempt made by Allen at reconstructing the texts within the pyramid of Unas is unique.[319] Allen tries to treat the material architecture as representation of the passage of the king from the underworld to the sky. Allen's analysis indicates that different spells with different content were placed on purpose in specific areas of the burial chambers of the pyramid, implying that the texts and architecture worked together to ensure an eternal life for the king. The individual spells within the pyramid chambers are grouped together in what he called sequences of the spells. The texts begin from the burial chamber (*dwꜣt*), and they proceed through the space to the antechamber (*ꜣḫt*) and then to the corridors and the doorway. The whole architecture of the Pyramid of Unas is simply representing the same theme that is represented on the walls of the New Kingdom tombs, referring to the path of the sun from the west to the east. The sun dies in the west, uniting with Osiris in the Duat and rising in the east.[320] The only difference between the Old Kingdom pyramids and the New Kingdom tombs is that the New Kingdom tombs are illustrated, while the Old Kingdom pyramids only present the texts for recitation.[321]

The same methodology was used by Vischak to argue that the same concordance occurs in the tombs of the elite of the Old Kingdom, exemplified in the case of the decoration of the tomb of Ankhmahor.[322] The only difference between the two methods is the use of mainly pictorial representations rather than presenting the texts recitations on the private tomb walls.

The Coffin and Coffin Texts

In the Coffin Texts, decorations, orientation of the texts, titles, rubrics and glosses are of great importance.[323] They provide evidence of how, when and by whom the ritual might be performed. In the Middle Kingdom coffins the decoration consists of text bands, and usually goes with the placing of the body of the deceased on its left side and thus facing east.[324] The long back west side is inscribed with texts for Anubis as the patron of the western desert, and thus good burial for the deceased in the west is ensured.[325] On the front eastern side, an invocation offering is inscribed for Osiris as provider of offerings and thus connected with the east. The east side of the coffin is the place of communication between the living and the dead. For that reason the offering formulae invoked for Osiris as Foremost of the West is inscribed on the east.[326] The place of the offering tables in Old Kingdom tombs was the east. The east was also the place of the sunrise. Osiris was also the god of resurrection, and the east was the place where the sun was born every morning.[327] From the reign of Sesostris I, Isis and Nephthys are depicted at the foot and head ends respectively. Willems argues that the placing of these two goddesses on these sides of the coffin has a ritual background, which is derived from their roles as female mourners or kites during the burial rites.[328] Isis as the widow of the deceased was represented on the coffin facing him; Nephthys protects him from behind and thus was represented on the back.[329]

During the reigns of Sesostris II and III, the four sons of Horus were depicted on the edge columns along the corners of the two long sides of the coffin as protectors of the deceased.[330] Imset and Hapi are connected with the northern (head) end, and Duamutef and Qebehsnuef with southern end (at the foot).[331] This is corroborated by the association of Imesty and Hapi with the two hands or arms of the deceased, and Duamutef and Qebehsenuef with the feet or legs. Imset and Hapy are equated with the souls of Pe (Buto in the north) and Duamutef and Qebehsenuef with the souls of Nekhen in the south (CT spells 157-158). They were later depicted wearing the crowns of Upper and Lower Egypt respectively.[332] The lid is identified with the sky goddess Nut and the four sons of Horus represent the poles that support the sky, which ensures the connection between the placing of the body within the coffin and the direction of the cosmos.[333]

---

317 Allen, *The Ancient Egyptian Pyramid Texts*, 6.
318 Allen, *The Ancient Egyptian Pyramid Texts*, 6.
319 Allen, in: *Hommages Leclant* I, 5-28.
320 Allen, in: *Hommages Leclant* I, 24.
321 Allen, in: *Hommages Leclant* I, 24-28.
322 Vischak, *JARCE* 40 (2003), 133-157.
323 For the importance of the titles to a ritual, see Willems, in; Willems (ed.), *The World of Coffin Texts*, 203-7.
324 Willems, *Chests of Life*, 122-4; *Heqata*, 364.
325 Willems, *Chests of Life*, 124.
326 Lapp, *Die Opferformel des Alten Reichs*, 233.
327 This back (west) and the front (east) sides of the coffin are not arranged in the same way on coffins from Asyut, but they replaced each other: Willems, *Chests of Life*, 118-122. This may have been done because the artists in Asyut noted that the orientation of their necropolis was not ideal, and they have to reverse the two sides of the coffin to go with the orientation of cosmos: Bleiberg, in: *Studies Redford*, 118-9.
328 Willems, *Chests of Life*, 134.
329 Willems, *Chests of Life*, 135.
330 Willems, *Chests of Life*, 140.
331 Willems, *Chests of Life*, 140-1.
332 Raven, *JEA* 91 (2005), 41-3.
333 The New Kingdom coffin places Isis at the head and Nephthys at the feet of the deceased. The only difference between the Middle Kingdom decoration schemes is that Imset and Duamutef are placed on the right while Qebehsenuef and Hapi are placed on the left: Willems, *Chests of Life*, 141; Von Falck, *SAK* 34 (2006), 126, 129-30.

Titles, as Willems argue, 'place the text to which it belongs in ceremonial context.'[334] Unfortunately de Buck was not interested in the titles of the spells and did not pay full attention to them. In the case of Shu spells for instance, de Buck argues, 'the using of titles to a spell is only of a limited interest for a proper assessment',[335] and they are, according to de Buck, later additions, which do not necessarily correspond with the original purpose of the text.[336] The titles and rubric can occur at the beginning or at the end of a spell. For instance CT spell 1082 (*CT* VII 354c) has the label 'Spell for being in Rosetau'.[337] These titles and labels explain what exactly the purpose of a spell is, but there are some explanatory labels that do not explain or identify themselves clearly. In this case the ancient editors of the Coffin Texts used some other language construction that helps in explaining the purpose of a spell.[338] To bring attention to something that needs to be stressed, they used, for instance, *jr* + a nominal construction, which puts stress on a particular nominal part of a spell. For instance in CT spell 1081 'As for anyone who is seen there alive, he cannot perish (*skj*)'.[339]

Glosses are also no less important than titles, and they can explain what might be obscure for a modern reader. CT spell 335, which occurs in 33 sources collected from different sites in Egypt, is the best example to be cited here. In *CT* IV 188-189a, the text reads 'I am the Great One who came into being himself'. A gloss on coffin B9Ca adds 'who is he, the Great One who came into being himself? He is Nun, the primeval water'. The explanatory glosses can in some spells take more space than the main text. For instance, CT spell 339 (*CT* IV 238a-239c), reads 'I raised the hair from the sacred *wḏ3t* Eyes in the time of the rage'. The glosses in most sources of the spell explain this in more detail 'what really is the sacred *wḏ3t* Eye in the time of the rage?' (And) 'Who actually raised the hair from it?' 'It is the right Eye of Re' is the answer.[340]

Not all Coffin Texts are provided with titles and glosses, and in this case the object frieze can give a clue to the ritual context of a spell. Jequier's fundamental study focuses on the individual objects rather than presenting the object frieze as a whole.[341] The object frieze is simply a register showing the items and the implements to be offered to the deceased during ritual. The objects within the register are usually depicted standing on a table, and they are accompanied by explanatory labels, which may occur in a register above the objects or distributed among them.[342] The object frieze and the placing of the spell on the coffin can provide information on the performance of certain rituals. It helps explaining the religious texts inscribed on the inner and outer parts of Middle Kingdom coffins.[343]

Jequier argues that the object frieze usually replaces other items which are not found among the tomb equipment. Willems rejects this suggestion arguing that the items represented within the object frieze are those used as funerary equipment of the deceased in his tomb.[344] Willems' argument seems convincing. For instance, the object frieze on the back of the coffin of Mentuhotep T1Be shows a headrest, and the spell inscribed below is for offering a headrest (CT spell 823).[345] Among the funerary equipment of the tomb of Mentuhotep, a headrest was found, which in turn can be evidence that the object frieze depicts the ideal tomb inventory. The object frieze is not the same on all coffins, and neither are the items represented. In many cases there is a locational relationship between the frieze objects on the sides of the coffin and the parts of the body buried in it. For instance, representations of a headrest on the head end of coffin B2BO, wigs on the head end of coffin S10C, and masks on coffin AIC are found.[346] However this arrangement of the objects is not the same on all coffins. For instance, the headrest on the coffin of Mentuhotep (T1Be) is depicted on the back of the coffin, which does not seem strange. The back of a coffin which is near the back of the head end can also be the right place exactly behind the head, and thus can be seen in relation with the headrest.

In some other CT spells, where titles and the object frieze do not exist, the stages of a particular ritual can be shown.[347] Spells simply stage direction indicating how a ritual should be performed. For instance, CT spell 925 deals with the offering of seven unguents and reads: '*smr* priest. The chest (*hn*) is opened; oil (*mrḥt*) is brought before this N'. Although the text does not give detailed directions of the performance of the ritual, it can be envisaged that a *smr* priest is the one who will perform this part of the ritual, and that the tools (the chest and the oil) needed for performing the ritual exist.[348]
This methodology brings together texts, actions and symbolic explanations from the material record.

The Cosmographical Location of the Lake of Knives

The Lake of Knives occurs in CT spell 823, and reads:

[334] Willems, *Heqata*, 276.
[335] Willems, *Heqata*, 197; *The World of the Coffin Texts*, 272.
[336] Willems, *Heqata*, 273; *The World of the Coffin Texts*, 198.
[337] Silverman, in: Allen et al., *Religion and Philosophy in Ancient Egypt*, 35.
[338] Silverman, in: Allen et al., *Religion and Philosophy in Ancient Egypt*, 35.
[339] *CT* VII, 354a (spell 1081).
[340] Silverman, in: Allen et al., *Religion and Philosophy in Ancient Egypt*, 37.
[341] Jequier, *Les frises d'objets des sarcophages du Moyen Empire*.
[342] Willems, *Chests of Life*, 202.
[343] Willems, *Chests of Life*, 200.
[344] Willems, *Chests of Life*, 209-211.
[345] *CT* VII, 231-24f (spell 339).
[346] Willems, *Chests of Life*, 209.
[347] Willems, *Heqata*, 151.
[348] Willems, *Heqata*, 151; for more examples of a similar relation between the Coffin Texts and the object frieze, see Willems, *Chests of Life*, 203-6.

r3 n rdjt wrs n N pn	A spell for giving a headrest to this N.
ʿḥʿ ḥr tp jbtyw	Horus stands at the head of the trappers.
nḥm=f N pn ḏd=f j nṯrw	He saves this N; he says, "Oh gods,
skdw m-ẖnw š ds	Sailing in the Lake of Knife,
ḥr=sn m ẖsfj.t	Whose attention is directed to the meeting,
ḥr jṯt jbw ḥsḳ tpw ʿnḫw	On the day of seizing the hearts, and chopping off the heads of the living,
nn wnt jrj=ṯn nw r=j n ḏd nṯrw	It is not possible that you do that to me because of what the gods say."
jnk ʿmʿm=f jrj ḏs=f št3w jrw	I am his throw stick,[349] who created himself, mysterious of shapes.
ʿnḫ=k jt=j wṯs=k tp=j	May you live, my father. May you raise up my head.
nn ẖpr ḏsw=ṯn r=j	Your knives will not exist against me.[350]

CT spell 823 refers to an offering of a headrest to the deceased, who is said to sail over the Lake of Knife. I will try to explain here the symbolism of offering a headrest, and the relation between the headrest and the horizon on one hand, and the Lake of Knives and the horizon on the other hand, in order to reach the cosmographical location of the Lake of Knives.

The Symbolism of the Headrest

The most famous headrest is the one found in the tomb of Tutankhamun (fig. 23). This headrest consists of a central figure of the god Shu, but the role he plays has been explained in three different ways. The most widely accepted opinion among scholars is that of Carter.[351] He has argued that the central figure represents Shu separating the sky goddess Nut from the earth god Geb.[352] According to Carter's explanation, the top part of the headrest represents the sky, while the bottom represents the earth. When the deceased puts his head on the upper part, he is then identified with the stars and the sky. Another opinion concerning the decoration of the headrest, and not completely different from that of Carter, assumes that the central figure is of Shu supporting the sky goddess Nut, and the base is not associated at all with Geb.[353] The third opinion is that of de Buck, who had suggested that the headrest is a symbol of the raising of the sun out of the netherworld by Shu.[354]

[349] *Wb* I, 186.2.
[350] *CT* VII, 231-24f (spell 823).
[351] For the complete list of references of the scholars who accepted Carter's suggestion, see Hellinckx, *SAK* 29 (2001), 63. n. 7; for a detailed discussion on Shu spells, see Willems, *Heqata*, 297-323; *World of the Coffin Texts*, 197-209.
[352] Carter, *The Tomb of Tutankhamun* III, 116.
[353] Reeves, *The Complete Tutankhamun*, 183.
[354] Hellinckx, *SAK* 29 (2001), 63.

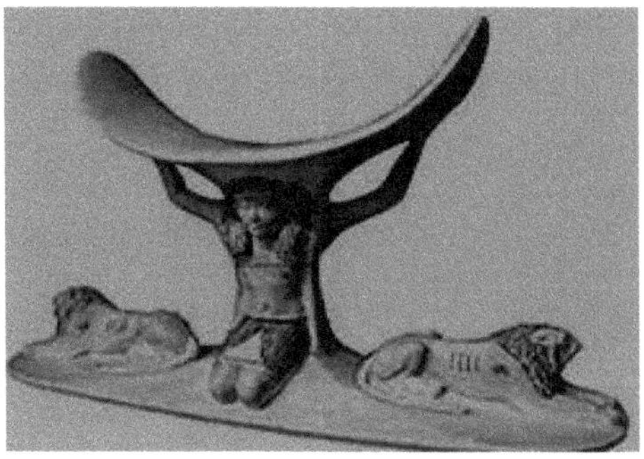

Fig. 23. A headrest from the tomb of Tutankhamun (after Wilkinson, *Reading Egyptian Art*, fig. 4, 68).

In the three different opinions, the two recumbent lions are identified with the two lions guarding the two mountain peaks of Manu and Bakhu, between which the sun sets and rises. It seems clear here that as the sun is flanked by the two mountain peaks, the headrest flanks the head of the deceased.[355] Some headrests from the Middle Kingdom bear the decoration of a pair of hands carved on the underside of the curved upper part.[356] In addition to the pair of the hands, some headrests were also decorated with a sun disk, which rests between two arms or hands carved on the upper curved part. These hands may represent the supportive function of the headrest.[357] The raising up of the head by the two hands symbolises the lifting up of the deceased's head to the sky.[358] Perraud argues that the two hands represent the two hands of the sleeper, who puts his two hands under his head when he is a sleep. She concludes that the sun disk on the upper curved part assimilates the head with the sun, and thus the headrest with the horizon where the sun rises and sets.[359]

The representation of the two hands on the curved upper part might also resemble the representation of the two hands that support the lower curved part in the Middle Kingdom headrests. So as the sun disk is lifted to the sky by the two hands of Shu and is received by the two hands of the sky goddess Nut, the deceased's head is lifted to the sky by the two hands of Shu and is received by the hands of the sky goddess Nut (fig. 24). This conclusion is supported by representation of New Kingdom images that show the sun being raised out of the underworld by two hands and is received by two hands of the sky goddess Nut. The representation of the god Shu as he is lifting up the ram headed god from the

[355] Wilkinson, *Reading Egyptian Art*, 138-9.
[356] Hellinckx, *SAK* 29 (2001), 69.
[357] Wilkinson, *Reading Egyptian Art*, 159.
[358] Sourdive, *La main dans l'Egypte pharaonique*, 255-7.
[359] Perraud, *Appuis-tête de l'Egypte pharaonique: typologie et significations*, 268-69 (quoted from Hellinckx, *SAK* 29 (2001), 69). The headrest can also be used as an amulet and applied to the neck of the deceased. These amulets can carry representations of the god Bes, who plays the role of the protector of the head of the deceased. For this type of amulet in the shape of headrest, see Konrad, *ZÄS* 134 (2007), 134-7.

netherworld also supports this hypothesis (fig. 25a-b).[360]

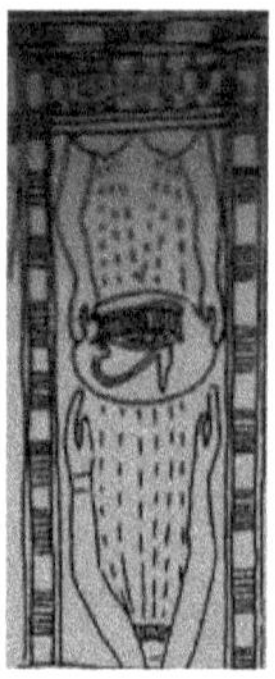

Fig. 24. The raising and receiving of the sun by the two pairs of arms (after Hellinckx, *SAK* 29 (2001), 70).

Fig. 25a-b. The raising of the sun out of the netherworld by Shu (after Hellinckx, *SAK* 29 (2001), 66. fig. 3a-b).

The headrest occupied by a head closely resembles the representations of Shu lifting the sun to the sky.[361] As the sun god Re is lifted up to sky to start his journey in the eastern horizon, the head of the deceased is lifted up by the headrest to pass the place of passage over the Lake of Knives.

Most of headrests found in the Old Kingdom and early First Intermediate Period were painted in red. Perraud argues that the red colour imitates the colour of wood, but at the end of her conclusion she argues that the red colour reproduces the red glow of the sun at its rising and setting in the horizon.[362] It seems possible that the headrest is painted red to enhance its horizon symbolism. The horizon was one of the places where the sun god Re defeats his enemies, so this colour may refer to the blood of the enemies of the sun god, or to the colour of fire.[363]

Some headrests from the Old Kingdom were also gilded or painted in yellow, which also has a solar symbolism. Gold in the New Kingdom texts is a metaphor of the light and rays of the sun god Re.[364] Painted yellow or red, the two colours have to do with the sun, whether in its rising or setting between the two horizons.[365] In all the three explanations of the functions of the headrest as representation of the sunrise and the sky-lifting, the deceased wishes to be lifted to the sky, to rise from death and start the journey across the sky like the sun god Re. The early drawing of the object frieze on the coffin of Mentuhotep made by Steindorf, shows that the headrest of Mentuhotep is painted yellow (fig. 26).[366]

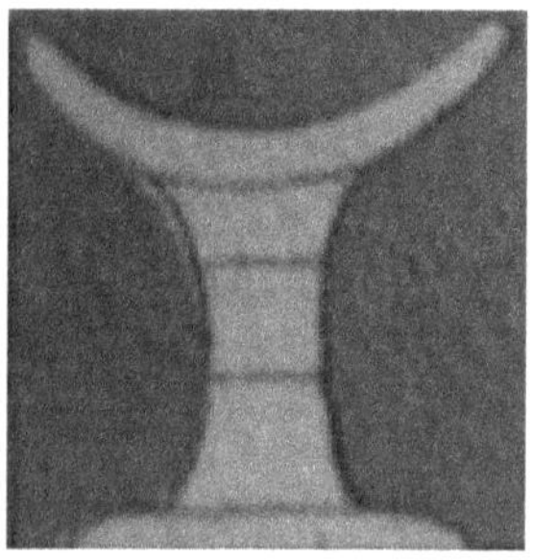

Fig. 26. The headrest on the object frieze of Mentuhotep (after Steindorf, *Grabfunde des Mittleren Reichs* I, pl. III).

Coffin Text spells associated with the headrest connect the head rising from the headrest with the sunrise. This connection equates the headrest with the sky.[367] These spells usually use the verb *wṯs tp* or *ṯsi tp* 'to raise up' or 'lift up' a head of a deceased.[368] Raising or lifting the head may refer to the lifting of the sky by Shu. In CT spell 366, there is a passage which reads:

ṯsj ḥ3t=j jn šw m-ʿ=f j3bt	My head is raised up by Shu with his left hand,
w3j=f pt jm=f	With which he supports the sky.[369]

The verb (*ṯs*) in this spell is written with the determinative of a headrest, which in the present context seems to suggest that the mythological conception of raising a head by Shu was associated with a headrest as early as the Middle Kingdom.[370]

As well as evidence for a connection between the headrest and the sky, religious texts express a relationship between the headrest and the horizon, and between the headrest and the Lake of Knives. The connection between the horizon and the headrest is found in a passage in Chapter 166 of the Book of the

[360] Konrad, *ZÄS* 134 (2007), 136.
[361] Hellinckx, *SAK* 29 (2001), 66.
[362] Perraud, *Appuis-tête de l'Egypte pharaonique: typologie et significations*, 90-91 (quoted from Hellinckx, 2001, 86).
[363] On the symbolism of the red colour in magic, see Pinch, in: Davies (ed.), *Colour and Painting in Ancient Egypt*, 182-5.

[364] Zandee, *Amunhymnus des Papyrus Leiden* I 344, verso I, 356-58.
[365] For objects found in the tomb equipment, as exemplified in pottery vessels, and can be related to rituals taking place before, at, or after burial, see Op de Beeck, *ZÄS* 134 (2007), 157-65.
[366] Steindorf, *Grabfunde des Mittleren Reichs* I, 10-24.
[367] Hellinckx, *SAK* 29 (2001), 88.
[368] *CT* VII, 136c (spell 934) and *CT* III, 300b (spell 232).
[369] *CT* V, 27a (spell 366).
[370] Münster, *Isis*, 100.

Dead, which is devoted to the offering of a headrest and reads:[371]

r3 n wrs	A spell for the headrest.
srs ṯw mnwt sḏr.tj	May the swallows awaken you when you are asleep
stj[372]*=sn tp=k r 3ḫt*	May they raise up your head to the horizon.[373]

On the vignettes of this chapter on the walls of the Theban tomb 290 from Deir el-Medina, a headrest is depicted on a building in the shape of a pylon (fig. 27).[374] The relationship between the pylon and the horizon is explicit, as both represent the place where the sun shines. The assimilation between the headrest and the horizon is now explicit, and in turn the headrest symbolises the horizon.[375]

Fig. 27. A headrest standing on a pylon (after Saleh, *Das Totenbuch in den thebanischen Beamtgräbern*, 86, fig. 111).

The (*3ḫt*) is the place where the sun rises and sets every day. It is also one of the places where the enemies of Re are necessarily overcome.[376] In CT spell 823, the theme of overcoming the enemies is obvious. The deceased begs the gods who sail over the Lake of Knives to save him on that day of the chopping off the heads and seizing the hearts. It seems that there is a strong symbolic relation between the headrest and the horizon on one side, and the Lake of Knives and the horizon on the other side. The celestial symbolism of the headrest is in fact connected with the wish of the deceased to be received after death by the sky goddess Nut, and to live perpetually with the stars.[377] The deceased's wish can be stressed by causing the sarcophagus, the tomb, the coffin, the funerary bier, and the headrest to symbolise the sky goddess Nut.[378]

The horizon symbolism of the headrest might also relate to the Egyptian conception of sleep.[379] Sleep to the ancient Egyptian was dangerous like death. The sleeping person was threatened by dangerous creatures such as snakes, and thus very close to the state of death.[380] The Egyptians also noted the parallelism between the sleeper and the night sun. In the evening the sun goes down to the world of the dead and succeeds in overcoming the enemies in the netherworld and shine in the morning. They looked for a way by which they could transport this to the world of human beings. The two methods they used are found in the headrest and the bed. Because of the similarity between the sun and the head on one side, and the headrest and the mountains on the other side, the headrest was liable to carry solar symbolism.[381] It is also interesting to note that the head resting in the headrest bears a strong resemblance to the hieroglyphic sign for *3ḫt* 'Horizon'.[382]

In the coffin of Mentuhotep (T1Be) the placing of CT spell 823 on the inner back, exactly behind the head, clearly points to an explanation of this sort for the relationship between the mythological and the ritual contexts of the spell.[383] The spell is placed on the back facing the eastern side which is the front of the coffin. The deceased overcomes his enemies while crossing the Lake of Knives. So, the Lake of the Knives is located in the eastern horizon.

A priest who is performing the headrest offering ritual places the headrest under the head of the deceased who faces east, and the headrest has its symbolism with the east. In CT spell 823 the Lake of Knives is envisaged as being situated in the eastern horizon, a place where the sun god Re sails every day before he rises in the sky.[384] As a place at the eastern horizon, the Lake of Knives is one of the places where the sun god Re defeats his enemies. On the ritual level, the Lake of Knives is a place the deceased wishes to sail over, and not to be threatened by these gods who chop off the heads of the unprepared dead. The mention of Horus as the one who sits at the head of the trappers also gives the Lake of Knives a celestial aspect. One of the roles of Horus as personification of the king and kingship is helping the deceased in his ascension to the sky. The ascension of the king takes place in the eastern horizon where he ascends a ladder to reach the sky.[385]

[371] Perraud, in: *Totenbuch-Forschungen*, 283.
[372] Willems suggests that this verb was written incorrectly and should be *ṯsi* and not *srs*: Willems, *Heqata*, 402. n. 68.
[373] Naville, *TB*, Kapitel 166, pl. CLXXXV, line 3. Hellinckx transliterated *sṯsi* as *srs* which is, as Willems says, wrong: Hellinckx, *SAK* 29 (2001), 88; Willems, *Heqata*, 402, n. 68.
[374] Saleh, *Das Totenbuch in den thebanischen Beamtgräbern*, 86.
[375] Hellinckx, *SAK* 29 (2001), 88.
[376] Assmann, *LÄ* III, 3-7; Jansen-Winkeln, *SAK* 23 (1996), 201-15.
[377] Hellinckx, *SAK* 29 (2001), 88.
[378] Assmann, *MDAIK* 28, 1(1972), 47-73.
[379] Szpakowska, *Behind Closed Eyes*, 1-2.
[380] Hellinckx, *SAK* 29 (2001), 68.
[381] Hellinckx, *SAK* 29 (2001), 93.
[382] See Gardiner's sign list N27.
[383] For the performance of the offering headrest ritual, see below, 85-6.
[384] Allen, in: *Mysterious Lands*, 27.
[385] Davis, *JNES* 36 (1977), 161-79.

2.4 .The Cosmographical Location of the Lake of Knives in the New Kingdom Sun Hymns and Book of the Dead

Hymns to the sun are the most frequent form of divine lyric in the Egyptian record.[386] They are common in New Kingdom private tombs, and they also appear in Mortuary Papyri. On the basis of his study of the Sun Hymns in the papyri of the New Kingdom, Naville argued that the Sun Hymns should have originated in a temple liturgy.[387] Stewart has noted that several copies of the Book of the Dead of the New Kingdom (in particularly 18th and 19th Dynasties) contain one or more complete Sun Hymns, which are identical with these found in the Theban liturgy of Amun Re as preserved in Papyrus Berlin 3055 (22nd Dynasty).[388] There is enough reason, according to Stewart, then to suppose, when parallels occur, that the source was a liturgical text.[389]

In 1949, T.G Allen published a number of Late Period Solar Hymns, which he identified as variants of the Book of the Dead Chapter 15. These new variants were labeled as BD Chapters 15A5, 15B 4-5 and 15H.[390] With the exception of 15H, Assmann has objected to attributing these solar hymns to Chapter 15 of the Book of the Dead.[391]

Hymns in private tombs and statue inscriptions may be described as prayers, to grant the deceased funerary requests connected with his afterlife. However the longest and most important hymns are found on Hibis Temple walls and also on papyri.[392] The text describing the crossing over the Lake of Knives occurs in a composite Sun Hymn from the New Kingdom.[393] The Lake of Knives also occurs in another Sun Hymn, which is depicted on the right hand side of the entrance of TT 102.[394] The Hymn reads:

jnḏ ḥr=k rˁ m wbn=k	Hail to you Re, at your rising,
jmn sḫm nṯrw	Amun, power of the gods,
wbn=k sḥḏ.n=k t3wj	You rise when you have illuminated the two lands.
ḏ3j=k ḥrt m ḥtp	You cross the sky in peace.
jb=k 3w m mˁnḏt	Your heart is joyful in the *Mˁnḏt* barque.
sw3=k ḥr ṯst n mr nḫ3wj	You pass over the Sandbank of the Lake of Knives.
sḫrw ḫftjw=k	Your enemies have been felled.
jw=k ḫˁj.tj m ḥwt šw	You have appeared in the House of Shu,
ḥtp.tj m 3ḫt jmntt	And have set in the western horizon.
šsp.n ḥm=k jm3ḫ	Your majesty has received veneration.
ˁwj mwt=k m s3 ḥ3=k	The arms of your mother protecting you,
m-ḫrt ḥr nt rˁ nb	Daily, everyday.
m33=j tw m ḥb=k nfr	May I see you in your beautiful festival,
m ḫnt=k nt ḏsr-ḏsrw	As in your Deir el-Bahri voyage.
ḫpr j3ḫw=k ḥr šnbt=j	May your radiance be upon my breast.
dw3=j tw nfrw=k m ḥr=j	May I worship you, (with) your beauty in my eyes,
dj=k ḥtp=j m ḥwt jrt.n=j	May you allow me to rest in the house I have built,
m ḥswt nt nṯr nfr	In the favour of the good god.

386 Assmann, *Liturgische Lieder*, 2; *STG*, 10; *Egyptian Solar Religion*, 1.

387 Naville, *TB*, Einleitung, 120.

388 Stewart, *JEA* 46 (1960), 83; in Chapter 15 of the Book of the Dead in Naville's addition, these Sun Hymns occur as part of this chapter. The text reads:

Adoration to your face
Maat embraces you, at the two times,
When you travel across the sky in joy,
The Lake of Knives has become in peace.
The Nik-serpent is overthrown and his arms are cut off.
The msktt-barque has received a good fair wind.
He who is in his shrine, his heart is pleased.

From the opening stanza of this text, one can conclude that it has been derived from a temple liturgy, where 'Maat embraces you' simply refers to the coronation ritual of the kings, which is one of the most common rituals during the New Kingdom, and is well-preserved on the walls of Karnak and Luxor Temples. In this ritual the king is usually represented offering Maat to the gods. It is also derived from Amun Ritual, and the Opening of the Mouth Ritual as seen in Hibis Temple: Assmann, *Liturgische Lieder*, 270.

389 Stewart, *JEA* 46 (1960), 83. Assmann has divided the Sun Hymns into three groups:

1- Texts of an Esoteric Body of Knowledge

These Sun Hymns were like the Underworld Books in that their knowledge, according to Assmann, was guarded in the New Kingdom by the royal class.

2- Standard Sun Hymn

Liturgical sun hymns used as a model by tomb owners who could not afford to generate new texts of their own. They originate in the cult, but are not esoteric or secret. Stewart defines traditional Sun Hymns by the fact that they occur more than once (Stewart, *JEA* 46 (1960), 84). Assmann adds one more aspect of these hymns, saying that they do not only occur more than once, but in more than one tradition. Assmann, *Egyptian Solar Religion*, 8.

3-Individual hymns

These hymns are distinct from the other two groups in relation to the expression of a traditional conceptual world. The individual hymns, in Assmann's definition, represent another conceptual world: Assmann, in: Assmann, A. (ed.), *Stimme, Figur Kritik und Restitution*, 114. The Lake of Knives occurs among the traditional Sun Hymns, which is group two.

390 Allen, *JNES* 8 (1949), 349-55.

391 Assmann, *Egyptian Solar Religion*, 5.

392 Assmann, *Egyptian Solar Religion*, 3. The textual transmission of these Sun Hymns in Assmann's words is 'dynamically active, which makes the understanding easier than in the case of the Book of the Dead, where the transmission of the text tends to be statically reproductive, which sometimes makes it impossible to understand. In the reproductive tradition the sole function is simply to copy a typical example. In this sense, the Book of the Dead has the character of a classic text of the Egyptian literary tradition, rather than that of a living literary form. To analyse the historical dimension of the texts of the New Kingdom Sun Hymns, one has to reconstruct the productive stage of their tradition. Religious tradition by its very nature tends towards reproductivity; for instance the process of canonisation, which transfers the holiness of an object to the discourse that has grown up around that object.' Assmann, *Egyptian Solar Religion*, 5-6.

393 For the sun hymn, see above, 10.

394 Assmann, *Liturgische Lieder*, 281-3; *STG*, 24; *Egyptian Solar Religion*, 13.

dj=k wn=j m-m šmsw=k	May you allow me to be among your followers,
ḥtp=kw m ḥrt nt dd=k	And resting in the tomb granted by you,
mj jrrwt n m3ʿtj tp t3	As is done for the righteous on earth.

The placing of the Sun Hymns on the New Kingdom private tombs walls plays an important role in identifying the cosmographical location of the Lake of Knives. The private tomb architecture tends to divide the tomb into two main parts: the funeral part, which leads to the burial chamber and was usually inscribed with funerary literature resembling texts found in the New Kingdom royal tombs,[395] and the cultic part which occupies the outer part of the tomb and leads to a chapel with the statue of the owner of the tomb. This second part of the private tombs serves in Assmann's opinion as an equivalent to the royal cult temple of the New Kingdom. So, the New Kingdom private tombs gathered the funerary function of the royal tombs and the cultic function of their (the royal tombs) mortuary temples.[396] The private tomb consisted of a number of chambers arranged on an axis, which was in theory at any rate oriented east-west, the entrance facing the rising sun. The thickness of the outer doorways during the early 18th Dynasty often showed the owner of the tomb on both sides facing outwards and worshipping the sun god. Later on it became customary to differentiate the two sides, showing on the left the deceased looking outwards and addressing a hymn to the rising sun and on the right turned inwards, adoring the setting sun.[397]

The deceased, while reciting these Sun Hymns, is facing east, the place of the sunrise, and facing west, the place of the sunset. The Sun Hymns were not placed on these sides of the tomb walls in a haphazard way, but the composer of the text considered the orientation of the cosmos in the first place. The ritual landscape in these Sun Hymns might also have been oriented in the same orientation of the performer or the worshipper. So, when the deceased is represented on the sides of the entrance of his tomb worshipping the sun god Re and faces east, the ritual landscape –the Lake of Knives– might also be oriented with the same orientation as the performer.

In these Sun Hymns, the Lake of Knives features as a place of passage for the barque of the sun in its journey across the sky. However it is difficult and sometimes impossible to envisage what was going on when the sun barque crossed the Lake of Knives. No detail is given, and the emphasis is on the act of passing.[398] The Sun Hymns, according to Assmann, might represent one of the several interpretations of what happens during the crossing of the barque of Re over the Lake of Knives, and not be a description of the journey itself.[399] This interpretation varies from one text to another. They also might be a description of the solar circuit and the cosmic process.[400] A priest reciting these Sun Hymns on the behalf of the deceased helps in cosmos maintenance.[401]

In the Book of the Dead, Sun Hymns are usually accompanied by vignettes showing a deceased worshipping the sun god Re at his rising or at his setting.[402] To pass safely over the Lake of Knives in the New Kingdom Book of the Dead, fair wind and good current are required. Fair wind and good current are typical Egyptian themes of traveling over the River Nile, which occur for instance in the New Kingdom Book of the Dead Chapter 15 A. III.[403] The good current occurs in the Book of the Dead Chapter 15. B I mentioned above.[404]

As argued above, the east-west axis is usually connected with the movement of the sun, but a problem occurs when a north-south axis is mentioned. Boats traveling over the River Nile to the south are traveling upstream and require fair wind, while these boats traveling to the north are traveling downstream and require good current. In his study on the depictions of the boat convoy in the Old Kingdom private tombs, Altenmüller argues:

1-The boat scenes in the Old Kingdom private tombs represent the journey of the deceased in rowing and sailing boats. In reality, the sailing and rowing boats represent the deceased's journeys over the River Nile, and on the symbolic level, the two boats represent the daily and nightly journeys of the sun god Re and the deceased across the sky.[405]
2-The journey of the deceased king during the Old Kingdom was also envisaged as a convoy of ships that is escorted by the day barque in the day journey, and by the night barque in the night journey. The pictorial evidence that supports that hypothesis is a depiction of a boat in the temple of Sahure in Abusir, which served as the daily journey of the deceased king across the sky. On the front section (*bow*) of the boat there is a depiction of a sun disk, which indicates that it was the day barque of the king (fig. 28).[406]

395 Assmann, *STG*, XVI-XVII.
396 Assmann, *STG*, XVI-XVII; for a detailed discussion on the placing of the Sun Hymns on private tomb walls, see Assmann, *STG*, XIV-XIX.
397 Stewart, *JEA* 46 (1960), 84.
398 Assmann, *Liturgische Lieder*, 272.

399 Assmann, in: Assmann, A. (ed.), *Stimme, Figur, Kritik und Restitution,* 114; more description for the journey of the sun god over the Lake of Knives is found in the Hour-Ritual texts. In these texts, the sun barque stops on the Sandbank of the Lake of Knives, the critical stage of the journey. The Book of Apep should be recited on this sandbank: Faulkner, *JEA* 24 (1938), 41-53.
400 Assmann, *Liturgische Lieder*, 273-4.
401 Assmann, in: Assmann, A. (ed.), *Stimme, Figur, Kritik und Restitution,* 114.
402 The vignettes of the papyrus of Ani show the deceased standing with both hands in the attitude of a prayer and accompanied by his wife.
403 For the text of BD 15 A. III, see above, 29.
404 For the text of BD 15 A. I, see above, 28-9.
405 Altenmüller, *SAK* 32 (2004), 11.
406 Borchardt, *Das Grabdenkmal des König Sahure* II, pl. 9; Altenmüller, *SAK* 32 (2004), 12-3.

Fig. 28. The day barque of Sahure and the sun disk on the bow of the boat
(after Borchardt, *Das Grabdenkmal des König Sahure* II, pl. 9).

3-The journey of the deceased's boat from the north to the south of the sky is envisaged as the daily journey of the sun god Re from the east to west (fig. 29).[407] It takes place in a boat that travels with the wind,[408] and is envisaged as a journey from the east to the beautiful west (*sḳdwt r jmnt nfrt*).[409]

Fig. 29. The journey from the north to the south in sailing boats from the tomb of Niankhkhnum and Khnumhotep
(after Moussa and Altenmüller, *Das Grab des Nianchchnum und Chnumhotep*, pl. 25).

The second journey of the deceased from the south to the north is envisaged as the night journey of the sun god Re from the west to the east,[410] and takes place in a rowing boat (fig. 30).[411] The destination of the deceased's journey from the south to the north is the Field of Offerings which according to the Pyramid Texts is located in the north-eastern side of the sky.[412]

Fig. 30. The journey of the deceased from the south to the north in rowing boats in the tomb of Niankhkhnum and Khnumhotep
(after Moussa and Altenmüller, *Das Grab des Nianchchnum und Chnumhotep*, pl. 30).

The north-south axis might also have stellar connotations, and the best example for this is the air shafts in the Pyramid of Kheops.[413] It is argued that the north shafts and the north entrance face the pole-star and the indestructible circumpolar stars, while the south shafts enable the deceased King to observe the passage of Orion or Sirius through the zenith.[414] The south might then refer to fertility and new life. It is the place from where the Nile comes. The north might then also be considered as place of resurrection where the Nile ends and fades out.[415]

In the Book of the Dead Chapter 153 the deceased wishes to ferry over the Lake of Knives to reach the northern sky.[416] The aim of the deceased's journey to the northern sky is to reach the Field of Offerings (*sḫt ḥtp*), the home of the Imperishable Stars (*jḫmw-sk*).[417] When the deceased says that he is travelling to the north that means his journey starts from the south, the place where the Fields of Reeds (*sḫt j3rw*) and the home of the Unwearying Stars (*jḫmw-wrḏ*) are located. The aim of the deceased's journey over the Lake of Knives and the Winding Waterway is to cross from the south of the sky to its north, where he can join the Imperishable Stars in the Field of Offerings.[418] On this evidence it seems plausible to argue that the Lake of Knives was located at the eastern horizon.[419]

---

407 Bickel, in: *Fs Hornung*, 41-56.
408 Altenmüller, *SAK* 32 (2004), 12.
409 Moussa and Altenmüller, *Das Grab des Nianchchnum und Chnumhotep*, 85-6.
410 In the tomb of Niankhkamun and Khnumhotep the journey of the deceased from the south to the north on the eastern wall runs from the left to the right, while the rest of the scenes on the same wall run from the right to the left: Moussa and Altenmüller, *Das Grab des Nianchchnum und Chnumhotep*, 90.
411 Altenmüller, *SAK* 32 (2004), 12.
412 Moussa and Altenmüller, *Das Grab des Nianchchnum und Chnumhotep*, 90-1; for the location of the Field of Offerings, see Barta, *Die Bedeutung der Pyramidentexte für den verstorbenen König*, 91-2; Krauss, *Astronomische Konzepte*, 279-82.

413 Raven, *JEA* 91 (2005), 39.
414 Stadelmann, *MDAIK* 50 (1994), 285-94.
415 For the placing of the text corpus of the Hymns to the rising sun and setting sun in the temple of Re at Medinet Habu, and how these texts were placed and oriented to fit in the Egyptian vision of cosmos, see Voß, *SAK* 23 (1996), 377-396.
416 For the text, see above, 29.
417 Krauss, *Astronomische Konzepte*, 14-27.
418 Krauss, *Astronomische Konzepte*, 14-27.
419 During the mummification ritual the body was placed on a north-south axis. This is confirmed by the vignettes in chapter 151 of the Book of the Dead. These vignettes have been described as a summary for the rituals taking place in the burial chamber of a tomb. However, as Raven argues, it might represent sets of rituals connected with mummification, revivification and funeral rites. In the vignettes of this chapter, Anubis is shown in the center while the deceased's head is directed towards the north and his feet are directed to the south. Isis is depicted at the foot end and Nephthys at the head end. The north-south direction is also connected with movement of the River Nile, which forms one of the most important

The Lake of Knives at the Edge of Cosmos

The Lake of Knives was also a place which witnessed the first appearance of the sun god from the primeval ocean Nun.[420] Nun was envisaged as limitless ocean and lies beyond the sky. Nun was also the source of the entire world's water.[421] The Lake of Knives was envisaged as a place that once contained the sacred egg from which the sun god Re appeared as occurs in the Magical Papyrus Harris BM EA 10042.[422]

The description of the Lake of Knives as located in the primeval ocean Nun is also found in the cosmology of Hermopolis. In a text in Hibis Temple Re is said to be born in the Island of Fire in the Lake of Knives.[423] In this text the Lake of Knives is envisaged here a place that is separated from the world of the living and the world of the dead. It is a place located at the edge of cosmos.

2.5. The Cosmographical Location of the Lake of Fire

The Lake of Fire in the Book of the Amduat

In the Book of the Amduat the Lake of Fire is depicted below the lower register of the Fifth Hour. The texts describe it as a place in the necropolis where no barque can sail over its water.

nwt j3kbjw nṯrw jmjw jmḥt	The waters of mourning of the gods in Imhet (necropolis),
n ʿpj n wj3 ḥr=sn	No barque can traverse over them.
n sḫm.n dw3tjw m mw=sn	The ones who live in the underworld have no power over their water,
wnn m ẖrt-nṯr pn	Which is in this necropolis.
wnn mw=sn r ntjw jm=s m sḏt	Their water for those who are in it is fire.[424]

The Fifth Hour in the Book of the Amduat represents the critical stage in the underworld journey of the sun god Re. The depiction of the landscape in the Kingdom of Sokar is interesting and can give clues to how the Egyptian cosmos was envisaged. The sun barque has to be dragged for hours over the mysterious ways and the sacred roads of the Kingdom of Sokar.[425] Robinson summaries the issues in the following way:

> The Egyptian cartographers who drew the scenes were following in a long tradition of describing the cosmological world around them. Like in much of their art, they seem to have used the experiences they gained from their environment, the cycle of the sunrise and sunset, the course of the Nile, the differences between the black land, *kmt*, and red land, *dšrt*, and even the rock formations in the hills around, to great effect. The landscape of the Amduat should be seen as a mirror image of this world, a metaphysical overlay, unknown and inaccessible to the living, yet laid upon, around and within the physical environment but known only to the divinities or solar visitors who nightly pass through its ways.[426]

This landscape found its way into the Books of the Netherworld in general. The sandy islands in the River Nile inspired the ancient Egyptian cartographers and they transferred the difficulties that the boat faces on the surface of the Nile to be depicted among the scenes of the Book of the Amduat.

The introductory passage of the Fourth Hour describes the area in the upper register as *w3t jrjt R3-st3w* 'a path belonging to Rosetau'. Rosetau is a name given to the Memphite necropolis, and it also designates the underworld. The Fourth and Fifth Hours of the Amduat conatin the crucial resurrection scenes of the journey of the sun god Re, as he is preparing himself for the coming dawn.[427] The introductory passages of the Fifth Hour relate that the sun god Re is towed along the ways of the netherworld.

sṯ3w nṯr pn ʿ3	This Great god is towed,
ḥr w3wt m3ʿwt nt dw3t	along the true ways of the netherworld,
m gs ḥrj ḳrrt št3t nt skr šʿj=f	In the upper half of the Secret Cavern of Sokar-who-is-upon-his-Sand.[428]

The texts in the Fifth Hour locate the cavern of the sun god Re in the west.

rn n ḳrrt nṯr pn jmnt	The name of the cavern of this god is West.
rn n wnwt nt grḥ sšmt nṯr pnʿ3	The name of the Hour of the night, which guides this Great god is,
sšmt ḥrjt-jb wi3=s	She-Who-Guides-in-the-Midst-of-Her-Barque.
w3wt št3wt nt jmnt	The secret paths of the West.[429]

So the Lake of Fire is here located in the west, and represents one of the stations of the sun god Re in his

features of the Egyptian landscape: Raven, *JEA* 91 (2005), 41; Willems, *Chests of Life*, 134-5; *Heqata*, 92.

420 Allen, *Genesis in Egypt*, 4.

421 Allen, in: *Mysterious Lands*, 25.

422 For the text, see above, 29.

423 Bickel, *Cosmogonie*, 28; for the text, see above, 10.

424 Hornung, *The Egyptian Amduat*, 171.

425 Rößler-Köhler, in: Gundlach and Seipel (eds), *Das frühe ägyptische Königtum*, 76-7.

426 Robinson, in: Wahllberg et al., *CRE* III, 55.

427 Hornung, *The Ancient Egyptian Books of the Afterlife*, 37.

428 Hornung, *The Egyptian Amduat*, 140.

429 Hornung, *The Egyptian Amduat*, 141.

night journey across the netherworld. The region occupied by the Fifth Hour represents the west, and includes all the essential elements of the realm of the dead.

The evidence which supports this hypothesis is a depiction of the grave of Osiris in the midst of the upper register flanked by two birds representing Isis and Nephthys.[430] The grave is guarded by Anubis. It is another image of the whole netherworld in which the sun god Re and Osiris unite during night and reappear as a scarab in the morning. Wilkinson points out that Isis and Nephthys are here goddesses of direction, symbolising north and south, while the goddess of the West had already been mentioned in the beginning of the Hour. This refers to the fact that the whole scene takes place in the west,[431] and in turn confirms that the Lake of Fire is located in the west specifically in this Hour.

There is a strong resemblance between the journey of the sun god Re over the Lake of Fire and his journey over the Sandbank of Apep in the Lake of Knives, but both time and space are different. The only difference between the two places of passage is that the texts in the case of the Lake of Knives are presented for recitation, while in the case of the Lake of Fire the texts are illustrated.

The Lake of Fire in the Book of the Gates

In the Third Hour of the Book of the Gates the Lake of Fire is described:

nṯrw jmjw š ḫbt	The gods who are in the Lake of Fire.
š pw wnn=f m dwꜣt	It is a lake: it exists in the Duat,
dbn=f m nn nṯrw	It is surrounded by these gods.
wnn=sn m ꜥꜣww	They are in wrappings,
wnn=sn m ꜥꜣf Variant	They are in linen cloth,[432]
tpw=sn ḥꜣj	And their heads are bare.
š[433] *pn mḥ m kꜣmwtt*	This lake is full with barley,
mw n š pn m wꜣwꜣt	And the water of this lake is fire.
ḫpp ꜣpdw mꜣꜣ=sn mw=f	The birds fly away when they see its water,
ssn=sn stj ntj jm=f	And smell the stench which is in it.
jn n=sn rꜥ	Re says to them:
ḫrt=ṯn n nṯrw m kꜣmwtt nt š=ṯn	Your share of gods is this barley of your lake.
kft tpw=ṯn	Your heads are uncovered,
štꜣw ḥꜥw=ṯn	Your bodies are hidden,
ṯꜣw n fnḏw=ṯn	Breathe with your noses!
ḥtpw=ṯn n=ṯn kꜣmwt	Your offerings belong to you, namely barley,
ꜣwt n=ṯn š=ṯn	Your offerings belong to you of your lake,
mw=f n=ṯn	Its water belongs to you,
jwtj tꜣw=f r=ṯn	Its heat is not against you,
jwtj hh=f r ẖwt=ṯn	Its blast is not against your bodies.
jn. n=sn n rꜥ	They said to Re:
mj r=k r=n ḏꜣj m wjꜣ=f	Come to us, the one who sails in his barque,
sttw n=f jrt=f tkꜣ	Whose eye ignites the flame for him,
sḥḏw n=f ꜣḫt=f dwꜣt	And whose bright eye illuminates the underworld for him
hj ꜥr=k ꜣḫ n=n	Oh, you will ascend, the Beneficial One to us,
nṯr ꜥꜣ stj m jrt=f	The Great god who burns with his eye.
ꜣwt=sn m t kꜣmwtt	Their offering is from bread of barley.
ḥnḳt=sn m kꜣmwtt	Their beer is from barley.
ḳbḥw=sn m mw	Their libation is from water.
jw dj n=sn ꜣwt	The one who gives them offerings,
m nb mꜣwt m š pn	Is the Lord of Regeneration in this lake,
m nb mꜣꜥ m š pn variant	Is the Lord of the Bank of this lake.[434]

The text refers to the Lake of Fire as a place that is located in the netherworld. It is surrounded by the gods who are wrapped in linen cloth and their heads are uncovered. The Lake of Fire is full of barley, and its water is fire. The birds fly away when they see its water and smell the stench that comes out of it.

The next stanza presents the speech of Re to the gods who reside over the Lake of Fire. Re says that their bodies are hidden, and the offerings that come from the Lake of Fire belong to them. The water of the lake is for the gods and its heat is not against them. The following passage presents the speech of the gods to the sun god Re, in which they ask him to come to them, as he is the one who illuminates the underworld with his bright eye. The gods then say that the offerings and the libation in the Lake of Fire belong to the sun god Re, and he is the Lord of Regeneration in the Lake of Fire.

The final stanza can give a clue to the cosmographical location of the Lake of Fire, where the sun god Re descends to the netherworld and illuminates it with his eye. So the Lake of Fire comes as the first station of the sun god Re into the netherworld. It is a place where he regenerates himself and a place where he will be united with his body or with Osiris.

To conclude, the funerary texts, tomb scenes, and their orientation can be used to build an image of how the

[430] Hornung, *The Egyptian Amduat*, 148.
[431] Wilkinson, in: Wilkinson (ed.) *Valley of the Sun Kings*, 74-80.
[432] *Wb* I, 167. 16.
[433] In the versions from the tombs of Horemheb, Seti I, and Set I's sarcophagus, (*jw*) Island is used instead of *š*.

[434] Hornung, *Pfortenbuch* I, 56-62, *Pfortenbuch* II, 80-84; Zeidler, *Pfortenbuchstudien* II, 52-57.

Egyptians envisaged the cosmographical locations of the Lake of Knives and the Lake of Fire. The two lakes do not have fixed locations, but their locations change from one context to another depending on the ritual performed and the orientation of the performer. As places of passage, they appear in the east where the sun god Re and the deceased identified with him are born in the morning. They can also be located in the west as transitional areas that take the deceased to an advanced stage in the netherworld.

Chapter Three

The Theme of Passage over Water in Ancient Egyptian Religious Texts

3.1. Introduction

A high proportion of ancient Egyptian texts belong to the rites of passage.[435] This passage often takes the deceased from one state to another, such as from the state of the living to the state of the dead.[436] Ritual texts focus also on the safe passage of order through chaos, as in the royal coronation rituals in the Ramessum Dramatic Papyrus,[437] or as in the Underworld Books which describe the passage of the sun through the underworld. In temple context, such rituals assert the continuing of cosmic order.[438] In funerary context,[439] they assert resurrection, rebirth and life after death.[440] The passage is re-enacted in mythical images and in ritual actions, and focuses on the safe journey of the deceased through the ordeals of the netherworld.[441]

The placing of the texts on the walls of the pyramids also represents this theme of passage. For instance, in the Pyramid of Unas, Allen has succeeded in recognizing the order of the texts on the walls and their relation with the rites of passage.[442] The same theme of passage is also clear in the ordering of the spells on the sides of Middle Kingdom coffins.[443] The texts inscribed near the head deal with the restoration and resurrection of the deceased,[444] and those inscribed near the feet deal with the restoration of feet for passage.[445] The texts inscribed on the east side of the coffin focus on the transition of the funeral rituals and offering ceremonies in order to contact the world of the living, while the spells on the back of the coffin focus on the passage in life beyond the tomb.[446]

The focus here will be on how such themes are represented in the deceased's safe passage over the Winding Waterway, as represented in the ferryman spells, and on the Island of Fire as a place of passage over water. The ritual aspects of the ferryman spells and the Island of Fire will be presented to show how they are related to ritual aspects of the Lake of Knives and the Lake of Fire.

3.2. The Ferryman Spells and the Passage of the Deceased over Water

The ferryman spells are attested since the Old Kingdom Pyramid Texts, and are devoted to the celestial ferryboat that transported a deceased along the Winding Waterway to an area near the eastern horizon.[447] These characteristics remain the same until the New Kingdom, with small variations. For instance, the ferryman spells in the Pyramid Texts are monologues or descriptive texts which present the content of the dialogue between the deceased and the ferryman.[448] The later versions of the ferryman spells are dramatic texts, in which different actors play different roles and lead different conversions. In the Pyramid Texts spells the king plays the prominent role, and by his authority he is able to stir the ferryman into an action.[449] The Coffin Texts versions do not only represent the journey over the Winding Waterway, but also describe a test that a deceased should undergo before he is allowed to enter into the ferry.[450] A type of the ferryman spells that was common in the Middle Kingdom was already found in the Pyramid Tomb of Ibi of the VIII Dynasty.[451] It is not completely different from the Middle Kingdom spells and it shares most of its characteristics with Middle Kingdom spells. The ferryman spells in the Pyramid Texts run as follows:

ḏd mdw	Recitation:
rs=k m ḥtp ḥr=f-ḥ3=f m ḥtp	Wake in peace Face-Behind-Him, in peace!
m3-ḥr=f m ḥtp	He-Who-Sees-Behind-Him, in peace!
mḫntj pt m ḥtp	Ferryman of the sky, in peace!
mḫntj nwt m ḥtp	Ferryman of Nut, in peace!
mḫntj nṯrw m ḥtp	Ferryman of the gods, in peace!
jj.n N ḫr=k ḏ3j=k sw	N has come to you, so that you may ferry him,
m mḫnt tw ḏ33t=k nṯrw jm=s	In that ferryboat in which you ferry the gods.
jj.n N n gs=f mj jwt nṯr n gs=f	N has come to his side as the god came to his side.
jj.n N n sm3=f mj jwt nṯr n sm3=f	N has come to his side as the god came to his side.
n srḫw ʿnḫ jr N	There is no accusation of a living person against N,
n srḫw mt jr N	There no accusation of a dead

[435] For the most recent discussion on ritual texts and how they were used in the form of liturgies performed for the deceased in the Coffin Texts, see Assmann, *Totenliturgien* I; *Totenliturgien* II for the New Kingdom liturgies; *Totenliturgien* III for the Late Period liturgies.
[436] On the opening of the mouth ritual as imagery of birth, see Roth, *JEA* 78 (1992), 113-47; *JEA* 79 (1993), 57-79.
[437] For the most recent comment on the reading and meaning of the Dramatic Ramesseum Papyrus, see Quack, *ZÄS* 133 (2006), 72-89.
[438] On the texts describing the daily cycle of the sun god Re and its function in keeping the cosmic in order in Medinet Habu, see Voß, *SAK* 23 (1996), 377-96.
[439] For how a single ritual can be employed in rituals of different settings, and on the relation between the temple offering ritual, the Opening of the Mouth Ritual and the Pyramid Texts offering rituals, see Hays, *SAK* 30 (2002), 153-67.
[440] Eyre, *Cannibal Hymn*, 50.
[441] Eyre, *Cannibal Hymn*, 50.
[442] Allen, *Hommages Leclant* I, 24-28; for the same ordering of the spells on the Old Kingdom tombs, see Vischak, *JARCE* 40 (2003), 133-57; for the whole Pyramid Complex, see O'Connor, in: *Fs Stadelmann*, 135-44.
[443] Willems, *Heqata*, 360-3.
[444] Willems, *Heqata*, 91-92, 101-2.
[445] Willems, *Heqata*, 109, 132-38.
[446] Willems, *Heqata*, 192-5, 196-9.

[447] Bidoli, *Fangnetze*, 27.
[448] Bidoli, *Fangnetze*, 28; Willems, *Heqata*, 157.
[449] Willems, *Heqata*, 157.
[450] Willems, *Heqata*, 157.
[451] Willems, *Heqata*, 158.

	person against N,
n srḫw st jr N	There is no accusation of a goose against N,
n srḫw ng3w jr N	And there is no accusation of a Long Horned Bull against N.
jtm=k jr=k ḏ3j N	If you do not ferry N,
stp=f (w)dj=f sw	He will jump up and put himself,
tp ḏnḥ n ḏḥwtj	On a wing of Thoth.
swt ḏ3j=f N jr gs pf	He is the one who will transport N to yonder side.[452]

In the Coffin Texts, the ferryman spells run as follows:

j mḫntj pw jnj n ḥr n jrt=f	Oh this ferryman, bring to (me) Horus for his eye!
jnj n stt n ḫrwj=f	Bring to (me) Seth for his testicles,
jnj n wj3 n ḥr	And bring to (me) the barque for Horus,
wᶜr=s ḫr=s m ḥsp=f	When it flees and falls down into his garden,
nḥm.t(w)(=j) m-ᶜ stš	I have been saved from the hand of Seth.
j mḫntj pn jni n=j nw	Oh this ferryman, bring this (the boat) to me.
ṯwt tr m	Who are you?
jnk mrr jt=f	I am one whom his father loves.
mrr ṯw jt=k jrj=k n=f jsšt	Your father loves you. What (things) will you do for him?
ṯsj.n=j ksw=f s3ḳ.n=j ᶜwt=f	(Because) I have tied together his bones and gathered together his members,
dj.n=j n=f t r mrr=j	And I have given to him bread at my will,
3ḫ n=f 3ḫ n tpjw-t3=f	It goes well with him, and it goes well with his survivors.
mḥ r=k wsḫt	Make the barge ready!
n šdj.t(w)=s	It has not yet been cut (the plank).
šdj s(y) spj s(y) dmḏ s(y)	Cut (the planks for) it, build it, and assemble it,
ḥnᶜ skr ḥnᶜ nb ḥnw	With Sokar, and with the Lord of the Henu-Barque.[453]

In the Ferryman spells, the deceased approaches the bank of the Winding Waterway, which he will cross to reach the Fields of Reeds.[454] He asks the ferryman, who in turn refuses to sail before the deceased is able to answer a list of questions. These questions include the aim of the journey, the ship used in sailing,

questions on the deceased's identity, and finally the question of who will bring him the ferry.[455] The deceased's answers carry indications of his knowledge of the sacred, and he can give the names of the parts of the ferry by the names they carry in the divine world.[456] At the end the ferryman gives him the permission to cross to the eastern side of the sky.[457]

The ferryman spells in the Coffin Texts are divided into three sections: the introduction, the list of the parts of the ship, and the conclusion. However this ordering of the contents of the spells is not always systematic. For instance, in CT spell 398 cited above, the conclusion follows immediately after the introduction and then follows the list.[458]

The Content of the Ferryman Spells

The Introduction

The ferryman spells open with a conversation between the deceased and the ferryman. In the texts cited above, the ferryman's name is Mahaf,[459] and in other ferryman spells Aken is another name given to him.[460] In PT spell 270 cited above,[461] the ferryman is given the epithets that he is the ferryman of Nut and the ferryman who transports the gods in his ferryboat. In CT spell 398 he is the one who brings to the deceased Horus for his eye and brings Seth for his testicles.[462] In the Pyramid Texts the deceased clarifies why he should be ferried in the ferryboat, since there is no accusation of a living person or a dead person against him. In CT spell 398 cited above, the deceased should be ferried across the Winding Waterway because of the acts he carried out for his father. The deceased is describing himself as the one whom his father loves and adds some acts that he has carried out for his father. He is the one who ties up his father's bones and gathers his members —mediates his resurrection— and finally presented offerings to him, which might refer to the rites he has performed for his father.[463] The deceased then asks the ferryman to prepare the vessel, but the ferryman replies that it has not been constructed yet. The introduction ends with the deceased request that the vessel should be brought for him. In the Pyramid Texts the deceased says that if the ferryman does not bring him the ferryboat, he will jump up and put himself on a wing of Thoth. In CT spell 398 this vessel will be constructed with the help of Sokar.[464]

---

[452]PT spell 270=*Pyr.* § 383a-387c; Allen, *Inflection of the Verb*, 124.

[453]*CT* V, 120a-124c (spell 398).

[454] Bidoli, *Fangnetze*, 28.

[455] Bidoli, *Fangnetze*, 29; Willems, *Heqata*, 156-8; Assmann, *Death and Salvation*, 132.

[456] Bidoli, *Fangnetze*, 32; Willems, *Heqata*, 157.

[457] Willems, *Heqata*, 158.

[458] Bidoli, *Fangnetze*, 36; Willems, *Heqata*, 156.

[459] For Mahaf, see Depuydt, *GM* 126 (1992), 33-38.

[460] In BD 99A, Aqen and Mahaf are the names of the ferryman.

[461] PT spell 270= *Pyr.* § 383a-387c.

[462] *CT* V, 120a-b (spell 398).

[463] Willems, *Heqata*, 161.

[464] *CT* V, 120a-124c (spell 398); Willems, *Heqata*, 161-2.

In CT spell 398 the deceased describes the ferryman as the one who brings Horus to his Eye. Jacq[465] argues that the Eye of Horus is an epithet designating the ferryboat, which is made explicit on coffins from Meir.[466] The ferryboat is also identified with the testicles of Seth.[467] The deceased here plays the role of the *s3 mrj-f* priest, which is made explicit when he describes himself as the one whom his father loves.[468]

In the texts cited above, the deceased has not yet resuscitated his father or opened his mouth. The acts performed by the son might be envisaged as taking place in a resurrection ritual, which might also be described to take place in the night of the vigil.[469]

The List of the Ship

This list with the names of the different parts of the ship does not occur within the ferryman spells in the Pyramid Texts. A complete list can be found in CT spells 398 and 399. In this part of the ferryman spells the deceased undergoes a test, in which he has to name the different parts of the ship by the names they have in the divine world.[470] Bidoli plausibly argues that this list resembles the list of the objects used in the Ramessum Dramatic Papyrus, where the names given to the different parts of the ship represent theological interpretation of concrete objects.[471] In the Ramessum Dramatic Papyrus the realm of the cult and the divine realm are connected together by ritual actions. In Assmann's words 'in the cultic realm, there are the king, priest officiants, and objects. In the divine realm, there are the gods and their actions and words. In the divine realm, it is the speeches of the gods that comprise the central element, while in realm of the cult it is the ritual actions. The commentary supplies the explicit correlation of the two levels of reference'.[472]

A similar principle underlies the ferryman spells, in which the deceased is asked about the divine or mythic meanings of the parts of the ship. These texts occur in the context of rituals of transition, or what is known as the rites of passage. Assmann describes these texts as 'initiatory examinations'.[473] In these spells the two worlds, the divine and the ritual, are also connected by means of mythic explanation. Two conceptual spheres occur here. The first one occurs in the real world, the world where the ritual is carried out, and the other occurs in the world of the gods. The names of the different parts of the ship are only available for the initiated person who has the password to pass the examination and the place of passage.[474]

Although Bidoli noticed the resemblance between the ferryman spells and the Dramatic Ramessum Papyrus,[475] the rest of his argument is not convincing. According to Willems, Bidoli argrees with Kees that there are two groups of ferryman spells: magical Group (*magische Gruppe*), and earthy Group (*irdische Gruppe*).[476] In the first magical group, the dialogue between the deceased and the ferryman focuses on the theological knowledge of the ferry and its parts. In the second earthly group, the ferryman uses a language far away of being magical. In other words, when the ferryman replies the questions of the deceased he uses a language that is common in the daily life of the shipbuilders' community. CT spell 398 cited above belongs to the second group.

Bidoli concluded that the ferryman spells were patterned on the ceremonials used in the initiatory organizations of the ferrymen on earth, and as a result he accepts Kees' argument of the earthly group of the ferryman spells. The deceased who intends to enter the ferry is interpreted as a beginner who wants to join the ferrymen ranks. He even argues that Mahaf and Aken are representatives of the ferryman organization, and they are in charge of examining the new candidates who want to join the ferrymen ranks.[477] For the deceased to join the ferryboat he should pass an examination in which his knowledge of the divine parts of the ship is tested, and that, as Bidoli argues, is found in the initiatory rites in which the new members are admitted to guilds in the modern world.[478]

Bidoli also concluded that the version of the ferryman spells found in the Pyramid of Ibi do not in fact belong to the ferryman spells, and the early part of the dialogue which presents the deceased as the son who resuscitates his father does not also belong to the interest of the ferrymen guild and they are later additions to the texts.[479] The addition of funerary aspcts to the ferryman spells is a later invention, and what is

[465] Jacq, *Le voyage dans l'autre monde selon l'Egypte ancienne*, 47. n. 278.
[466] Coffin from Meir replaces the Eye of Horus with the ship in M6c: *CT* V, 120c (spell 398).
[467] Te Velde, *Seth*, 50-8.
[468] Bidoli, *Fangenetze*, 29. In CT spell 397 the son says: 'I am the one whom his father loves, the one whom his father loves greatly! I am the one who awakens his father when he is asleep. O Mahaf, awaken Aken for me, as you are endowed with life; see, I have come. (Mahaf) Did you say you would navigate to the eastern side of the sky? With what aim will you navigate? (Son) That I may raise his head, that I may lift his brow: *CT* V, 79a-80a (spell 397). Another variant occurs in the Pyramid of Ibi and reads: 'I am the one whom his father loves, the one whom the father of his father loves. I am the one who awakens him for you when he is asleep. I am the one who raises his head for you. I am the one who opens his mouth for you': Willems, *Heqata*, 163.
[469] See below for the ritual aspects of the ferryman spells.
[470] For the complete list of spell 397 and 398 with commentary, see Willems, *Heqata*, 427-443.
[471] Bidoli, *Fangnetze*, 28; Goyon, *Ritual funeral*, 72; Gillam, *Performance and Drama*, 49; Assmann, *GM* 25 (1977), 16-18; *Death and Salvation*, 351; Parkinson, *Voices from Ancient Egypt*, 124-5.
[472] Assmann, *Death and Salvation*, 351.
[473] Assmann, *GM* 25 (1977), 17-8; *Death and Salvation*, 352.
[474] Assmann, in: Allen et al., *Religion and Philosophy in Aancient Egypt*, 145.
[475] Bidoli, *Fangnetze*, 28.
[476] Willems, *Heqata*, 158.
[477] Bidoli, *Fangnetze*, 31; Willems, *Heqata*, 159.
[478] Bidoli, *Fangnetze*, 31. For initiation in handcraft jobs in ancient Egypt, see most recently, Von Lieven, *SAK* 36 (2007), 147-55.
[479] Bidoli, *Fangnetze*, 29-30.

not used in the initiatory examinations of earthly guilds does not belong to the genre of the ferryman spells.[480] Willems rejects Bidoli's argument on social groups. He argues that here:

> Although it is possible that social groups comparable to the European guild existed in Egypt, no clear evidence to this effect emerges from Bidoli's work. This makes it very hard to accept that the ferryman spells were patterned on the ceremonials used in the initiatory rites of the organizations. Nor can I accept the history of the texts reconstructed by Bidoli. There is no reason to believe that the model of the original compositions differed in any significant degree from the ferryman spells that have actually survived.[481]

The Conclusion

The conclusion comes from CT spell 398 and reads:

jḫt nbt sḫmt.n=j m mḫnt tn	Anything I have forgotten of this ferry,
njs.t(w)n=j r=s jn nṯrw jpn jm=sn	And on account of which I am called upon by these gods who are in them.
ntsn pw šdj=sn m pr-šnꜥ pw	It is they who will take (things) from this storeroom,
šdj.n=sn n ḥr nb	And they have taken (them) for Horus the Lord,
m prt=f r pt špt r rmṯ	At his departure to the sky, angry against Mankind.
dj.n=k r=k m-m sšsšt=s	You have placed (yourself) among its *sšsšt,*
r sj bw[482]	To which place?
r jmjtj[483]	To *jmjtj.*
jšst pw jmjtj ptn jjt.n=k jm	What are these two *jmjtj* from which you have come?[484]
m sḫt ḥtp ḥnꜥ sḫt jꜣrw	From the Field of Offerings and the Field of Rushes.
jj n=k r=k ꜥ=ṯn	Your document comes to you,
jj.n=j ww ww	And I have come (from) the two *ww* towns.
sṯ wj m-ꜥ=sn nṯrw	I am being in their hands, the gods,
jmj=sn nḥm=sn nn rdj.n=sn n=j tp š	May they not take away this which they have given to me on the lake,
r šꜣr jꜣrw	To *šꜣr(?)* ......rushes.
sfḫ jpw nṯrw gm=j sn ksw=sn	These seven gods, I found them bowed down,
ꜣsḫ=sn bdt kꜣmwt	While they reaped emmer and barley.
ks=k sꜣḳ.n=j jmjt mntjw=sn	Bow down! I have gathered what is between their thighs,
r prt n=sn n ḫrw jm	For an invocation offerings for them there,
m ḫd r ḫm m ḫsfw mꜣ-ḥꜣ-f	When travelling downstream to Khem, at the approach of Mahaf.
jnj n=f dpt ꜣḫ pw ꜥpr	Bring the boat for him, for he is an equipped spirit.[485]

After being able to give the names of the parts of the ship by the names they bear in the divine world, the deceased now states that if he has forgotten some parts of the ship, he pleads the gods to bring substitutes from their storerooms.[486] The text then tends to take another direction. The deceased is asked about the aim of his journey. The deceased replies that he is on his way to the two towns.[487] Willems argues that these two towns are the Field of Offerings and the Field of Reeds,[488] and they are situated in Heliopolis, where a variant in CT spell 397 places Heliopolis instead of *jmjtw*.[489]

The deceased says that he will be handed a document, which might give him the right to pass the passage, when the ferrymen approach him from these two cities. At the beginning of the spell, the deceased claims that he is the son whom his father loves because of the rituals acts he carries for his father. He is the eldest son who is responsible for carrying out the rituals for his father, and the one who will inherit from him. In Ancient Egypt the idea of 'who buries inherits' is common in funerary literature. For the son to inherit from his father, he should bury him.[490] This document will be given to him in the two towns, which are in Heliopolis. This reminds us of the document which Horus was given when he was vindicated against Seth in the Great Temple of Heliopolis.

The deceased is now in the hands of the gods, who are not only Mahaf and Aken, but other seven gods. These seven gods are reaping emmer and barley with the deceased. The deceased is doing so in order to present offerings to the gods. This act is said to take place while the deceased is travelling downstream to Letopolis. Mahaf gives the orders that the ferry is brought for the deceased to cross the Winding Waterway, because he is an equipped spirit.[491]

[480] Bidoli, *Fangnetze*, 30.
[481] Willems, *Heqata*, 160.
[482] Faulkner's translation is 'for going to *jmjt*' considering *sbjw* as infinitive of *sbj*: Faulkner, *Coffin Texts* II, 35. Willems rejects this translation, and argues that the infinitive of *sbj* is *sbjt*. He considers this as one of the ferryman questions to the deceased: Willems, *Heqata*, 420, n. h.
[483] For the reading of *jmjtj* as the two towns, see Willems, *Heqata*, 420, n. j.
[484] This reading is found on the coffins from Meir.
[485] *CT* V, 150a-154b (spell 398). The translation uses Willems, *Heqata*, 418-9.
[486] *CT* V, 150a-150c (spell 398).
[487] *CT* V, 150f (spell 398).
[488] Willems, *Heqata*, 166.
[489] *CT* V, 113c (spell 397).
[490] This is also mentioned in connection with the Lake of Fire in the Book of the Two Ways, where the son of the deceased says that he will inherit the way after his father; see below, 75.
[491] *CT* V, 154a-b (spell 398).

The seven gods occur also in CT spell 409, in which the deceased is addressing the parts of the ship and picturing them as gods forming the seven tribunals of Osiris. These seven gods might be identical with the seven gods in CT spell 398. CT spell 409 reads:

sm3ꜥ-ḫrw=k [3ḫ n N] pn r ḫftjw=f	May you justify the [spirit of] this N against his enemies,
m pt m t3 m ḏ3ḏ3wt sfḫ jptw	In the sky, on earth, in these seven tribunals,
m ḏ3ḏ3wt wsjr	And in the tribunals of Osiris.[492]

A tribunal of seven *3ḫw* occurs also in CT spell 335, where the deceased says:

jnḏ ḥr=ṯn ḏ3ḏ3t ḥ3t wsjr	Hail to you, tribunal which is behind Osiris,
dd šꜥt m jsfwt	And who put terror in evil-doers.[493]

From the texts cited above, it seems that these seven gods play different roles. They reap emmer and barley with the deceased. They are also pictured as the seven tribunals of Osiris, who protect the body of the god.[494] The activites of these seven gods take place in the *Stundenwachen*, in which the bier was envisaged as a vessel, while the acts of those participating in the vigil were a ceremonial rendering of the judgment of the dead.[495]

The Ritual Aspects of the Ferryman Spells

The most important points referred to in the ferryman spells cited above are the actions performed by the son for his father. The aim of the son's journey is to reach the place of embalming where his father is, but before he is doing so, he undergoes a test. He has to give the divine names of the parts of the ship.[496] The aim of having this test is simply to enable the deceased to pass the place of passage, which is here the Winding Waterway. The test is led by the two ferrymen, Mahaf and Aken. The ferryman Mahaf is also the gatekeeper of Osiris. In PT spell 519 the deceased says to the ferryman:

ḏd mdw	Recitation:
j ḥr=f-ḥ3=f jrj-ꜥ3 wsjr	O Face-Behind-Him doorkeeper of Osiris:
ḏd n wsjr dj jn.t(j) n N pn wj3=k pw	Say to Osiris “have this boat of yours brought to its N,
ḏ33 wꜥbw=k jm=f	In which your Pure Ones ferry,
jr ššp n=k ḳbḥw	To receive for you cool water,
ḥr wꜥrt tw nt jḫm skw	On that region of the Imperishable Stars,
ḏ3j=f jm=f	That he may ferry in it,
ḥnꜥ sšd pw n wḏ3t n jdmj	With this bandage of green and red linen,
st3j m jrt ḥr	Which was woven from the Eye of Horus,
jr wt ḏbꜥ pw n wsjr sj mr	In order to bandage this finger of Osiris that has gone sick,
šm rf N pn ššw ššw	So this N will go freely freely”,
s3w sw š3wt š wr	And the destiny of the Great Lake will guard Him.[497]

The deceased's aim in crossing is to reach the place of his father.[498] He takes with him green and red linen in order to bandage the finger of his father that has gone sick. The son is doing that with the protection of the Great Lake. Mahaf and Aken are not only the gods who will meet the deceased on the bank of the Winding Waterway, but he will meet seven other gods as mentioned above in CT spell 398. These gods and the deceased will reap emmer and barley to make invocation offerings to present to the gods in Letopolis.

In his journey from this life to the next, the deceased should face ordeals in the shape of a boat that the deceased uses to cross a body of water. In the ferryman spells this body of water is the Winding Waterway. The journey of the deceased over the Winding Waterway can be interpreted on two levels: mythical and ritual.[499] On the mythical level the deceased is featured as the sun god crossing the Winding Waterway. On the ritual level, the deceased is featured as Osiris in the place of embalming while the acts of the participants in the vigil are interpreted as ritual acts. The bier on which the body of Osiris is lying was envisaged as the ship, which the sun god Re uses in his daily journey across the sky.[500]

3.3. The Island of Fire as a Place of Passage over Water

The Island of Fire as a Place of Creation

The Island of Fire occurs in the Old Kingdom Pyramid Texts and in the Middle Kingdom Coffin Texts as a place of the primordial creation, where the sun god Re emerged from the waters of chaos. In the Pyramid Texts the deceased king is described as the god that emerged from the primeval water and restored the cosmic order in the Island of Fire.[501]

---

[492] *CT* V, 227g-h (spell 409). The seven gods occur also in CT spell 400, and are called seven *3ḫw* ‘O you seven spirits, ferrymen of the sky; O Mahaf, come and bring me the ferryboat in its name *k3jt*-boat’: *CT* V, 171a-b (spell 400).
[493] *CT* IV, 253c-254b (spell 335).
[494] Willems, *Heqata*, 168.
[495] Willems, *Chests of Life*, 154-9.
[496] Willems, *Heqata*, 169.

[497] PT 519=*Pyr.* § 1201a-1203b.
[498] Roeder argues that the main aim of the deceased's crossing the Winding Waterway in the ferryman spells is to purify his father, where the water of the Winding Waterway might be considered as the water that the son will use to purify his father: Roeder, *LingAeg* 3 (1993), 110-1.
[499] For the connection between myth and ritual, and how myth was enacted in ritual, see Baines, *JNES* 50 (1991), 81-105.
[500] Willems, *Chests of Life*, 156.
[501] Assmann, *GM* 140 (1994), 98; *Ma'at*, 216-7; *Liturgische Lieder*, 271-3.

N pj nw n sšsš wbn m tꜣ	N is these *sšsš* plants that rise from the earth.
wꜥb ꜥ N jn jrj st=f	The hand of N is cleaned by the one who made his throne.
N pj r šrt sḫm wr	This N is at the nose of the Great Power.
jj.n N m jw nsjsj	N has come from the Island of Fire,
wdj.n N mꜣꜥt jm=f m st jsft	N has put the right in it in the place of wrong.
N pj jr sšrw sꜣꜣ jꜥrwt	This N is toward the linen garment, which the serpents guard,
grḥ pw n ꜣgbj wr pr m wrt	(In) this night of the Great Flood that comes from the Great One.[502]

In Coffin Texts spell 317, Khepri is said to be born in the Island of Fire.

sj pw nṯr msj m mjn	Who is it the god who is born today?
ḫprj jj m jw nsjsj	Khepri has come from the Island of Fire.[503]

On the stelae of King Ramesses IV from Abydos, the King says:

ꜥnḫ=j m mrr nṯr	I live on what the god loves,
m mswt=f m jw nsjsj	On the day of his birth in the Island of Fire.[504]

In the Fayum Book the Island of Fire is envisaged as a part of the Great Lake.[505]

sw rꜥ ḥms m ḏt=f ḏs=f	One day the sun god Re sat with his own body;
jꜣw ḳsw=f m ḥḏ	having become old, his bones were of silver,
ḥꜥw=f m nbw	His flesh was of gold, his hair
šnj=f m ḫsbḏt	was of lapis lazuli,
jrtwj=f m wꜣḏw	His two eyes were of Wadj stone ,
jtn nfr m mfkꜣt	And (his) beautiful sun disk was of turquoise.
wnn=f ḥr sjꜣ kꜣ	He recognized the (bad) plan,
n rmṯw nṯrw m ḥwt-nswt	Of the gods and people in Herakleopolis.
rnp ḥꜥw=f m tr n ꜣbd 12	While he was renewing his flesh in the 12 months,
prj=sn ḫr gnw	They came out bringing trouble,
wr ꜥšꜣ=sn r=f m jw nsjsj	Great was their multitude against him in the Island of Fire.[506]

The Great Lake in the Fayum Book was envisaged as the primeval ocean Nun, from which the sun god Re emerged in the primeval times.[507] According to the Fayum Book, the Island of Fire is described as a place at the eastern horizon where the sun god refreshes himself everyday in the water of the primeval ocean Nun before he appears in the sky. While Re was renewing himself in the Fayum Lake, people and gods came against him in great number in the Island of Fire bringing trouble.[508] The Fayum Lake was also envisaged as the place of the Ogdoad:

st pw nt ssnw	This is the place (Fayum Lake) of the Ogdoad,
ꜥnḫ rꜥ jm ḥtp wsjr jm	Re lives there and Osiris rests there.[509]

When Re came out from the water of the Fayum Lake he was called *ḥrj-š=f* (He-who-is-upon-his-Lake). In the Hermopolitan myth of creation the sun god Re appeared from the water of the Lake of Knives on primeval hill of Hermopolis in the Island of Fire, and then ascended upon the Ihyt cow to the sky. [510]

On the stela of King Nectanebo I from Hermopolis, the king says that he built a temple for the goddess Nehmetaway, the gods of Hermopolis and the Ennead. He declares that the sun god Re came forth from the Great Lake of the Island of Fire.

rꜥ prj m š ꜥꜣ jw nsrsr	Re who has come out from the Great Lake of the Island of Fire,
ḫmnw wrw pꜣwtj	The Ogdoad, the Great Primeval gods,
nḥmt-ꜥwꜣj m ḫnw pr wr ḥwt-ꜥꜣ	Nehmetaway in the interior of the Great House of the Great Temple,
njt jhjt tꜣ wrt msj rꜥ	Neith Ihyt the Great One who gave birth to Re,
psḏt ꜥꜣt jmjw ḫmnw	And the Great Ennead Who are in Hermopolis.[511]

[502] PT 249=*Pyr.* § 264b-265e.

[503] *CT* IV, 110g-h (spell 317).

[504] *KRI* VI, 23, lines 9-10. Being the place where *Mꜣꜥt* and *Jsft* existed side by side in the primeval times, the Island of Fire is a place that is distinguished from both the world of the living and the world of the dead: Assmann, *GM*, 140 (1994), 98-9; for how the world was divided between *mꜣꜥt* and *jsft* and the act of the creator god to establish *mꜣꜥt*, see Frandsen, *GM* 179 (2000), 9-34.

[505] Vernus, *Cadernos de Filosofi* 10 (2001), 14-15.

[506] Beinlich, *Das Buch von Fayum* I, 148-149, lines 110-115.

[507] Beinlich, *Das Buch von Fayum* I, 314-19.

[508] Beinlich, *Das Buch von Fayum* I, 315.

[509] Beinlich, *Das Buch von Fayum* I, 152, line 148. The same myth of the sun god Re and his rebellion occurs also in the Book of the Heavenly Cow from the New Kingdom: Hornung, *Der Ägyptische Mythos von der Himmelskuh*.

[510] Cruz-Uribe, *Hibis Temple* I, 135. For the text see above, 9-10.

[511] Roeder, *ASAE* 52 (1952), 413, line 33. Petosiris the high priest of Thoth at Hermopolis states that he built a temple of Re, the nursling in the Island of Fire, 'I stretched the cord and released the line to build the temple of Re in the Great Park. I built it of fine white limestone, inlaid with Asian copper. I made Re reside, the nursling in the Island of Fire': Lefebvre, *Le tombeau de Pétosiris*, Inscription 81; Lichtheim, *AEL* III, 47; Menu, *BIFAO* 94 (1994), 311-327; *BIFAO* 95 (1995), 281-295; *Recherches sur l'historie juridique, économique et sociale de l'ancienne Égypte* II, 261-2.

The Island of Fire as a Place of Passage

Being a place of creation, the Island of Fire is envisaged in Egyptian mortuary literature as a place at the edge of cosmos where the vision of fire is both dangerous and positive.[512] As a place of birth and creation, the Island of Fire is envisaged as a gateway or a passage that leads to the hereafter.[513] It is also associated with the idea of releasing magical powers. Releasing the magical powers, as food, and passing over the Island of Fire, is a repeated theme in Egyptian Texts.[514] For the deceased to pass safely over it, he fills his body with magic, and gets rid of his enemies whose bodies are full of magic. In the Pyramid Texts, the deceased king is described as a bull, who eats the innards of those who come with their bellies full of magic from the Island of Fire.

jw kꜣw W ḥꜣ=f	The *kas* of Unas are behind him,
jw ḥmswt=f ḫr rdwj=f	And his *hemsut* are under his feet.
jw nṯrw=f tp=f	His gods are upon him,
jꜥrwt=f m wpt=f	And his Uraei are at his brow.
jw sšmwt W m-ḥꜣt=f	The guiding-snake of Unas is at his forehead:
ptrt bꜣ ꜣḫt n ṯbs	The spier-out of *ba* (s), the fiery snake for burning.
jw wsrw W ḥr mkt=f	The powers of Unas are protecting him.
W pj kꜣ pt nhd m jb=f	Unas is the Bull of the sky, aggressive in his nature,
ꜥnḫ m ḫpr n nṯr nb	Living on the manifestation of every god.
wnmw zmw=sn	Eating the innards of them,
jww mḥ ẖt=sn m ḥkꜣw m jw nsjsj	Who come with their bellies full of magic from the Island of Fire.[515]

The Island of Fire is a place of destruction and creation. For the king, it is a bright place where he needs fear no darkness. The king as a sacrificial bull of the sky burns his enemies with the uraei on his forehead, and he is not burnt with fire. He is not devoured, but he is a devourer with the aid of the flames, that is cooking and also burning.[516] The king's body filled with the necessary powers, he takes precedence over the powers already there in the Island of Fire. The same theme also occurs in CT spell 37, where a deceased visits the Island of Fire and acquires all the magical powers, leaving nothing for those living there. As a result, he overcomes the dangers of the place of passage.

mk ḥm=k jj ꜥpr.n=f ꜣḫ nb	Look! Your majesty has come, and acquired all power,
n sp m-ꜥ=f m jw nsrsr	And nothing from him is left in the Island of Fire.
mḥ.n=k ẖt=k m ḥkꜣw	You have filled your body with magic,
ḥtm.n=k jbt=k jm=f	And you have quenched your thirst with it.[517]

This theme of opposition in the Island of Fire is alluded to when it is described as a place of creation. Both *isft* and *mꜣꜥt* are there in the Island of Fire, the place of passage and by coming into the Island of Fire, the king restores the order of cosmos and places *mꜣꜥt* in the place of *isft*. The theme of creation and destruction is found in PT spell 273 mentioned above.

The same can be said about the Island of the Shipwrecked Sailor, a place standing at the edge of cosmos, where the safe passage of the sailor is assured after fire descended from the sky.[518] On the Island of the Shipwrecked Sailor, fire has both positive and negative aspects. The sailor burns his offerings with fire, and he is threatened by fire. The sailor receives assurance of his life renewal and restoration of cosmic order after passing the place of passage.[519]

The Island of Fire is a place where the deceased receives his offerings (*ꜣḫw* and *ḥkꜣw*), and at the same time he is threatened by fire. A deceased will renew his life by getting the offerings from the Island of Fire and his safe passage over it.[520] As a place of creation, the Island of Fire is separated from the world of the living and the world of the dead. It is a transitional place, and a place of crisis that stands at the edge of cosmos.[521] For the deceased to be reborn again, he should leave the created world, and here lies the Island of Fire, a transitional area between the two worlds. In the Coffin Texts, the Island of Fire is an ordeal that the deceased has to pass before he gains access to the hereafter. As a result, it represents one of the places where the judgment of the dead takes place.[522] In CT spell 149,[523] a deceased says:

jnk wnnt bjk rmṯw	I am a human falcon,
mdw m tpḥt nt wsjr	Who speaks in the cavern of Osiris.
mdw=j r-gs wsjr	I speak in the presence of Osiris,
mj mdw=j m jw nsrsr	As I spoke in the Island of Fire.
ꜣḫw sw nṯr pn j.jn wsjr ḫntj-jmntjw r=j	'He is a spirit, this God' so said Osiris the Foremost-of-the-Westerners about me.

[512] Eyre, *Cannibal Hymn*, 81.
[513] For the Island of Fire as a gate to the Netherworld where the (*bas*) live on its food, see Hornung, *Das Buch von Pforten* II, 208-213, Ninth Hour, upper register, scenes 55-56.
[514] For instance, *CT* I 148a-149c (spell 37), *CT* II, 112b-113a (spell 105), and *CT* V, 176f (spell 402).
[515] PT 273=*Pyr.* § 396a-397c; the translation is after Eyre, *Cannibal Hymn*, 7.
[516] Eyre, *Cannibal Hymn*, 81-3.
[517] *CT* I, 148b-149c (spell 37).
[518] Eyre, *Cannibal Hymn*, 82.
[519] Baines, *JEA* 77 (1990), 62-4.
[520] Eyre, *Cannibal Hymn*, 83.
[521] Bickel, *Cosmogonie*, 69-70.
[522] Grieshammer, *Jenseitsgericht*, 101-3.
[523] On the function of the spell in referring to the judgment of the dead, see Roeder, *Mit dem Auge sehen*, 23-6.

jj.n=j mjn	I have come today,
jw.n=j ḥr ḫftj pf	And I have cried out because of that enemy.
jw wḏ m ḏꜣḏꜣt jw wḥm r-gs mꜣꜥt	It is decreed in the tribunal, and repeated in the presence of Maat,
rdj.t(w) sḫm=j m ḫft=j	That I be caused to have power over my enemy.[524]

The Island of Fire is also described as a place of vindication.

ꜥḥꜥ.n N tn m jw nsjsj	This N has stood in the Island of Fire,
mꜣꜥ-ḫrw=s	That she might be vindicated.[525]

As a passage to the hereafter, the Island of Fire was a place for the judgment of the dead. In CT spell 650, the deceased says:

jnḏ ḥr=k jtrw n ḫt nb bꜣw ꜥꜣ ꜣḫw	Hail to you River of Fire, Lord of Souls, Great of Spirits,
wr r nb=f ꜥꜣ ḫnmwt[526] nb jtrw wr r nw	Greater than its Lord, Great of Wells, Lord of Rivers, greater than Nu.
dj=k swꜣ=j jj.n=j m jw nsjsj	You will let me pass (because) I have come from the Island of Fire,
mḥ.n=j ḫt=j m ḥkꜣw	And I have immersed my body in magic.
ḏd.ḫr=f swꜣ=k wḏꜣ ḥtp	He will say, "It has been commanded, that you pass safely
m sbt wꜣt m nn wꜣwt	In travelling a path from these paths",
ḏd.ḫr=k ḥrt-jb mꜣꜥt pw	And you will say "This is what is in the heart of Maet",
ḏd.ḫr=f swꜣ r=k ḥr wꜥt mrt=k jm	(And) He will say "Travel on the one you like there".[527]

For the deceased to pass safely, he will tell the truth, which refers to the judgment of the dead as the ritual context of the spell. It is interesting to note the decorations on the back of GIT coffin where the spell occurs.[528] The back is decorated with what can be described as a plan for the topography of the netherworld. It is also inscribed with a group of spells dealing with the safe passage of the deceased through an area of ordeal which occurs only on this coffin.[529] This group of spells includes CT spells 646-655. In these spells, the deceased asks the guardians, whose names occurs in CT spell 649, to let him pass for he is coming from the Island of Fire. They hold knives in their hands and are ready to attack the unprepared. The decoration programme on the back of this coffin resembles that on coffin floors from Deir el-Bersha. This recalls the same situation of the deceased in the Book of the Two Ways, where before gaining entrance to the Lake of Fire, the deceased performs some rituals to be able to proceed to the hereafter. The area around which the deceased performs his rituals to gain entrance to the hereafter is surrounded by obstacles, and by the performance of these ritual, the deceased mediates his passage and passes the area of ordeal.

The deceased will stand and not be opposed in the tribunal of Osiris, for he has come from the Island of Fire. In Chapter 22 of the Book of the Dead, a deceased says:

wbn.n=j m swḥt jmj tꜣ štꜣ	I have risen from the egg which is in the secret land.
rdjw. n=j rꜣ=j	I have been given my mouth,
mdw=j jm=f m-bꜣḥ nṯrw dwꜣt	So that I can speak with it in the presence of the gods of the netherworld.
nn ḫsfꜥ=j m ḏꜣḏꜣt nt nṯr ꜥꜣ	My hand will not be opposed in the tribunal of the Great God,
wsjr nb rꜣ-stꜣw m tp ḫtjw	Osiris Lord of Rosetau who is on (his) platform.
jj.n=j jrj.n=j mrrt jb=j m jw nsrsr	I have come and I have done what my heart desires in the Island of Fire.[530]

From what is cited above, the Island of Fire appears to represent a place in the netherworld where the judgment of the dead takes place. It is also a place of passage, which the deceased has to pass before he gains entrance to the next station in the underworld.

The Aim of the Deceased's Journey over the Island of Fire

In Coffin Text spells 31-41, Willems argues that the deceased's journey starts from the Island of Fire, which represents the mortuary chapel of his tomb.[531] In CT spell 33 the deceased says:

jnḏ ḥr=ṯ jmnt nfrt	Greetings to you Beautiful West!
mṯ jt=j pf ꜥḥꜥw=j pf	Look, that father of mine, that helper of mine,
ḥꜣj=j pf hꜣ.n=j n=f pf	That protector of mine, that one to whom I have descended.
jj ḥr=ṯ jnḏ=f ḥr=ṯ	Has come to you that he may

[524] *CT* II, 247b-250c (spell 149).
[525] *CT* VI, 164l-m (spell 566).
[526] The reading of this word is not obvious. Faulkner suggests that it may be read as *ḫnmwt*, which fits in the context of the spell: Faulkner, *Coffin Texts* II, 225.
[527] *CT* VI, 272d-n (spell 650).
[528] Lesko, *Index*, 56.
[529] The decorations on the back of this coffin were studied by Willems, *Heqata*, 52, but he did not pay attention to the location of the Island of Fire in these spells.

[530] Naville, *Tb*, Kapitel. 22, lines 3-6; Faulkner, *BD*, 31.
[531] Willems, in: Willems (ed.), *Social Aspects*, 253-72.

rꜥ-nb	greet you every day.[532]
sꜣ=ṯ js sḏt=ṯ js ms.n=ṯ n wsjr	Your son, your child whom you have born for Osiris,
jj.n=f nḏ=f ḥr=ṯ m jw nsrsr	He has come that he might greet you in the Island of Fire,
dr.n=f ẖmw=f r=f	After he has removed his dust from himself,
mḥ.n=f ẖt=f m ḥkꜣw	After he has filled his body with magic,
ḫtm.n=f ibt=f jm=f	After he has quenched his thirst with it,
sdꜣ.n=f wrš=f im=f mj ꜣpd	After he has trembled and spent the day in it like a bird.[533]
ꜥpr.n=f tꜣ m rḫt.n=f	He has mastered the land by means of what he knows,
mj hꜣ.n=f n=sn	Like those to whom he has descended.
m ḏd=f ḫft=s	Being what he says to her [534] (the Beautiful West).
jnḏ ḥr=ṯ jmnt nfrt	Greetings to you Beautiful West,
m šmsw wsjr ṯs pẖr	In the following of Osiris and *vice versa.*
jj.n wsjr N pn ꜥꜣ mr.n=f	This Osiris N has come here as he desired,
dr.n=f nkn n wsjr	He has removed the injury of Osiris,
snwr=f ḫftjw=f	So that he makes his foes tremble.
ḫpj m ḥtp nḥm=j ṯw	"Travel in peace, and I protect you",
j.t(w) jn jmnt nfrt r jt=j pf	So is said by the Beautiful West in the case of that father of mine,
ꜥḥꜥw=j pf r ḥꜣj=j pf	That helper of mine, in the case of that protector of mine,
hꜣ.n=j n=f pf	That one to whom I have descended.[535]

The son of the deceased is addressing the Beautiful West, saying that his father is the son whom the goddess (the Beautiful West) has born for Osiris. The deceased had removed the dust from himself, had filled his body with magical powers, and finally quenched his thirst. The father has then come in the Island of Fire to greet the goddess. The aim of the deceased's journey is to remove the injury of Osiris and to dispel his enemies.[536]

In the preceding CT spell 32, the aim of the deceased's journey was also to soften the pain of Osiris and to perform the embalming rites for him.

wsjr m ḏdw jj.n jt=j pf	O Osiris in Busiris, that father of mine has come,
ꜥḥꜥw=j pf ḥꜣj=j pf	That helper of mine, that protector of mine,
hꜣ.n=j n=f pf	That one to whom I have descended,
r bw ẖr ḥm=k jm	To the place where your majesty is,
dr=f jhj=k snwr ḫftjw=k	That he may remove your pain, and make your enemies tremble.[537]

The sequence of events in the above mentioned CT spell 33 can be summarized as follows:

1- Before the deceased reaches the Island of Fire, he gets rid of his dust, fills his body with magic and quenches his thirst. Then the deceased reaches the Island of Fire.[538]

2- The deceased leaves the Island of Fire and arrives at a locality which is not identified.[539]

3- Osiris asks the Beautiful West to welcome the deceased and to let him in.

4- The Beautiful West asks the deceased to travel to the place of Osiris under her protection.

5- The son of the deceased, who plays the role of a priest, asks the gods to rejoice at the meeting of his father.[540]

6- Then the son of the deceased directs a speech to the Beautiful West, giving the aim of the journey of his father. The father is doing this journey in order to perform rites for Osiris.

The content of CT spells 30-37 have been extensively studied by Egyptologists.[541] Ogdon describes this group of spells as a liturgy to be performed on the day of funeral.[542] The liturgy is to be performed by recreating the situation to be encountered by the deceased in the netherworld.[543] Ogdon's use of the term drama means that there are different actors performing this liturgy, and playing different roles, but

532 This only occurs on coffins from Deir el-Bersha, B12C, B13C, and B16C, while the other versions do not describe the father as the defender and protector of his son.

533 This passage concerns the provision of the deceased with food on the Island of Fire, and compares it with food-stuff the earth provides for a bird. This reference to the bird and food might refer to the migrant birds that come from beyond the Egyptian cosmos and feed on the products of the Nile water, lakes and islands.

534 As occurs on S1C and S2C: *CT* I, 119c (spell 37).

535 *CT* I, 115d-121b (spell 37).

536 *CT* I, 120e-f (spell 37).

537 *CT* I, 103a-104b (spell 32).

538 The deceased does not get rid of his dust in the Island of Fire, as Willems argues, but before he reaches it: Willems, in: Willems (ed.), *Social Aspects*, 254.

539 *CT* I, 120c (spell 37), where the deceased says that 'I have come here' without giving a name to the place where he is.

540 This occurs in *CT* I, 111c-113a (spell 33), which reads 'The gods who are in Endlessness and the Ennead who are in secrets! See him, you gods, the divine spirit, whom Osiris has conceived as his son, whom Isis has conceived as her child. Oh, you two crews, give adoration to him! Rejoice at meeting him.'

541 Ogdon, in: *L'Egyptologie en 1979* II, 38-43; De Jong, *SAK* 21 (1994), 141-157; Willems, in: Willems (ed.), *Social Aspects*, 253-372.

542 Jürgens argues that coffins from Assiut tend to transmit spells 30-32 together with spells 345 and 609 without spells 33-37. He thus argues that spells 30-37 do not belong together. Jürgens, *Grundlinien*, 193-94; on the criticism of Willems to the approach of Jürgens, see Willems, in: Willems (ed.), *Social Aspects*, 248.

543 Ogdon, in: *L'Egyptologie en 1979* II, 38-43.

this is not evident in this group of spells. Only one person, as Willems argues, is clearly profiled as a priest living and functioning on earth.[544] So it is only one person who is uttering a monologue and bringing different persons and parties to life. This person is most probably the eldest son of the deceased, who is functioning as a priest on earth and perform these sets of different rituals for his father. Jürgens uses the same adjective 'dramatic', with reference to spells 30-37, but he argues that the priest (the eldest son of the deceased) is the only person who is alive.[545]

Willems argues that spells 30-41 form a mortuary liturgy to be recited during seasonal feasts. He supports his argument by the fact that on two coffins[546] the title of the spell is 'Causing that the West loves a man, and causing that the West rejoices about a man by all that is done for him in the course of all of the seasonal festivals of the necropolis.' He also argues that this liturgy was performed in the tomb during seasonal feasts, when relatives and professional priests commissioned by the relatives came to the tomb.[547] Yet the title of this liturgy in CT spell 30, which connects it with seasonal feasts, occurs only on two coffins, which are not included in Willems' argument. He dealt with the latest versions of the spells on coffins from Deir el-Bersha.[548]

The Island of Fire here, according to Willems, designates the tomb chapel.[549] Willems based his argument on a passage in CT spell 35, which reads:

jnk sꜣ=k ꜥnḫ tp tꜣ	I am your living son on earth,
jr n=k prt-ḫrw tp tꜣ	Who makes an invocation offerings for you on earth,
m pr=k nt m jw nsrsr	In your house which is in the Island of Fire.[550]

Willems argues that this ritual is taking place in the tomb of the deceased on earth, which is the Island of Fire. It is, however, not clear that Willems' interpretation of the Island of Fire as a physical place rather than symbolic is supported by his evidence. He maintains that the deceased consumes the *ꜣḫw* and *ḥkꜣw* powers, which are the offerings presented for him in his tomb chapel, and then he departs to reach the place where the abode of Osiris is.[551] Removing the dust from the body does not occur on the land of the living, in this spell the Island of Fire, it occurs in a resurrection ritual, which takes place after the end of the mummification and offering rituals. For instance, in the Book of the Dead Chapter 68 removing the dust occurs in a resurrection ritual. The text reads:

sṯsj (=j) wj ḥr jꜣbj=j	(I) raise up myself upon my left side,
dj=j wj ḥr wnmj=j	I put myself upon my left side,
sṯsj (=j) wj ḥr wnmj=j	(I) raise up myself on my right side,
dj (=j) ḥmsj.kw ꜥḥꜥ=j	(I) sit down and stand up,
wḫꜣ=j ḫmw=j	I throw off my dust.
jmj-r[552]=j rꜣ=j m šmw spd	And my tongue and mouth are in the following of the Wise One.[553]

Grieshammer plausibly argues that the Island of Fire is a mythical and spiritual place of contact that separates this world and the next. It is not a concrete earthly location, but a liminal area of contact between this world and the next.[554] It is a place at the edge of cosmos. As mentioned above, it is the place of creation, and this place should be distinct from this world and the next.[555] To be reborn again in the netherworld, there is a need to leave the created world.[556]

In CT spell 346, the deceased is said to have come from the land of the living from the Island of Fire.

hꜣ N pn wꜥb ṯw ḥr ḏs=f m š ḳbḥj	O this N! Horus himself will cleanse you in the pool of cold water,
ḥbs ṯw jnpw m wt=f tpj	And Anubis will wrap you in his best bandage.
ḏḥwtj swꜥb=f n=k wꜣwt nfrt nt jmnt ḫr wsjr	Thoth will cleanse for you the fair paths of the West before Osiris,
jrj ddwn sṯj=f m jmjw=k	Dedwen will make his perfume of what is in you,
wpj=f n=k wꜣwt nt mꜣꜥ-ḫrw	He will open for you the fair paths of justification,
nmj ṯw(sic) nw	So that you may traverse the sky.
jn wpwꜣwt sšm=f ṯw r wꜣwt nfrt nt jmnt	It is Wepwawet who will guide you to the fair paths of the West.
jrj n=f nṯrw hnj	The gods shall make a praise

[544] Although Ogdon's argument does not seem convincing, he is right when he argues that there was a dramatic performance for the liturgy: Willems, in Willems (ed.), *Social Aspects*, 253.
[545] Jürgens, *Grundlinien*, 189-90.
[546] The title of CT spell 30 (*CT* 1, 83d-g) occurs only on S1c and S2c coffins, and indicates that the whole liturgy is to be performed on seasonal festivals.
[547] Willems, in: Willems (ed.), *Social Aspects*, 254. Willems argues that the tomb is not the only place where mortuary rituals for the deceased after burial took place, but they can be carried out at home or in shrines in settlements on the days of the festivals: Willems, in: Willems (ed.), *Social Aspects*, 255.
[548] Willems, in: Willems (ed.), *Social Aspects*, 255.
[549] Willems points out that CT spells 33 and 34 constitute different ritual acts, starting with the presentation of invocation offerings, which takes place in the chapel. The main priest is the eldest son of the deceased, who was dependent on his father during his lifetime. Furthermore, many of those who were around the deceased, his family or friends may participate in this ritual: Willems, in: Willems (ed.), *Social Aspects*, 292-3.
[550] *CT* I, 129f-g; 130g; 131g; 132g; 133g; 134h (spell 35).

[551] Willems, in: Willems (ed.), *Social Aspects*, 292,
[552] *Wb* I, 74.11.
[553] Lapp, *Ppayrus of Nu*, pl. 18, lines 14-5.
[554] The first to argue that the Island of Fire might represent an earthly place is Kees, *ZÄS* 78 (1942), 41-53.
[555] Eyre, *Cannibal Hymn*, 82.
[556] Hornung, *Conceptions of God*, 161-2.

	for him,
m33=sn sw jj	When they see him coming,
m t3 ꜥnḫ m jw nsrsr	From the land of the living from the Island of Fire,
r swt nt m3ꜥ-ḫrw ḫr wsjr	To the places of vindication before Osiris.
N jj m šmsw jt=f wsjr	N has come in the following of his father Osiris,
m ḥtp m ḥtp	In peace, in peace.[557]

Wepwawet assists in the funeral procession of the deceased.[558] He is the one who opens the paths for the deceased. The ritual acts in this spell should have taken place in the *Stundenwachen*, where priests playing the roles of the gods mentioned in the spell above perform their acts for the deceased. This text also represents a part of the Osiris secret rituals which were enacted for the deceased in the *Stundenwachen*. Willems is not right to treat *m t3 ꜥnḫ* and *m jw nsrsr* as apposition, referring to a single place. It is also important to note here that the place of Osiris' judgment is in the Island of Fire. It plays the role of a place of vindication and a place for the judgment of the dead. This is the one of the roles of the Island of Fire as a place of passage. The spell relates that the deceased is coming in the following of his father Osiris, which might refer to the place of the abode of Osiris in the Island of Fire. It is not the place of embalming in the land of the living, but it is a place in the netherworld where the deceased wishes to participate in the treatment of the body of Osiris.[559] As the place where the abode of Osiris is, CT spell 465 reads:

wnn m ḥtp nb sḫt ḥtpt	To be Hetep, Lord of the Field of Offerings.
ḥr nw	This is Horus,
jw=f m bjk mḥ ḫ3 pw m 3w=f	H is a falcon and he is thousand cubits long.
jw ꜥnḫ ꜥpr m ꜥ=f	Life and equipment are in his hand.
šm=f jw=f r mrrt jb=f	He comes and goes as his heart wishes,
m šw=s m njwwt=s	In its lakes and in its towns.
wbn=f m msḫn nṯr	He rises in the birthplace of the god,
ḥtp=f m ꜥnḫ m ḳnḳnt	And he rests in life in *ḳnḳnt*.[560]
jrj=f ḫt nbt jm=s	He does everything in it (he will perform every rite in it),
mj jrrt m jw nsrsr	As is done in the Island of Fire.
n wnt nhm nb jm=s	There is no shouting in it at all,
n wnt ḫt nbt ḏwt jm=s	There is nothing bad or evil in it.
ḥtp nw šm=f ḫtḫt sḫt=f tw	This Hetep who walks through this countryside of his.
sm3=f rḫt nbt m msḫnt nṯr	He unites the whole knowledge in the birthplace of the god.
jr ḥtp=f m ꜥnḫ m ḳnḳnt	If he is satisfied with life in *ḳnḳnt*,
jrj=f ḫt nbt jm=s	He will do everything in it,
mj jrrt m jw nsrsr	Like what is done in the Island of Fire.
n wnt nhm nb jm=s	There is no shouting in it at all,
n ḫt nbt ḏwt jm=s	And there is no evil in it at all.[561]

The spell tells about Hetep, who performs every ritual in the birthplace of the god and in the Island of Fire, and he rests in *ḳnḳnt*.[562] It is interesting to note *jrj ḫt* which simply means that the deceased will be able to carry out rituals in the Field of Offerings, in the Island of Fire and in *ḳnḳnt* .[563] *jrj ḫt* and the placing of the spell on the front panel of the coffin where the table of offerings is depicted might give clues to the interpretation of the whole spell.[564]*jrj ḫt* is not only connected with the food offerings but also with other ritual performed by the deceased or for the deceased by his family and relatives.

In CT spell 465, Horus will perform every ritual in the Field of Offerings as being performed in the Island of Fire. It is also important to note that his life and equipment are in his hands, which might refer to the fact that he is personally performing the ritual in these two places and so uses his hands. The Field of Offerings and the Island of Fire are the places where there is no shouting. The place where there is no shouting is no doubt an expression which designates the place where the body of Osiris is. Shouting is not allowed in the abode of Osiris.[565] It might be the place where Horus as son of the deceased will perform the rites for his father Osiris, but it is not a must that this place is the place of embalming as Willems argues.[566] It might also represent the otherworldly place of embalming where Horus should enter to the place

[557] *CT* IV, 377a-378d (spell 346).

[558] For the role of Wepwawet in the funeral procession and in the *Stundenwachen* ritual, see Willems, *Heqata*, 225-7.

[559] Willems' interpretation of this group of spells is based on his belief that the Island of Fire is an earthly place, which represents the tomb chapel of the deceased, and in turn it can feature as the place where the rituals concerned with the resurrection are carried out for the deceased in his sarcophagus chamber which carries all the characteristic of the place of embalming. It is true that the Island of Fire in this group of spells represents the place where the deceased will participate in the ritual concerned with the resurrection of Osiris, but that will take place in the netherworld and not in the land of the living as Willems argues.

[560] This translation is after B3L, *CT* V, 349c-d (spell 465).

[561] *CT* V, 348b-351c (spell 465).

[562] An island in the Netherworld: *Wb* 5, 56.13-14.

[563] *jri ḫt* as a term refers to the performance of a ritual by a lector priest. One of the roles of the lector priest in the Old Kingdom is connected with the preparation of the food offerings. For instance, in the Mastaba of Mereruka, there is a caption which depicts men slaughtering cattle and they tell each other to work hard because the lector priest is coming to perform the rite, 'Hurry the lector priest is coming to perform rites': Duell, *The Mastaba of Mereuka* II, 109.

[564] It worth noting that Coffin Texts spells 646-647 are inscribed on the front panel on the eastern side of the coffins from el-Bersha. The decoration on this side include a false door, offering table and then follows this group of texts, which, as Willems argues, are devoted to the Field of Offerings and thus he locates the events to take place in the eastern side of the sky: Willems, *Heqata*, 258.

[565] On the different kinds of shouting in the place of Osiris, see Frandsen, in: *Studies Quaegebeur*, 974-1000.

[566] For how Willems envisaged the abode of Osiris as his tomb or his place of embalming, see Willems, *Heqata*, 153, 315-6, 326, and 347-8,

where the abode of Osiris is to treat him. Willems supports his argument by a passage in CT spell 847, which reads:

jj.n wsjr N pn m jw nsjsj	This Osiris N has come into the Island of Fire,
wr N pn m33 (=f) wsjr N pn	This N is great when (he) sees this Osiris N,[567]
sꜥḥ N pn m nb	This Osiris is ennobled as a Lord.[568]

Seeing Osiris is not always in the place of embalming, particularly in this spell. Osiris can also be seen in the place of the judgment of the dead as in CT spell 847 cited above.[569] Osiris is ennobled as a Lord when he is vindicated against his foes in the judgment of the dead. As a place of passage, the deceased asks the ferryman to launch his vessel and ferry to the Island of Fire. In CT spell 402 the deceased says:

j jnj mḫnt n rꜥ	O you who bring the ferryboat to Re,
srwd ꜥk3=k	Strengthen your rope,
mḥ mḫnt=k	launch your vessel,
d3j=k r jw nsrsr	So you may cross to the Island of Fire,
jsṯ dmḏ.n=j ḥk3w=j pn	For I have collected this magic of mine.[570]

The Island of Fire is a place which the deceased has to visit to acquire the magical powers which will help him overcoming the place of passage.

The Island of Fire in Shu spells

In CT spell 75, which belongs to a category known as Shu spells,[571] a deceased says:

km3.n=j b3=j ḥ3=j		I have created my *ba*, which is behind me,
km3.n=f n=j b3=j ḥ3=j	variant	He has created for me my *ba* which is behind me.[572]
n ns.n b3=j ḥr ẖt=j		My *ba* does not burn over my corpse.[573]
n ns=f ḥr ẖt=j	variant	It has not burnt over my body.[574]
n s3w.n.tw b3=j jn jrjw ꜥwt wsjr		My *ba* is not restrained by the guardians of the members of Osiris.
jw=j sṯj=j jw b3=j sṯj=f		I ejaculate and my *ba* ejaculates,
sṯj b3=j m rmṯw jmjw jw nsrsr		My *ba* ejaculates in the people who are in the Island of Fire,
sṯj=j ḏs=j m nṯrwt		And I myself ejaculate in the goddesses.[575]

Shu spells enable the deceased to be Shu.[576] CT spell 75 mentioned above describes how someone's *ba* is said to be created behind or around him. The *ba* does not burn over the corpse of the deceased. The *ba* is also not restrained by the guardians of the members of Osiris, which might refer to the guardians of the room of the body of Osiris.[577] In CT spell 49 the guardians of the room light torches and divide the hourly protection around Osiris.

sḥḏ tk3 jrjw ꜥt	Light a torch! O guardians of the room,
nṯrw jmjw snkt	The gods who are in darkness!
dj s3=ṯn ḥr nb=ṯn	Set your protection around your lord!
psš wnwt ḥr nb ḥḏt	Divide the hours on the Lord of the White Crown,
r jjt ḥr m jwnw	Until Horus comes from Heliopolis.[578]

CT spell 49 forms a liturgy to be recited in the place of embalming.[579] In this spell the guardians of the room are the gods who stood watching over the corpse of Osiris in the embalming place designated here as a room (*ꜥt*). They light torches and divide the hours of the night among themselves, which is known as the *Stundenwachen*.[580]

CT spell 75 describes how Shu is created by Atum. The deceased on his bier might represent Atum, and the *ba* of the deceased, at least in this spell, is Shu as son of Atum, which is evident when the deceased says:

km3.n=f n=j b3=j	He has created for me my *ba*

[567] Faulkner says that Osiris N is simply Osiris. This makes sense, because Osiris N is the deceased, and he will see Osiris. On Osiris NN and Osiris of NN see Smith, in: *Totenbuch-Forschungen*, 325-36.

[568] *CT* VII, 51q-r (spell 847).

[569] Roeder, *Mit dem Auge sehen*, 38-40.

[570] *CT* V, 176b-f (spell 402). The same theme occurs also in BD 32, and reads 'O you who bring the ferryboat of Re, strengthen your rope in the north-wind. Ferry upstream to the Island of Fire beside the realm of the dead': Faulkner, *BD*, 32. The Island of Fire occurs also in CT spell 403 in which the deceased asks the ferryman to bring him the ferryboat to travel to the realm of the dead: *CT* V, 180b-d (spell 403).

[571] This group of spells includes spells 75-83.

[572] In *CT* I, 362a on T3C (spell 75).

[573] *CT* I, 362c (spell 75).

[574] Willems translation is 'it (my *ba*) will <not> burn over my corpse': Willems, *Heqata*, 474.

[575] *CT* I, 362a-366b (spell 75).

[576] Coffin Texts spell 75 has the title of 'spell of the ba of Shu' (*r3 n b3 n šw*), becoming Shu (*ḫprw m šw*): *CT* 1, 314a (spell 75). On the textual history of the spell, see Jürgens, *GM* 105 (1988), 27-39; Zandee, *ZÄS* 97 (1971), 155-62; *ZÄS* 98 (1972), 149-55; *ZÄS* 99 (1973), 48-63.

[577] Willems, *Heqata*, 308.

[578] *CT* I, 216e-217b (spell 49).

[579] Assmann, *Totenliturgien* I, 266-76.

[580] Assmann, *Totenliturgien* I, 272-3. In CT spell 76, the eight *Heh* gods are also called *jrjw ꜥwt pt* 'keepers of the members of the sky': *CT* II, 1a (spell 76). They watch over the legs of the celestial cow, which lifts the deceased to the sky.[580] Therefore, these guardians can also be envisaged as priests performing rituals around the bier of the deceased, and they play the same role as the guardians of the members of Osiris: Willems, *Heqata*, 309.

ḫ3=j	which is behind me.[581]

The speaker is Shu and the one who created his *ba* for him is no doubt Atum. When the deceased says that the his *ba* does not burn over his body, this may refer to the fact that the guardians of the members of Osiris, while they are lighting torches and performing the *Stundenwachen* around the body of the deceased, will not burn the *ba* that comes to see the deceased.[582] The *ba* might also be that of Horus as son of Osiris.[583] So Horus as the *ba* of the deceased approaches the place where the body of Osiris is, and he is not restrained by the guardians.[584] Horus here plays the role of the deceased's son as his active *ba* that guarantees the continuity of his father's posterity on earth.

jw=j sṯj=j jw b3=j sṯj=f	I procreate and my *ba* procreates,
sṯj.n=j b3=j m rmṯw jmjw jw nsrsr	Myself and my *ba* have procreated in the people who are in the Island of Fire,
sṯj=j ḏs=j m nṯrwt	And I procreate in the goddesses.[585]

variant

snṯ[586]*=j jm b3=j*	I procreate in the (form) of my *ba*,[587]
snṯ b3=j m rmṯw jmjw jw nsrsr	And my *ba* procreates in the people who are in the Island of Fire.
snṯ b3=j ḏs=j m nṯrwt	My own ba procreates in the goddesses.[588]

The deceased procreates in the goddesses while his *ba* procreates in the people who are in the Island of Fire. Willems argues that the people who are in the Island of Fire are the living people on earth, and it is the role of the *ba*, representing the living son, to ejaculate in the living people on earth, who are in the Island of Fire.[589] The Island of Fire is a place of creation separated from the land of the living. It is not a physical earthly place, as Willems argues, but a marginal one.

The *ba* is also active in marginal areas, which in this text is the Island of Fire. The deceased is differentiating between the divine world where he is, and the world where his *ba* is. That is obvious from the fact that he procreates in the goddesses while his *ba* procreates in the people who are in the Island of Fire. The *ba* is the only creature that can enter and leave the realm of the dead.[590]

In CT spell 96, the deceased goes out into the day in the shape of his *ba*, and he copulates by means of it.

dj=j sḫt ḥw m ḫnt st ḥr n ʿr ḥrt	I place the Field of Hu (?) in front of the seat (on) the day of ascending the sky,
n-ntt jnk b3 pw ʿ3 n wsjr	Because I am this great *ba* of Osiris,
wḏ.n nṯrw nk=f jm=f	In which (form) the gods have commanded that he copulates,
ʿnḫ=f jm=f ḥr k3 m ḥr	In which (form) he lives on him high by day,
jrj.n wsjr m rḏw jmj jwf=f	Whom Osiris has made from the efflux which is in his flesh,
mtwt prt m ḥnn=f r prt m ḥr	The seed which comes out from his phallus to go out by day,
nk=f jm=f	That in him he might copulate.
pr nk=k m b3=k ʿnḫ	Go, and you will copulate as your living *ba*.[591]

The deceased does not ejaculate in his *ba* as Willems argues.[592] The *ba* is not the female partner of the deceased, at least in CT spell 75.

CT spell 75 concerns the transformation of a deceased into the soul of Shu, so the *ba* might represent Geb as son of Shu.[593] CT spell 80 may also give an answer to this question. Like other Shu spells, the spell recounts the creation of the world and the roles of both Atum and Shu in the creation process.[594] The text reads.

dwd[595]*.n=f wj r bʿnt=f*	He (Atum) has set me on his neck,
n rdj.n=f ḥrj=j r=f	And he did not let me be far from him.
ʿnḫ=j rn=j s3=j nṯr p3wtyw	I, my name, my son, and the primeval god live.
ʿnḫ=j m bsnw jt=j jtmw	I live on the natron[596] of my father Atum.

---

[581] *CT* I, 362a on T3C (spell 75).

[582] Willems, *Heqata*, 312.

[583] The *ba* can also be considered as manifestation of the power, and in this case Horus is the manifestation of Osiris: Roeder, in: Dücker and Roeder (eds), *Text und Ritual*, 190-1.

[584] Willems, *Heqata*, 308-9.

[585] This occurs on coffin M5C: *CT* I, 365b-367a (spell 75).

[586] On both coffins, A1C and G1T, the verb *sṯj* is replaced by the verb *snṯ* with a penis determinative. Willems argues that the verb is attested in some Graeco-Roman Period texts and is used to describes the sexual ability of a bull, which fits in this context: Willems, *Heqata*, 483, n. bo.

[587] The deceased does not procreate in his *ba* as Willems argues (Willems, *Heqata*, 474), but in the form or in the shape of his *ba*. Willems' translation was adopted by Barta, *Das Gespräch eines Mannes mit seinem Ba*, 72. This translation was then questioned by Assmann who argues that if the *ba* of the deceased is his living son on earth, it does not seem convincing to say that he is ejaculating in his son: Assmann, *Death and Salvation*, 430, n. 24.

[588] This variant occurs on Coffins G1T, and A1C: *CT* I, 365b-367b (spell 75).

[589] Willems, *Heqata*, 313.

[590] Englund, in: *Studies Wente*, 101-109.

[591] *CT* II, 76b-78d (spell 96).

[592] Willems, *Heqata*, 311-12.

[593] The transformation spells are wide spread in Egyptian religious texts. In these spells the deceased takes different forms (*ḫprw*) in his ascent to the sky. For the transformation spells in the Coffin Texts, see Buchberger, *Transformation und Transformat*; for the transformation spells in the Book of the Dead, see Lüscher, *Die Verwandlungssprüche*.

[594] Bickel, in: *Hommages Leclant* I, 93.

[595] Faulkner argues that *dwd* is a combination of the two related words '*dw*' and '*wdj*', and which can be translated as 'set' or 'place' and 'he has set me on his neck' means 'he carries me on his shoulder with my arm around his neck': Faulkner, *Coffin Texts* I, 87, n.34.

[596] Faulkner translated *bsnw* as a name for something edible: Faulkner, *Coffin Texts* I, 87, n. 36. Bickel translated it as 'Natron': Bickel, in: *Hommages Leclant* I, 86.

ꜥnḫ=j jrj bꜥnt=f swꜣḏ ḥtt	I live and (I am) the protector of his neck, who causes *ḥtt* (?) to be green,
jrj jtmw m npr	Whom Atum made as Neper,
m shꜣt=f wj r tꜣ pn r jw nsrsr	When he caused me to go down to this land, to the Island of Fire,
m ḫpr.n=j m wsjr sꜣ gb	When I became Osiris, son of Geb.[597]

This text can be interpreted on two levels. On theological level, the deceased's identification with Shu will guarantee the full capacities of life after death and divine status in the netherworld. The deceased will also obtain physical existence in the otherworld. At the end of this passage, the deceased says that his father Atum has made him as Neper. The deceased is thus constituted as the personification of the corn, symbol of any subsistence, and securing the certainty to have food eternally, since he is the god of food himself.[598]

This text provides a clue to the previous CT spell 75. A deceased is here identified with Atum, god of life, who created his son Shu who clings on his neck to provide him with air. The deceased also identifies himself in this spell with the god Shu, personification of life. This identification of Shu, in the shape of an amulet applied on the neck of his father Atum, guarantees full life for the deceased after death. Shu is sent by Atum to spread life among human beings, and he is the one who is responsible for the continuity of his father's life. The deceased is sent down to earth to spread life among human beings and to provide them with food as Neper, the Grain god. When the deceased is reduced to the ground, he becomes Osiris son of Geb. The identification of the deceased with Neper and his going down to the Island of Fire, which is here in the world beyond, refers to the fact that the deceased will overcome the dangers of the place of passage. The deceased as Neper will be able to save for himself the food that is essential for him to pass the place of the passage in the Island of Fire.[599]

On the funeral level, the passage might allude to an offering of an amulet to the deceased during the mummification ritual. The ritual can be constructed in the following way. First the deceased on his bier is Atum, and Shu is the son who clings on his father throat to provide him with air to breath. In the mummification ritual, the priest would apply an amulet on the deceased's neck. The amulet is in the shape of Shu.[600]

It can be concluded that the Island of Fire is not connected with death or the rituals taking place immediately after death, but it is connected with what happens when the deceased enters the netherworld. As a primordial place, the Island of Fire represents a place where the world came into existence. As a place in the netherworld, the Island represents a passage that a deceased wishes to pass in his journey to the hereafter. It is a marginal place that is separated from the world of the living and form the world of the dead. It is also one of the places where the deceased can see Osiris, where it features as a place where the judgment of the dead takes place.

[597] *CT* II, 40b-h (spell 80).
[598] Bickel, in: *Hommages Leclant* I, 93.
[599] Bickel, in: *Hommages Leclant* I, 94.
[600] Willems, *Heqata*, 295.

Chapter Four

Crossing of the Lake Ritual

The representations on the private tomb walls of the Old Kingdom include crossing of a lake as a part of the deceased's funeral procession from his house to his burial place. In the Old Kingdom Pyramid Texts and Middle Kingdom Coffin Texts, the deceased is warned against crossing over the Great Lake. This lake is also described as being a place which leads to the *3ḫw* and to the *mwt*. In the New Kingdom Sun Hymns, the deceased's journey over the Lake of Knives is described as a dangerous one. In the Book of the Two Ways the Lake of Fire is described as a true passage and also as a place where the sinners are punished by fire. The same theme occurs also in the Book of the Gates where the Lake of Fire is described as a place of food and nourishment for the righteous, and its water is fire for the sinners. Pictorial and textual evidence will be presented to show how the crossing of a lake in Old Kingdom private tombs and Old and Middle Kingdom texts can be related to the deceased' crossing over the Lake of Knives and the Lake of Fire.

4.1. Old Kingdom Evidence

Pictorial Evidence from Old Kingdom Private Tombs

Pictorial evidence comes from Old Kingdom Mastaba D 62 of the vizier Ptahhotep I at Saqqara.[601] The funeral procession of the deceased is depicted on the western wall of the pillared hall.[602] In the middle register on this wall, a boat is depicted with a man designated as *wt* putting his hand on a shrine, while his second hand lies flat on his knee. Behind this man stands a helmsman. Above the two men is a text which reads:

m ḥtp m ḥtp ḫr wsjr	In peace in peace before Osiris.

In front of the boat there is a man raising his right hand in recitation,[603] and beneath him there are two men and two women depicted beating their chests. This gesture is called *hnw* and is always translated as praising of a god and jubilation.[604] It is not a sign of happiness, but a sign of grief for the loss of a deceased.[605] *hnw* was accompanied by recitations of a lector priest, most probably the priest above the seated men and women as shown on fig. 31.

The lower register shows on the left hand side a helmsman, a seated woman most probably symbolising a kite, and an embalmer. At the prow of a boat a man designated as *ḫrj-ḥbt* is shown putting his hand on his chest in *hnw* gesture. A woman beside him is designated as a kite (*ḏrt*). A label in front of them reads *s3ḫw* 'performing *s3ḫw*'. It is important here to note that the crossing is accompanied by recitations of *s3ḫw*.

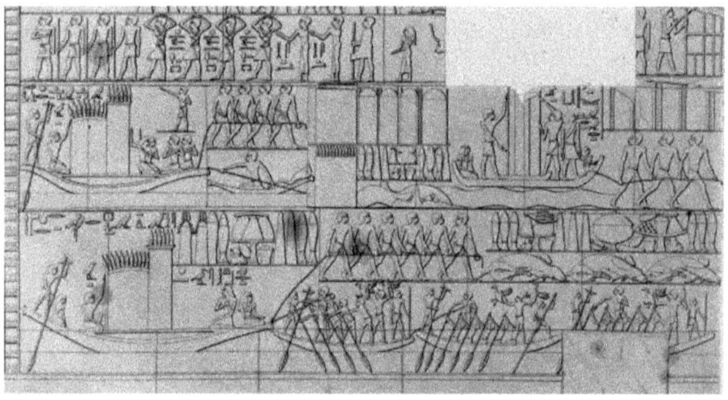

Fig. 31. The crossing of the lake from the Mastaba of the vizier Ptahhotep I (after Lepsius, *Denkmäler*, Band IV, Abteilung II, pl. 101).

Another instance is found in the tomb of In-Snefru-Ishetef (fig. 32). A scene on the upper register shows a boat with a shrine is towed across the water. The shrine, most probably, houses a statue of the deceased. At the prow of the boat sits a kite (*ḏrt*), two undesignated men, and a lector priest with containers holding his equipment. There is a woman sitting at the back of the boat near the helmsman. At the bottom, a boat seems to sail or rest on sand. Above the boat there is a label and reads:

ḏ3jt wrt	Crossing of the *Wrt*-boat

A kite is represented facing a priest, who stands in a canopy and reads from a papyrus roll. There is also a kite sitting at the back of the boat with a man designated as an embalmer (*wt*). The text accompanying the scene reads:

sšm ḥb m mw	Conducting a ritual in water,
jn ḫrj-ḥbt jjmḥ	By the lector priest Iimeh.

The rest of the scene shows three men towing a boat, offerings being presented and figures of men slaughtering an ox.[606]

[601] The mastaba of Ptahhotep I was discovered by Mariette. He referred to it briefly in his Book on the mastabas of ancient Egypt: Mariette, *Mastaba de l'Ancien Empire*, 351-6. Later Selim Hassan got the permission to start clearing the mastaba and the shafts around it, but he did not publish all the scenes on the walls of the mastaba including the one on the western wall of the pillared hall mentioned above: Hassan, *Excavations at Saqqara*, vol. II, 25-61. A recent study on the mastaba of Ptahhotep II (D64) has been done by Harpur and Scremin, *The Chapel of Ptahhotep*.

[602] *LD* II, vol. 1, 101; *LD Ergänzungs*, vol. 1, 43b.

[603] Dominicus, *Gesten und Gebärden*, 61-5.

[604] *CDME*, 159; Dominicus, *Gesten und Gebärden*, 60-4.

[605] Assmann, *Totenliturgien* I, 14.

[606] Wilson, *JNES* 3 (1944), 208.

Fig. 32. The funeral procession of In-Snefru-Ishetef at Dahshour
(reproduced by Wilson, *JNES* 3 (1944), pl. XIV from de Morgan, *Fouilles en Dahchour* II, pl. 22).

In the second register in the first corridor on the north wall of the tomb chapel of Hetepherakhti, a shrine with a statue of the deceased is shown transported to the tomb on a papyrus boat (fig. 33). At the back of the same boat sits a man without designation, and a woman designated as a kite (*ḏrt*).[607] In front of the boat sits a lector priest and an undesignated man. The text above this scene reads:

ḫnt sšm ḥb jn ḫrj-ḥbt	Sailing and conducting ritual, by the lector priest.

Fig. 33. The funeral procession of Hetepherakhti
(after Mohr, *The Mastaba of Hetep-Her-Akhti*, pl. 1).

In all these scenes the physical crossing and the recitations run together and the aim of both is to mediate the passage of the deceased to another state, the state of being an *ꜣḫ*.[608]

Textual Evidence from Old Kingdom Private Tombs

In the tomb of the vizier Ptahhotep from Saqqara, the text which describes the crossing of a lake is inscribed at the lower right side of the tomb's false door. The text is accompanied by a scene in which the deceased is shown seated in a shrine facing a lector priest who reads from a papyrus roll. The text reads:

hꜣjt r pr=f n ḏt m ḥtp nfr wrt	Going down to his house of eternity in very great peace,
wn jmꜣḫ=f ḫr jnpw ḫntj-ḫrt-nṯr	That he might be provisioned by Anubis-Foremost-of-the-Necropolis,
m-ḫt pr n=f ḫrw ḥr tp ḳrrt	After an invocation offering is brought to him on the top of the tomb,[609]
m-ḫt nmi.t(j) š	After the lake was crossed,
m-ḫt sꜣḫ.t(j)=f	After he has been made an *ꜣḫ*,
jn ḫrj-ḥbt	By the lector priest.[610]

According to the inscriptions on the false door of Ptahhotep, as Wilson argues, 'it is possible to argue that there were successive acts; crossing the water, landing on the west bank, entering the necropolis and finally the burial'.[611] What is explicit is that during crossing the water, there was a ritual conducted for the deceased.

On the false door of the tomb of Tepemankh at Saqqara, crossing the lake is described as:

prt r tp ḏw n jmnt	Going out to the top of the mountain of the west,
m-ḫt nmj.t(j) š	After crossing the lake,
js sꜣḫ jn ḫrj-ḥbt	During making into an *ꜣḫ* by the lector priest,
jrj n=f ḫt	And the rite was carried out for him,
jn wt ḫr inpw	By the embalmer before Anubis.[612]

The inscription states that the deceased reached the west after he had crossed a lake. The crossing was accompanied by a fully equipped ritual, conducted for him by a lector priest. The inscription maintains the acts of the lector priest by relating that:

sšm r js=f n jmnt	A procession to his tomb of the west,
m-ḫt ḫnt=f m wrt	After rowing him in the *wrt*-boat,
sšm n=f ḥb ꜥpr	And a fully equipped ritual had been conducted for him,
ḫft sš n ḥmt ḫrj-ḥbt	According to the writing of the craft of the lector priest.[613]

On the right inner jamb of the false door of the Mastaba of Neferseshemre at Saqqara, crossing a Firmament (*bjꜣ*) and traversing a lake occur.

ḏꜣjt bjꜣ m ḥtp nfr wrt	Crossing the Firmament in very great peace.
prt jr tp ḏw n ḫrt-nṯr	Going out to the top of the mountain of the necropolis.

---

[607] Mohr, *The Mastaba of Hetep-Her-Akhti*, 37-8.
[608] On the history of *sꜣḫw*, see Assmann, *Totenliturgien* III, 26-30.

[609] For the ritual taking place on the roof of the tomb in the Old Kingdom, see Alexanian, in: *Fs Stadelmann*, 4-22.
[610] Sethe, *Urk* I, 189, lines 4-6.
[611] Wilson, *JNES* 3(1944), 209.
[612] Sethe, *Urk* I, 190, lines 8-9; other instances describing the landing of the coffin after crossing the firmament are found in the tomb of Harkhuf at Aswan, and the tomb of Tetiankh and Meru at Sheikh Said: Wilson, *JNES* 3 (1944), 208.
[613] Sethe, *Urk* I, 190, lines 12-13.

nḏrt ꜥ=f jn jtw=f	His hand is grasped by his fathers,
[...] *tp nb jmꜣḫ*	[And...] Lords of *jmꜣḫ*.
prt-ḫrw n=f	An invocation (is brought) for him,
ḥr tp ḳrrt m pr=f n ḏt	On the roof of the tomb in his house of eternity,
sk sw jꜣwt [nfrt wrt ḫr wsjr]	When he has reached [a very good old age before Osiris].
hꜣt r pr=f ḏt m ḥtp nfr wrt	Going down to his house of eternity in very great peace,
wn jmꜣḫ=f ḫr jnpw ḫnty-ḫrt-nṯr nb-tꜣ-ḏsr	That he might be venerated before Anubis-Foremost-of-the-Necropolis, Lord-of-Sacred-Land,
m-ḫt prt-ḫrw [n=f] ḥr tp ḳrrt	After an invocation offering has been brought [for him] on the top of the tomb,
m-ḫt nmj.t(j) š	After traversing the lake,
m-ḫt sꜣḫ.t(j)=f jn ḫrj-ḥbt	After he has been made into an *ꜣḫ* by the lector priest.[614]

In tomb of Mehu at Saqqara, crossing a firmament is described as:

ḥtp dj nswt ḥtp dj ḫntj-jmntjw nb tꜣ wr	An offering which, the king and Khentamentiu Lord of the Great Land give,
smꜣ=f tꜣ ḏꜣj=f bjꜣ	That he may land, that he may cross the firmament,
jꜥ=f n nṯr ꜥꜣ	That he might ascend to the Great God,
m smjt jmntt	In the western cemetery.[615]

Crossing a lake takes place while the deceased is made into an *ꜣḫ*. In other words, a lector priest was reading or reciting texts while crossing the water was in process. In Wilson's words 'there was great deal of physical, ritual, and religious activity necessary to make the deceased a blessed and fully effective immortal. Priestly ritual and utterance are involved in this *sꜣḫ* beatifying'.[616] *sꜣḫw* texts included liturgies recited in the night before burial and at the day of funeral,[617] and their aim is to mediate the passage of the deceased to become an *ꜣḫ*, and to pass the place of passage safely.[618]

Pyramid Texts Evidence

On the eastern wall of the burial chamber of King Pepi I, a part of the resurrection ritual is inscribed and the crossing of the lake occurs. PT spell 603 reads:

ṯs ṯw jt=j	Raise yourself my father!
ṯs n=k tp=k	Raise for yourself your head,
[sꜣḳ] n=k ꜥwt=k	And assemble for yourself your limbs.
wṯs ṯw [m] rdwj=k	Raise yourself with your legs,
sšm ṯw jb=k	So that your heart will lead you.
sḫs jnw=k	Your messengers have run,
ntꜣj ḥwwt=k	Your heralds have hastened,
jj smj=k n=[k] m ꜣḫt	And your report has come for you in the horizon.
jj jnpw ḫsf=f jm=[k]	Anubis has come to meet you.
dj.n n=k ḥtp ꜥ=f	The Contented One has given you his hand.
nḫn.n nṯrw	The gods have rejoiced,
[j]ḥ[ꜥꜥ] [šmsw-ḥ]r	And Ho[rus followers] have celebrated.
jj ꜣḫ m ꜣḫ=f jn psḏtj	'An akh has come in its status of being an akh,' says the Dual Ennead,
[ḏ]ꜣ.n=f š nmj.n=f d[ꜣ]t	When he has crossed the lake and has traversed the Duat.[619]

The spell starts with a call for the deceased to raise up himself, which refers to the common goal of all rituals, aimed at the activation of the deceased from the embalming process to the mortuary offerings. It is a wakeup call intended to awaken the deceased from his unconscious state, and alludes to the fact that he is undergoing the resurrection ritual.[620] The deceased will gain his ability of movement, and mediate his passage with the recitation of these texts and the crossing of the lake which comes at the end.

In the Pyramid Texts raising up oneself and uniting the limbs is often connected with an invitation to receive offerings, especially libation offerings.[621] They consist of series of inter-related and complicated rituals, and sometimes it is not easy to figure out which ritual comes first. The aim of these rituals is to mediate the passage of the deceased to become an *ꜣḫ*, which allows him to escape the realm of death and join the realm of *ꜣḫw*.

The evidence discussed above comes from Old Kingdom royal and private tombs, and in both, crossing of the lake goes closely together with becoming an *ꜣḫ*, mediated by a lector priest who recites liturgies from the papyrus roll. Crossing a lake whether this lake is given a name or not, lies in a resurrection ritual context in which libation offerings are presented to a deceased.

Libation offering is envisaged as crossing a of lake, and the libation water is a body of water which should be crossed by a deceased. This is reinforced by some Old Kingdom libation basins which were decorated

[614] Kanawati, *Teti Cemetery* III, 35-6, pl. 58.
[615] Hawass, *LingAeg* 10 (2002), 221; Kloth, *Die auto-biographische Inschriften*, 48; Altenmüller, *Grab des Mehu*, 89; Lapp, *Opferformel*, § 98.
[616] Wilson, *JNES* 3 (1944), 210.
[617] For the representations of funeral processions on the Old Kingdom private tombs, see Bolshakov, *GM* 121 (1991), 31-54.
[618] Assmann, *Totenliturgien* III, 26-31.
[619] PT spell 603=*Pyr.* § 1675a- 1677b; Allen, *Inflection of the Verb*, 680.
[620] Assmann, *Death and Salvation*, 332
[621] Assmann, *Death and Salvation*, 332.

with boats crossing over water. On one of the offering table from Abydos, there is a depiction of four boats carved on the narrow step of the offering basin, which indicates that these basins were used as replacements of the lakes and rivers over which the deceased can travel to the netherworld.[622] Another instance is also found on the offering table of the Ankh Wedjes now in Louvre Museum. This offering table consists of three basins with lotus flowers carved into the stepped inner sides of the basins. The decoration on the long outsides shows a deceased sitting in a boat being offered ducks while sailing is in progress (fig. 34).[623]

Fig. 34. Offering table Louvre E 25369 (after Mostafa, *Opfertafeln*, pl. XXXI).

In the Pyramid Texts the lake is called the Great Lake, and the deceased has to avoid its dangers. It is also a passage which leads to the *ꜣḫw*.

hꜣ N pw [sꜣ ṯ]w š wr pw jr ꜣḫw	O this N beware of this Great Lake, which (leads) to the *ꜣḫw*,
ḫns pw jr mwt	This water course which (leads) to the dead,
sꜣ tw rmṯ jptf nt pr bꜣ-pf	Beware of those people of the house of *Bꜣ-pf*,[624]
ḫrt-ḏꜣt m rn=sn pw n ḏꜣtt	Terrible-Opponents in this their name of 'Female Opponents',
jmj=sn nḏrw ꜥ=k jr pr bꜣ-pf	Let them not to take your hand towards the House of *Bꜣ-pf*,
sw sw mr sw nh sw jꜣb sw	It is dangerous, it is painful, it is nasty (?), and it is foul-smelling.[625]

The Apis Bull Procession over the Lake of the King

Crossing of the lake in Old Kingdom private tombs goes well with the description of the Apis Bull procession over the Lake of the King in the Ptolemaic Period. The Lake of the King was a place where a kiosk was put up for the funeral rites of the Apis Bull, which was conveyed by a boat before burial. During the journey across the lake, the Opening of the Mouth Ritual was performed according to the demotic Papyrus of Vienna 27.[626] The Apis procession to the sacred lake takes place while nine holy books are read aloud. The text which describes this episode of the ritual reads:

> The Apis is carried in procession to the sacred lake. Journey to the Sacred Lake, while nine holy books are read aloud. They bring the....priests to the Wrapping-Room. They lay the beginning of the cord of the coffin in their hands. They draw (the coffin) out. The *wꜥb* priests draw (the coffin) in, while all people raise a great lamentation. They cry woe upon the god in the big house. The *wꜥb* priests take the beginning of the cord out of the hand of the Great Ones of the House of the Inundation of the Nile. They enter the lake with Isis and Nephthys before him (the Apis), with 2 *bs*-vessels filled with natron in their hands, 10 *mnḫt* cloths, white cloth and a blue cloth, Wepwawet of Upper Egypt, Horus, and the Bed of Ptah, are before this god. They make the god rest on the bank of sand, his face turned south. The *wꜥb* priests, who enter the shrines, go to the lake. They mount upon the Barque of Papyrus. They provide themselves with rowers. They read aloud nine books on the Barque. Their titles:
> I. Ritual of the Journey of the First Day
> II. The Protection of the Sacred Barque
> III. The Protection of the Barque
> IV. The Plan of your Face
> V. Glorification of Osiris, the Floating One
> VI. The Protection of the Holy Barque
> VII. Warding off
> VIII. Good Fortune
> IX. The Opening of the Mouth[627]

In this ritual, two priests are brought to the place of embalming, and with the help of the rope they pull the coffin containing the mummy of the Apis outside. After the mummy with the coffin is taken outside the embalming house, two *wꜥb* priests pull the rope from the hand of the Great Ones of the House of the Inundation of the Nile. During this process, loud lamentations take place. The coffin is then placed in a boat and the Apis is transported to the Lake of the King accompanied by Isis, Nephthys, Wepwawet of Upper Egypt, Wepwawet of Lower Egypt, Horus and Thoth. When the procession reaches the lake, the Apis is placed on a platform and his face is pointed southwards. After that the Apis mummy sails across

[622] Hölzl, *Ägyptische Opfertaflen und Kultbecken*, 67.
[623] Hölzl, in: *L'acqua nell'antico Egitto*, 313-4. For a similar type of offering tables but with no boat scenes, see Hölzl, *Ägyptische Opfertaflen und Kultbecken*, 14-8; Mostafa, *Opfertafeln*, 110-14. On the offering tables with basins in the Hermitage, see Bolshakov, *Studies on Old Kingdom Reliefs and Sculpture in the Hermitage*, 187-230.
[624] House of the *ba* is a place that the dead should avoid in the Netherworld: Zandee, *Death as an Enemy*, 209; Assmann, *Totenliturgien* I, 338.
[625] PT spell 666B=*Pyr.* § 1930c-1933b; Allen, *Inflection of the Verb*, 691-2; Assmann, *Death and Salvation*, 143; *Totenliturgien* I, 339.

[626] Published by Vos, *The Apis Embalming Ritual*.
[627] The translation is that of Vos, *The Apis Embalming Ritual*, recto IV, lines 14-19, 52.

the lake, and the priests read aloud the nine sacred books until they reach the purification tent, where the Opening of the Mouth Ritual is carried out for the Apis.[628]

Vos describes the procession across the lake as an episode from the Osiris secret rituals and drama, in which the resurrection of Osiris is made manifest. He supports his argument with a passage from Clement of Alexandria, a Christian writer who described one of the Egyptian funeral processions.[629] Clement described how four golden statues were carried in a procession, with two dogs, a falcon and an Ibis. Vos argues that when a comparison is made between this procession and the Apis procession over the lake, it seems that the two dogs can represent Wepwawet of Upper and Lower Egypt. The Falcon is Horus symbol of the sun, and the Ibis is Thoth. Vos maintains that the procession across the lake can be seen as a symbolic depiction of the journey of the sun god in the sun boat, and the route followed by the procession represents the path followed by the sun god Re in his journey. The Osiris resurrection and the solar procession are equated together in the Apis procession over the Lake of the King.[630] The papyrus boat (*wjꜣ*) of the Apis is identical to the sun boat in which Re sails over Nun and it is also equated with the (*nšmt*) barque of Osiris.[631] Osiris on his bier is equated with the sun god in his barque.[632] The deceased on his bier is threatened by Seth, and the sun god Re in his barque is threatened by Apep. The sun god Re overcomes his primeval enemies, and the Bull's resurrection will be achieved by reciting the nine books which are read aloud while sailing over the Lake of the King.[633]

In the Apis Bull procession across the Lake of the King, the procession is accompanied by Isis and Nephtys, which reminds us of the two kites in the funeral procession in Old Kingdom mastabas across the lake mentioned above. Goyon[634] argues that there were two categories of ritual books known in Egypt; the first category royal or Osirian books aimed at the protection against the enemies, Seth and Apep. The second category is the *sꜣḫw* books which were used in the mystery of the resurrection of Osiris and mediate the passage of the deceased to become an *ꜣḫ*. Vos argues that from the titles of the nine books to be recited while the Apis procession was crossing the lake, both categories appear to be represented.[635]

Diodorus Siculus' Description of Crossing the Lake Ritual

Crossing the lake as a ritual was fully described by Diodorus Siculus. He reports that when the body of the deceased was ready to be buried, the family announces the day of interment and affirms that the deceased is about to cross the lake. Officials and dignitaries were among the forty two assessors representing the gods who sat in judgment in the afterlife and acted as a court. The people stand in front of this court, and anyone has the right to denounce the deceased, while the boat waits empty at the river for the judgment to finish. If there were no hostile voices, the coffin was placed in the boat.[636]

During the Old Kingdom, the journey of the deceased was apparently across the river, but Wilson noted that there is no specific evidence, and the crossing is not described as a journey to Abydos.[637] Furthermore, the texts concerning crossing the lake are not only found in the private tombs of Saqqara, but other texts describing this ritual were found in the tombs of Harkhuf and Meru at Aswan, which supports the argument that crossing the lake was not an actual crossing, and not only connected with the private tombs in Saqqara. It was symbolic crossing, and the deceased's crossing over the lake might refer to his spiritual crossing of the sky on his way to the netherworld.[638]

The evidence that the crossing was a symbolic one is obvious from the inscriptions of the mastaba of Neferseshemre mentioned above. In this text, crossing a lake is compared with crossing a firmament. The deceased is said to cross a firmament to the mountain of the necropolis. Then the offerings are presented to him at the top of his tomb after he has crossed a lake. It is still not explicit what is meant by crossing a firmament, but this crossing is always compared with the crossing of the sun god Re to the sky.

Crossing the firmament, in Assmann's words, 'is a formally established turn of expression for the sun god's crossing the sky and it is at the same time basic principle of Egyptian mortuary belief.'[639] The funeral procession mentioned above thus might be explained as crossing the sky and not merely crossing a body of water whether this body was a lake, a river or a firmament.

[628] Vos, *The Apis Embalming Ritual*, 159-60.
[629] The most recent discussion on Clement of Alexandria is that of Hägg, *Clement of Alexandria and the Beginnings of Christian Apophaticis.*
[630] Altenmüller, *Synkretismus*, 42-6.
[631] Vos, *The Apis Embalming Ritual*, 162.
[632] Willems, *Chests of Life*, 156-8.
[633] Vos, *The Apis Embalming Ritual*, 166.
[634] Goyon, in: *Hommages Champollion* I, 73-81.
[635] Vos, *The Apis Embalming Ritual*, 166.
[636] Oldfather, *Diodorus of Sicily* I, 92.
[637] Wilson, *JNES* 3 (1944), 208.
[638] Wilson, *JNES* 3 (1944), 209; Bolshakov, *GM* 121 (1991), 37.
[639] Assmann, *Death and Salvation*, 291.

Middle Kingdom Evidence

Coffin Texts Evidence

Crossing a lake occurs in Coffin Text spell 62, which reads:

dj=j jrj=k ḫprw ḥnꜥ ḏwjt	I cause that you make manifestations with the *ḏwj.t* bird (?).
dj=j ḏꜣj=k ptrwj ḏꜣj=k š	I cause that you cross the *ptrwj* (?)[640] and cross the lake,
nmj=k wꜣḏ-wr (m) ṯbt	And traverse the sea (in) sandals,
mj jrj.n=k tp tꜣ	As you had done on land.
ḥkꜣ=k jtrw ḥnꜥ bnw	You will rule the river with the heron,
nn rḳw=k r wꜥrt[641]	And no opponent will be against you at the district of water.
dj=j wḏ=k m smꜥ n mḥ 40	I cause that you progress with a sounding-pole of 40 cubits,
m srd n ꜥš n kbn	Of planted wood of cedar of Byblos,
ꜥḥꜥ.tj m wjꜣ n rꜥ	As you stand in the Barque of Re,
ḏꜣj.n=k š n rḫjt	And you have crossed the Lake of *rḫjt*.
smꜣꜥ-ḫrw=k ḥr wḏꜥ-mdw	You will be vindicated (on) the day of judgment,
m ḏꜣḏꜣt nt nb gmwt	In the tribunal of the Lord of Suffering.
šd n=k ḫbs tꜣ	A liturgy of Hacking up the Earth will be recited for you,
ḫsf n=k sbj jj m grḥ	And the enemy who comes at night will be driven off for you.[642]

This spell occurs only on the outer coffin of Amenemhat, nomarch of el-Bersha. The text was recorded five times on the coffin, which was published in de Buck's edition as B10C. Willems dates the coffin to the end of the reign of Sesostris I and the beginning of the reign of Amenemhat II.[643] CT spell 62 is a liturgy by itself.[644] It is a speech by Horus to his father Osiris, containing three mortuary liturgies to be recited in the context of a wake.[645] This long speech of Horus to his deceased father resembles the speech of the goddess Neith on the lid of the sarcophagus of Merenptah.[646] The text belongs to the *sꜣḫw* texts and is aimed at the restoration of the deceased's social and physical aspects.[647] The spell begins with an address of Horus to Osiris describing the ritual acts carried by the son for his father.

jnḏ ḥr=k jt=j wsjr	Greetings to you, my father Osiris
mk wj jj.kw jnk ḥr	Behold, I have come, I am Horus.
wpj=j rꜣ=k ḥnꜥ ptḥ	I will open your mouth with Ptah,
sꜣḫ=j ṯw ḥnꜥ ḏḥwtj	I will spiritualize you with Thoth.[648]

Horus will carry out the Opening of the Mouth ritual for his father and he will make him an *ꜣḫ* with Thoth. Horus causes his father to make manifestations with the bird, and to cross the lake. After passing safely through the mummification and becoming an *ꜣḫ,* the deceased will have the ability of free movement over water.[649] By means of crossing the water, the deceased will mediate his passage and escape the realm of death, become an *ꜣḫ,* and steer the barque of the sun god Re. The next verses show the roles of the deceased in the sun boat, and because of the changing levels of the water of the Nile, the depth of water has to be measured constantly. The deceased will stand at the prow of the sun barque measuring the water level, as he was doing in his daily life. The deceased crosses the Nile knowing where the sandbanks are, and he is doing the same act on the boat of the sun god Re.[650]

The lake is also described as the Great Lake, and the deceased has to avoid its dangers. CT spell 67 reads:

jꜣ N pn sꜣ ṯw š wr	O this N, beware of the Great Lake.[651]
jr mwt nh=k sw	As for death, you will escape it.
ꜣb=k wꜣt r=f	And you will avoid the route to him.
jmj=sn jṯj ṯw r pr bꜣ-pf	They shall not drag you off to the house of *Bꜣ-pf,*
jmj=sn jrj ḏꜣjt r=k	And they shall not make opposition to you,
m rn=sn n ḏꜣjw	In their name of Opponents.[652]

The journey of the deceased starts with a warning against crossing the Great Lake. CT spells 62 and 67 form parts of the *jj-ṯhb-wr* Liturgy.[653] In this liturgy,

640 Faulkner translated *ptrwj* 'Waterway of the Sky-Windows': Faulkner, *Coffin Texts* I, 58.
641 A body of water in the hereafter: *Wb* I, 288.6-7.
642 *CT* I, 266h-268g (spell 62).
643 Willems, *Chests of Life*, 74-5.
644 Assmann, in: Willems (ed.), *The World of the Coffin Texts*, 18-9; *Death and Salvation*, 270: *Totenliturgien* I, 39.
645 Assmann, *Totenliturgien* I, 40-1.
646 Assmann, *MDAIK* 28 (1972), 47-73, 115-139.

647 His physical status will be restored by undergoing the mummification ritual, while his social status will be restored by passing safely through the judgment of the dead: Assmann, *Death and Salvation*, 270-6.
648 *CT* I, 265a-d (spell 62).
649 Assmann, in: Willems (ed.), *The World of the Coffin Texts*, 5-10.
650 Assmann, *Death and Salvation*, 274.
651 The same warning of crossing the Great Lake occurs also in PT spell 214=*Pyr.* § 136a, PT spell 447= *Pyr.* § 827d, and PT spell 619= *Pyr.* § 1752c.
652 *CT* I, 284e-285a (spell 67).
653 This liturgy occurs on some Middle Kingdom coffins; one coffin from el-Bersha, three coffins from Thebes and one coffin from Saqqara. It is also found in the tomb of Senenmut TT 353 from the time of Hatshepsut: Assmann, *Totenliturgien* I, 333.

the warning against crossing the Great Lake, as Assmann points out, might refer to the deceased's return into his tomb, while he is already in the world of the dead, to partake of the offerings presented to him in his tomb. The *jj-ṯhb-wr* Liturgy was recited in the morning before sunrise at the conclusion of the night rituals.[654] So crossing the Great Lake might refer to the deceased joining the solar barque and the partaking of the offerings presented to him. The deceased who is already in the netherworld returns to his tomb and in his way back to consume the offerings he is threatened by crossing the Great Lake. The consumption of the deceased's offerings is envisaged as traveling across the sky and joining the barque of the sun god Re.[655]

4.3. New Kingdom Evidence

Crossing the Lake in New Kingdom Private Tombs

In New Kingdom private tombs, particularly in Ramesside tombs, crossing to the west is described as 'the Great Ferry". For instance, in TT 133 the boat which carries the coffin is equated with the Great Ferry which the deceased uses for the transition from the realm of death to the underworld.[656] Thus, the crossing of a river or any other body of water was interpreted as a passage which was only granted for the righteous. The text in TT 133 reads:

[ḏ3] mẖnt wrt nt jmntt	Fare across, Great Ferry of the West.
mj ḏ3 m ḥtp r jmntt	Come! Fare in peace a cross to the West.
jw dj (=j) t n ḥḳr mw n jbw d3jw n ḥ3w	I gave bread to the hungry, water to the thirsty, and clothing to the naked.[657]

Here the deceased says that he has given bread to the hungry and water to the thirsty, which are required for his safe passage to the west. The deceased before giving this food stuff to the hungry, he was in the pre-liminal or marginal stage, which separates between the marginal and post-liminal stages, and by providing the hungry and thirsty with food and drink, he mediates his passage to the west and leaves the marginal state and enters the post-liminal state, the state of being an *3ḫ* which comes after his crossing to the west.[658]

It seems reasonable to equate a boat carrying a statue of a deceased with the *Neshmet* Barque of Osiris. In TT 347 the barque of the deceased is that of Osiris. The statue of the deceased, priests and mourners are shown on the boat, while Isis and Nephthys are depicted at the foot and the head of the deceased.[659] This depiction of the boat reminds us of the Old Kingdom tombs representations of a boat crossing a lake mentioned above, where an embalmer, kites, and lector priests are depicted in a boat traversing a lake. So crossing to the West in New Kingdom private tombs might be described as a ceremonial or symbolic crossing as it was in the Old Kingdom. The text describing crossing to the West in TT 347 reads:

ḏd n p3 ꜥš-ḥꜥt ntj m ḥ3t n t3 nšmt	Speech of the pilot at the prow of the N*eshmet* Barque,
jmj-wrt jtḥ r jmntt	To the West, tow (your boat) to the West,
p3 dmjt n m3ꜥtj ẖft-ḥr- nb=s njwt jmn	The Town of the Righteous, That-Which-in front-of-its-Lord, the city of Amun.
wḏ=f sw n NN t3 mnj gr=k	He (Amun) has given it over to NN, the mourning land of your Silent One,
wnf.wj st m ẖnw=s	How the place (the tomb) rejoices at it!
ḥt-ḥr ḥnwt jmntt t3 mḏ3t n jmj-wrt	Hathor, Mistress of the West, the Protector of the Western Side,
t3 jr… n m3ꜥtj nb	She [who prepares a place] for every Righteous,
šsp=s NN m ḳnw=s	May she take NN in her embrace.[660]

Crossing to the West is envisaged as a transition or a passage into a sphere of security and divine presence that is only granted to the righteous. It is not a mere physical transfer of a corpse from one place to another, but rather a ritual procession.[661] As a result, crossing over a lake or over a river is not connected with the geographical location of the necropolis as it might be thought, Saqqara in the Old Kingdom and the West of Thebes in the New Kingdom, but with the ritual enacted on the day of traversing the lake.

Rituals in the Garden and Crossing the Lake Ritual

In some New Kingdom tombs at Thebes and Memphis, there are scenes showing rituals conducted for the deceased in a garden in front of his tomb.[662] In these tombs the deceased is represented sitting or standing on the *Neshmet*-boat of Osiris and crossing a lake or a pond. For instance, in the tomb of the vizier Rekhmire

[654] Assmann, *Totenliturgien* I, 133.
[655] Assmann, *Death and Salvation*, 336-7.
[656] Barthelmess, *Der Übergang ins Jenseits*, 19.
[657] Barthelmess, *Der Übergang ins Jenseits*, 19.
[658] Franke, *ZÄS* 133 (2006), 106-7. For the three stages which charcterise the rites of passage according to Victor Turner, see below, 80.
[659] Barthelmess, *Der Übergang ins Jenseits*, 20.
[660] Barthelmess, *Der Übergang ins Jenseits*, 20-1. When the goddess Hathor embraces the deceased that simply means that she is receiving and protecting him: Versiljević, *SAK* 37 (2008), 368.
[661] Assmann, *Death and Salvation*, 304-5.
[662] Geßler-Löhr, in: Assmann (ed.), *Das Grab des Amenemope*, 162; Bonnet, *RÄRG*, 97. For a comparison between the funeral procession of the deceased from his house to his tomb as occurs in the New Kingdom private tombs and New Kingdom royal tombs as exemplified in the tomb of Tutankhamun, see Beinlich, *SAK* 34 (2006), 17-31.

TT 100 (fig. 35), the deceased is shown standing in an open shrine on a boat and crosses a lake or a pool. The boat is towed by two groups of men. Two water bearers are depicted at the corners, while at the bank stands a priest with incense waiting for the boat. On the boat two priests are depicted, the one in front of the shrine holds an incense pot in one hand while with the other hand he holds a vessel of water.[663] There is another person standing beside him raising his right hand in recitation. It seems as if while the crossing over the lake is in progress, recitation, fumigation with incense and the purification with water take place.[664]

Fig. 35. The crossing over the lake in the tomb of Rekhmire
(after Davies, *Rekhmire* II, pl. CX).

4.4. Crossing the Lake of Knives

When the *mꜥnḏt* Barque of the sun god Re crosses the Lake of Knives, it is said that the barque is in *hnw*.[665] In the Old Kingdom the family and relatives receive the funeral procession of the deceased in lamentation, and the Book of the Dead Sun Hymn mentioned above alludes to the same situation. Here the gods gather and greet the sun god Re in his barque when he crosses the Lake of Knives. It is the barque that carries the image of the sun god Re, with whom the deceased is identified. The aim of the deceased's crossing the lake in Old Kingdom private tombs was to reach the west, which is the same aim of the barque of the sun god Re's journey over the Lake of Knives.

The journey over the Lake of Knives is not always safe. The sun god Re is threatened by the snake of the primeval waters Apep, who tries hard to hinder the solar barque from sailing over the Lake of Knives and stops its progression through the *dwꜣt* as occurs in Chapter 15 A. III of the Book of the Dead.[666]

As the deceased is warned against crossing the lake in the Pyramid Texts and Coffin Texts, the sun god Re is threatened by Apep while crossing the Lake of Knives. Nine books are read aloud while the Apis crosses the Lake of the King, and the Book of Apep should be recited when the sun god Re crosses the Lake of Knives. In one of the New Kingdom composite Sun Hymns mentioned above,[667] the journey over the Lake of Knives and the Sandbank of Apep can be described as follows:

The first stanza in the hymn is adoration to the sun god Re at his rising and setting. The sun god rises and illuminates the two lands, and crosses the sky in a joyful heart. Then, the hymn mentions the crossing of the sun god Re over the Sandbank of the Lake of Knives, in which the enemies of the sun god Re have been felled. The hymn then moves to the description of the movement of the sun in the sky. The sun is protected by the two arms of the sky goddess Nut.

The next stanza deals with the beating of the sun on the chest of the deceased. In a recent article, Bommas argues that the motive of the morning sun beating on the breast of the deceased can be considered as the first sign for the funerary procession. It marks the end of the rituals which have taken place in the embalming place, and the beginning of the deceased's funeral procession to the forecourt of his tomb. It refers also to the deceased's wish to cross the borders from this world to the next by means of rituals. Horus is envisaged as a sun disk protecting the ways of his father from the embalming chamber until he reaches the open forecourt of his tomb.[668] This theme is also well known in the Underworld Books of the New Kingdom and is connected with the deceased's wish to go out by day and to take part in the daily solar cycle.[669]

Although this Sun Hymn may belong to a different text genre, it still retains most of the themes mentioned in the texts connected with the mummy's transition to the tomb. The funeral procession from the place of embalming to the tomb forecourt includes crossing the Lake of Knives. The journey of the deceased is parallel to the sun god's Re journey from the east to the west. The sun shines in the east and on its way to the west it crosses the Lake of Knives. It is also important to note that the sun's journey from the east to the west in this hymn is envisaged as a procession in the Beautiful Festival. It is not surprising here to say that the deceased's procession is also envisaged as a procession in which crossing the Lake of Knives takes place.

4.5. Crossing the Lake of Fire

The texts of crossing the Great Lake give an explanation to the two spells which occur in the Book

[663] Geßler-Löhr, in: Assmann (ed.), *Das Grab des Amenemope*, 165.
[664] Other instances are found in the tombs of Minnakht TT 87, tomb of Hatiya TT 324.
[665] For the text describing this event, see above BD Chapter 15B.I, 28-9.
[666] For Chapter 15 A. III, see above, 29.
[667] For the sun hymn, see above, 40-1.
[668] Bommas, *SAK* 36 (2007), 15-22.
[669] Bommas, *SAK* 36 (2007), 15; the motive of the sun beating on the chest of the deceased has also been dealt with by Assmann, *Death and Salvation*, 317-24; *Totenliturgien* II, 523-28; for the relation between the funeral procession and the transition of the deceased's mummy from the place of embalming to his tomb, see Assmann, *Totenliturgien* II, 264.

of the Two Ways and concern crossing the Lake of Fire. CT spell 1054 reads:

š n sḏt ᶜꜣtyw rn=f	The Lake of Fire, its name is Aatiu.[670]
n wnt s nb rḫ ᶜḳ m sḏt	There is no man who can enter in the fire;
šnᶜ.t(w)=f jm	And then he is repelled from (it).
šnᶜ=f jm variant	And then escapes (?) from it (?)
iw=f iwᶜ[w]	He is succeeded (by his heir).
iwf iwᶜ(=f) variant	Flesh of (his) heir (?)
wꜣt pw r n š mꜣᶜ	This is the way: the entrance of the true lake.[671]

And CT spell 1166 reads:

š nw n sḏt ᶜꜣtyw rn=f	This is the Lake of Fire; its name is Aatiu.
n wnt s nb ḫr m sḏt	There is no man fallen in the fire,
šnᶜ.t(w)=f jm=f	And can be repelled from it.
šnᶜ(t)=f sw (im)=f variant	And can save himself (from) it.
nmtyw 4 iwᶜt pw rn=f š mꜣᶜ	Oh four opposers (enemies),[672] its name is inheritance, the true lake.[673]

In both spells, the deceased is threatened by crossing the Lake of Fire. It is a place that the deceased should avoid while crossing Rosetau in the Book of the Two Ways. When a comparison is made between these two spells and the spells of crossing the Great Lake in the Pyramid and Coffin Texts, it seems that they have the same purpose. Zandee argues that the Great Lake is the Lake of Fire, and the deceased should avoid it in his journey to the netherworld.[674] Crossing the Great Lake as mentioned above means that the deceased should pass safely through the mummification and purification rituals, and the rituals accompanying the mummification also involve the presentation of offerings. The same themes occur in these two spells. The deceased is followed by his heir who is his son and the one who performs the rituals for his father.[675] The deceased is threatened by the House of the *Bꜣ-pf* while crossing over the Great Lake in the Pyramid Texts, and he is threatened by the four opponents in the Lake of Fire. It is worth investigating the word *jwᶜ* in the Book of the Two Ways for a better understanding of these two spells.[676]

Since the Pyramid Texts, the word *jwᶜ* has to do with the succession of the son to his father. Being an heir is a theme that occurs in the Pyramid Texts where Unas is Horus who inherits his father:

ḏd mdw	Recitation:
j gb kꜣ nwt	O Geb Bull of the sky,
ḥr pj Wnjs jwᶜ it=f	Unas is Horus, the heir of his father.[677]

jwᶜ occurs in three spells in the Book of the Two Ways. For instance, in CT spell 1063 the deceased is allowed to pass and row the barque because he is the heir of the Great One (the sun god Re).[678]

jwᶜ.n N tn ꜣḫt nt rᶜ	This N has inherited the horizon of Re.
jsṯ N tn js nb-tm	This N is indeed the Lord of All.
N js jtmw nb n nspw variant	N is indeed Atum, Lord of Wounds.[679]
N js jtmw nb knst variant	N is indeed Atum; Lord of Kenest.[680]
N tn sn.n=f ḏdt	This N, he has imitated what has been said.
N tn iwᶜw ꜣḫt	This N, (he is) the heir of the horizon.
jrj wꜣt n rᶜ ḫnj=f	Make a path for Re when he lands!
ᶜwnt rḫ.n N tn rn=ṯ	O heiress, whose name this N knows![681]

In the Old Kingdom texts of crossing the lake, direct references are made for the one who is making the deceased into an *ꜣḫ*, and in the Book of the Two Ways spells cited above, the son as heir of the deceased is the one who performs the ritual for his father. This spell constitutes a screenplay of a ritual drama enacted on the funeral. It is obvious that one person is profiled as a priest living and functioning on earth. This priest should be the eldest son of the deceased who is performing the ritual for his father.

Crossing the Lake of Knives and the Lake of Fire might also allude to crossing the Great Lake and the firmament, and might also allude to the mummification and purification rituals. It is known that the mummification ritual was accompanied by presentation of offerings and at some stage followed by purification ritual or offering libations. All these themes are found in texts dealing with crossing over the Lake of Knives and over the Lake of Fire. For instance, CT spell 823 describes an offering of a headrest to the deceased while crossing the Lake of Knives.[682] CT spell 823 lies within a mummification ritual context.[683] When the deceased crosses the Lake of Knives he is frightened that his head will be chopped off, but crossing the Lake

[670] *ᶜꜣtyw* is not quite obvious how to translate; Faulkner translated it 'Lake of Fire of the Knife-wielders' (*Coffin Texts* III, 138). In all versions the Lake has the determinative of a knife.
[671] *CT* VII, 306d-g (spell 1054).
[672] *Wb* II, 271.20.
[673] *CT* VII, 508e-h (spell 1166).
[674] Zandee, *Death as an Enemy*, 171-2.
[675] *CDME*, 12.
[676] See also Backes, *Das altägyptische Zweiwegebuch*, 259-60.

[677] PT 260=*Pyr.* § 316a.
[678] Note that in this particular case, the deceased is female.
[679] As occurs on B1C: *CT* VII, 321b (spell 1063)
[680] As occurs on B2C: *CT* VII, 321b (spell 1063).
[681] *CT* VII, 321a-322b (spell 1063).
[682] For the spell see above, 36-7.
[683] For the ritual context of the spell, see below, 84-5.

of Knives is also necessary for him to pass the place of passage.

It can be concluded now that crossing the lake is a ritual enacted at the day of the funeral. The funeral procession of the deceased over the lake in the Old Kingdom was accompanied by the recitation of *s3ḫw*, which runs at the same time with the crossing over the lake. The Apis Bull procession over the lake was also accompanied by recitation of nine sacred books, and the title of one of these books is *s3ḫw*. The offering of libation in the Old Kingdom Pyramid Texts was envisaged as crossing over water, and while the ritual was taking place the spells were recited. In the New Kingdom, the deceased is shown crossing a lake that is located in a garden in the forecourt of his tomb. In the tomb of Rekhmire, crossing the lake is also accompanied by priests holding incense and water and there were recitations taking place while the boat crossed over the lake.

Crossing over the lake of Knives was also accompanied by recitation of the Book of Apep. The crossing over the lake as a rite of passage was parallel to the sun god Re's crossing over the waters of the sky, and also to the crossing of the *wrrt* boat of Osiris. The deceased, who is equated with both gods, crosses the two lakes, equipped with recitation of texts which will mediate his passage from the world of the dead to the world of *3ḫw*.

Chapter Five

The Lake of Fire in the Book of the Two Ways

5.1. The History and Description of the Book of the Two Ways

The Book of the Two Ways will be briefly investigated in order to construct the journey of the deceased until he reaches the Lake of Fire. It is not my aim here to study the whole composition, but to concentrate on the lower land way. I will avoid the argument over the orientation of the two ways, which is outside the scope of my study, and it is inconsequential to the research here, but I will try to show what other scholars have written about it. I will start the lower land way from the left western side. The texts under discussion here are CT spells 1072-1054, which occur in sections III and IV in Lesko's edition of the Book of the Two Ways. The focus of my study will be on the spells occurring in the two long versions A and B, with a comparison with those occurring on the short version C when necessary.

On many Middle Kingdom coffins the lid is decorated with a representation of the sky goddess Nut spreading her wings over the deceased's mummy. This theme of lid decoration continued until later periods.[684] The floors of el-Bersha coffins were used for sets of texts dealing with the maps of the underworld and known as the Book of the Two Ways.[685] The ancient Egyptians treated the corpus as a book, with a beginning and an end, which is made explicit from the colophons occurring in CT spell 1031.[686] There are also different versions of the Book. The deceased can use any one of them, and sometime can have more than one version inscribed on the floor of the coffin. For instance, the deceased Sepi has the long version B on the inner of his coffin, encoded as B2P in de Buck's edition of the Coffin Texts (plan 11), while on the floor of his outer coffin (B1P) he has the short version C (plan 15). The outer coffin of the physician Sen (B4L) is an exception, where the short version C and the long version A are drawn on the same floor of his outer coffin (plan 12).[687]

The Book of the Two Ways has been described as the first Egyptian cosmography.[688] It was investigated early in the 20th Century by Schack-Schakenburg, who published the texts from the coffin of Sen in the Berlin Museum and facsimile copies of the texts on the bottom of this coffin.[689] Later, Lacau published similar texts from coffins in the Egyptian Museum.[690]In this book there are two pictorial routes taking zigzags shape, and the map section generally takes up about one-third of the whole book.[691] The other two thirds of the book are occupied with texts, and within the texts there are numerous gateways of darkness and of fire.[692] The Book of the Two Ways is a modern name. Like later hereafter texts from the royal tombs in the Valley of the Kings, the Book of the Two Ways can be envisaged as a guide to the hereafter, which enables the deceased to travel safely through the realm of the dead to achieve his or her ultimate goal of an existence in the company of the gods.[693]

Assmann asserts that the Book of the Two Ways and the Amduat belong to different text genres; the Book of the Two Ways is a funerary book while the Amduat is cosmography belonging to the Heliopolitan solar cult.[694] Assmann's discussion raises some different issues. For instance, there are some texts in the Amduat which include rubrics showing that they were intended for recitation, and in turn might have served as funerary texts. The Book of the Two Ways published by Lesko includes many spells (the long version has 101 separate spells and the short version 54), and instructs the deceased, among other themes, on the routes and paths through the land of Rosetau and the netherworld. Lesko began a critical analysis of the Book of the Two Ways using various textual elements and detailed plans of the coffins published by de Buck in his edition of the Coffin Texts. Lesko was able to identify and sub-divide the Book of the Two Ways into nine sections. These nine sections are divided into four versions: long A and B versions, the short version C and a small version A-B.[695] The long versions include group of the spells 1029-1130 (*CT* VII, 252-471), while the short version includes the group 1131-1185 (*CT* VII, 472-521), CT spell 513 (*CT* VI, 101), and CT spell 577 (*CT* VI, 192-193).[696] Section II only occurs in the short.[697] The short version C, according to Lesko, is

[684] The coffin lid was sometimes inscribed with texts dealing with speeches of the gods and goddesses. In the Old Kingdom above all Nut and Geb addressed and welcomed the deceased as their son. In the New Kingdom, the most splendid speeches are afforded by Neith, whose speech fills the entire lid of the outer sarcophagus of Merenptah. In later periods of the Egyptian history, divine speeches developed in another form. In those new genres of texts, the gods who stood watch over the hours of the wake address the deceased. Most of their speeches are taken from Book of the Dead chapter 169, which dates to a coffin liturgy; the well known liturgy of Coffin Text spell 335. The divine speeches of this chapter were placed later on coffins dating to the Saite Period: Assmann, *Totenliturgien* I, 13-8.

[685] Hermsen, *Die Zweiwege des Jenseits*, 100.

[686] Lesko, *The Book of the Two Ways*, 134.

[687] Hermsen, *Die Zweiwege des Jenseits*, 101; the numbers here refer to the plans numbers in de Buck's edition of the Coffin Texts, vol. VII, plans, 1-15.

[688] Hornung, *The Ancient Egyptian Books of the Afterlife*, 11.

[689] Schack-Schakenberg, *Das Buch von den Zwei Wegen des seligen Toten*.

[690] Lesko, *The Book of the Two Ways*, 3.

[691] Robinson, in: *Mysterious Lands*, 142.

[692] Lesko, *The Book of the Two Ways*, 4.

[693] Lesko, *The Book of the Two Ways*, 135; in all versions sailing with Re and living beside Osiris are the main aims of the whole journey of the deceased.

[694] Assmann, *Egyptian Solar Religion*, 7; for the difference between the Book of the Two Ways and the other Underworld Books, see Hermsen, *Die Zwei Wege des Jenseits*, 100-1.

[695] For how Lesko divided the Book of the Two Ways, see Lesko, *The Book of the Two Ways*, 135-7.

[696] The same division is accepted by Hermsen, *Die Zwei Wege des Jenseits*, 101.

[697] Hermsen, *Die Zwei Wege des Jenseits*, 102.

the oldest version.[698] De Buck records the Book of the Two Ways from 15 coffin plans. In addition, Lesko includes two additional examples in his analysis. These 17 copies are found within 40 coffins from el-Bersha.[699]

The texts of the Book of the Two Ways are usually placed on the floor of the coffin, but in two cases the texts are preserved on tomb walls. Spells from section VIII of the Book of the Two Ways were discovered on the western wall of the tomb chapel of *ḫsw* the Elder from Kom el-Hisn in Western Delta.[700] The upper section on the west wall contains scenes from daily life, and below the scenes are three registers of texts arranged in vertical columns. The inscriptions include four hundred lines of texts. One hundred and ten lines are from the texts of the Book of the Two Ways, corresponding to section VIII of Lesko's edition, and representing spells 1100-1113.[701] Spells from the Book of the Two Ways were also placed on walls in el-Bersha tombs. In the tomb of Nehri II, the texts are carved close to the tomb entrance.[702] This may indicate that these texts are the older equivalents of the New Kingdom Books of the Underworld.[703] Although they may belong to different genres of text, as Assmann argues,[704] both texts show the deceased the ways through the underworld.

Lesko attribution of the Book of the Two Ways to el-Bersha is based on the fact that most of the texts of the Book of the Two Ways came from there. Lesko's argument is open to debate. It is difficult to depend on a toponym or a deity to determine and identify the origin of a text,[705] and that is what Lesko did in his chronology which has been questioned later by Willems.[706]

The Layout of the Book of the Two Ways

The layout of the Book of the Two Ways, according to Lesko, can be best described as an image with two main bands. The shorter C version opens with Lesko's section II, an image of a ground plan of a palace and shrine with high walls of darkness and flame. These features take up most of the upper band of text. The longe A and B versions start with a description of the rising sun upon the eastern horizon, indicating perhaps the sky based nature of this section of the text. The deceased here is about to board a solar or a lotus barque of Re to begin his or her journey.[707] In both versions the next section contains the actual two pathways: one blue, upper way, and the other a darker lower way, which comprises section III and IV respectively. These two pathways are separated by a red band representing the Lake of Fire.[708] However, the two pathways meander and wind around in their sections. In some cases, we see multiple paths and areas surrounded by paths crossing the main ways. These features represent geographical landscapes that the deceased has to cross.[709] One of the most important features of the Book of the Two Ways are the maps showing the landscape of the netherworld, with points of entry and gateways leading the deceased to different destinations in the netherworld. There are also rites connected with these passages to allow the deceased to proceed safely on the ways of the land of Rosetau. The rites performed in front of or within these gateways initiate the deceased into the afterlife, and were marked by a number of barriers in his metaphysical journey to the netherworld. One of these gateways or passages to be crossed is the Lake of Fire. Being a passage to the netherworld, the Lake of Fire in the Book of the Two Ways features as a place which should be known by the deceased before crossing over it.

In the texts dealing with Book of the Two Ways and its topography, the emphasis is on the act of passing, and not on charting the underworld landscape. In all Egyptian funerary texts with maps, the texts do not make explicit the relations between the different geographical locations of the underworld, but in all cases the deceased should be initiated to attain the knowledge to pass safely through the obstacles of the netherworld.[710]

The Upper Waterway and the Lower Land Way

Here is a brief investigation of what the scholars of Egyptology have written about the two ways in a historical order (fig. 36).

[698] Lesko, *The Book of the Two Ways*, 134.
[699] Willems, *Chests of Life*, 20-1.
[700] Silverman, in: Allen et al., *Religion and Philosophy in Ancient Egypt, 35*.
[701] Silverman, in: Willems (ed.), *The World of the Coffin Texts*, 133.
[702] For the dating of the Coffin Texts in the tomb of Nehri II, see Willems et al., *Dayr al-Barsha*, 83; *Chests of Life*, 74. Silverman argues that the texts of the Book of the Two Ways in the tomb of Nehri II represent the earliest version: Silverman, in: Willems (ed.), *The World of the Coffin Texts*, 132. For the placing of the Coffin Texts on the tomb walls of the Late Period, see Gestermann, *Die Überlieferung ausgewählter Texts altägyptischer Totenliterature („ Sargtexte"),* 2 vols.
[703] Assmann, *Re und Amun*, 83-4.
[704] Assmann, *Egyptian Solar Religion*, 7, n.32.
[705] Hoffmeier, in: Willems (ed.), *The World of the Coffin Texts*, 48.
[706] Willems, *Chests of Life*, 235, although the name of the god Thoth, the patron of Hermopolis, occurs more than 20 times within the long version in spells grouped together; 1089, 1092, 1903, 1096, 1098 and 1099, Hoffemier states that these occurrences do not refer by any mean to Hermopolis, the name of which does not occur within the Book of the Two Ways. Even the Ogdoad of Hermopolis does not feature in the texts of the Book of the Two Ways: Hoffmeier, in: Willems (ed.), *The World of the Coffin Texts*, 49.
[707] CT spells 1029-1030.
[708] Hermsen, *Die Zwei Wege des Jenseits*, 135.
[709] Lesko, *JAOS* 91 (1971), 33-43; Robinson, in: *Mysterious Lands*, 146.
[710] Quirke, in: *Mysterious Lands*, 173-5.

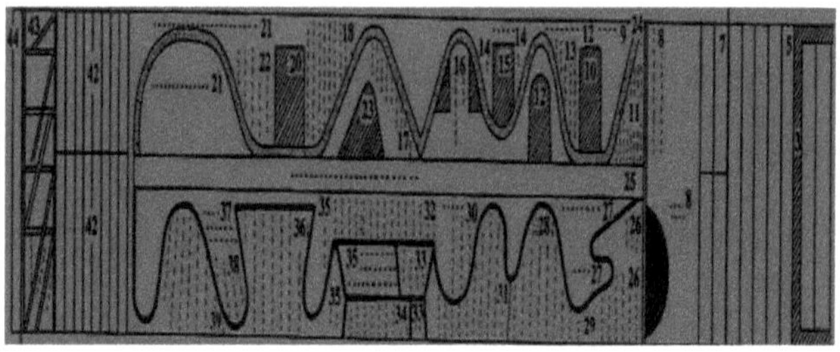

Fig. 36. A plan for the two ways (after de Buck, *CT* VII, pl. 7).

Kees

Kees designated the various places which occurred within the composition as goals. He treated each plan drawn at the bottom of each coffin as a unit trying to reconstruct the journey of the deceased until he reaches the aim of his journey. The plans and the texts are related to the idea of 'a Guide to the Hereafter', but he also admitted that texts and plans are sometimes not related to each other very well, since the texts which occur after the plan of the two ways places the land way on top and the waterway below (CT spell 1074, and its parallel spell 1184). Although this is the opposite orientation to that seen in the plan, Kees followed the orientation of the text rather than the plan. He also argued that the two ways lead to the Field of Offerings in Rosetau, which also causes a problem since the Field of Offerings seem to occur half unnoticed along the upper way in the middle of the Book (CT spells 1049-1160). Kees ended by saying that since the two ways have the same aim of reaching Rosetau, there is no need to say that one way has the priority over the other, but both ways can be used as alternative possibilities of travel.[711]

Grapow

Grapow referred to the Book of the Two Ways as a group of texts and not a book like the Amduat. It serves as a map for the deceased, guiding him to the hereafter ways, and as a magic book for the living. He gave no indication of how the Book might be approached.[712]

Zandee

The two ways were only part of the whole complex. There are two aims of the deceased's journey on the two ways: to serve Osiris and to accompany Re at the end.[713]

Müller

Müller argued that the upper way represents the daily waterway for the barque of Re, and ends by the Field of Offerings at the back of the Lake of Fire, according to CT spell 1053 (305a-e), which reads: 'This is the way to the cities of those living on [sweets]. This which is before is a spell for passing on it, a spell for passing the cities of 'Those of the Knives' and 'Those loud of Voice', and a spell for passing 'Those of Flame'.[714] Müller argued that this title of the spell refers to the upper way as the flame or fire way, while the lower land way is the way of 'Those of the Knives' and 'Those Loud of Voice'. He states that the lower way belongs to the Lake of Fire, which does not take an oblong or rectangular shape, but its windings are protected by demons and guardians on its long sides. Along the distance of this way, the solar barque might have been dragged. On a formal basis (the reading of the texts from the upper side to the bottom side on some of el-Bersha versions and the arrangements of the spell on B1Bo and B4Bo), the lower land way might be considered as a continuation of the upper waterway, which runs from right to left. The black dark colour of the lower land way is evidence that it was used as the returning way of the barque of the sun god Re. The dark and the red or the fiery gates (CT spell 1037) at the right end of the upper waterway is the meeting point of both ways. The red gate belongs to the upper way, and the dark gate belongs to the lower way. He also argued that there are three groups of guardians that meet and stop the deceased in the form of Osiris on his way to Rosetau. These guardians occur in CT spells 1070-1071.[715]

Lesko

Lesko argues that the easiest and the most obvious part of the Book to be isolated is the plan of the two ways, which occurs in all versions. He concludes that if the two ways are the essential part of the book, then all the rest of the composition serve as introduction and conclusion to the two ways, and the whole composition would be 'a unified guide to the regions through which the deceased would pass to his goal with a possible choice between the two ways themselves.'[716] The two ways comprise sections III and IV in Lesko's edition. Sections III and IV on both A and B long versions include spells 1036-1082, and are paralleled by the C version spells 1147-1185.[717]

Lesko starts the two ways from the upper waterway on the right hand side, and then follows the right-left direction until he reaches the left hand side of the Book. The beginning of the two ways is at the gate of spells 1036/1037. Then the upper waterway turns and meets the lower land way at the far western end in an area he described as the zigzags. The lower land way then follows the left-right direction or east west orientation. It is a continuation of the water way leading the deceased, who accompanies Re, back to his starting point. It is likely that the deceased will expect to travel on each as the circumstances demand, or to

[711] Kees, *Totenglauben*, 293-5.
[712] Grapow, *ZÄS* 46 (1909), 77-81.
[713] Zandee, *Death as an Enemy*, 26.
[714] *CT* VII, 305a-e (spell 1053).
[715] Müller, *BiOr* 20 (1963), 248-50.
[716] Lesko, *JAOS* 91 (1971), 36.
[717] Lesko, *The Book of the Two Ways*, 40.

make a circuit of the two ways.[718] He also proposes that the two ways are combined together and meet at the far end of the two compartments. Lesko argues that here:

> The two ways apparently meet and do touch on one coffin B3C at the far end of the two compartments, but, since this is not at the Field of Offerings or any other significant place, this can also be used as evidence for a combination of the ways.[719]

Hermsen

The two ways are included in sections III and IV and they should be read from right to left. The waterway represents the night and the day sky. At the end of the waterway, most probably in the east, lies the Field of Offerings of Osiris and there the waterway winds into the Lake of Fire. In the lower land way, the deceased plays a prominent role of the sun god Re. Like the waterway, the land way ends in the Lake of Fire, and as a result the Lake of Fire represents the aim of the deceased's journey on both ways.[720]

Rößler-Köhler

Rößler-Köhler treated the two ways in the short version C as a self-standing composition without considering the rest of the floor decoration. She called the two ways 'das eigentliche Zweiwegebuch', which includes Coffin Text spells 1036-1072. She started the two ways not from the right eastern side, but from the western left side which comprises the texts and the vignettes of CT spell 1072. She argues that the vignettes and the texts give the essential and the necessary information on the ways of Rosetau and marks the beginning of the two ways. Rößler-Köhler also argues that the two ways run in the opposite direction, and the deceased cannot pass them without knowing the spells inscribed on their sides. The actual starting point of the two ways is on the left or the western side, which comprises CT 1068. The spell is a greeting spell and the stress is on the beginning of the night journey of the sun god Re on the lands of Rosetau. [721]

Backes

The two ways are the ways of Rosetau. The deceased travels on the upper waterway to reach the abode of Osiris. He identifies himself with Thoth or as a follower of Thoth, who cures the body of Osiris in Rosetau. The upper waterway represents the night sky in which the stars wait the sun to rise in the morning from the eastern horizon. The lower land way represents the path followed by the sun god Re from the west to the east in his night journey through the underworld. The deceased as Re starts his journey from the right side of the lower land way until he reaches the Field of Osiris, which represents the point of contact between Re and Osiris and comprises CT spells 1118-1124. The two ways end in the Lake of Fire, which represents the abode of Osiris and the place of sunrise.[722]

5.2. Section IV and the Lower Land Way

The lower way occurs within section IV in Lesko's edition of the Book of the Two Ways. This section in the long version begins on the left hand side with an area where a zigzag is drawn in the vignettes at the far end. A representation of a red band designating the Lake of Fire is depicted above the main part of section IV, separating it from the body of section III. This upper section includes the upper water way, on top, forming section III, while the lower section IV contains the lower land way. Section III on the long version ends directly at the gates of section I, and forms with section I the right portion of the Book of the Two Ways. Section IV begins on the right hand side with a door which belongs to section III, and includes spells 1055-1069 on the long version and spells 1167-1179 on the short one. On the short version the same depiction occurs. The blue path meets the black way at the far end of the compartments.[723]

The main interpretation of all the spells inscribed on the lower land way in section IV is connected with the Lake of Fire. In all these spells, the keepers are said to guard a bend of a lake, which refers to the Lake of Fire at the far right end of this section. We can consider all these spells as an introduction to CT 1054, which occurs at the far end of this section and marks the end of section IV and the beginning of section III. The lower land way is full of curves and resembles in its topography the Fifth Hour of the Amduat.[724]

One of the most important features of section IV on the lower land way is the occurrences of the names of different demons and guardians whom the deceased has to pass in his way to the Lake of Fire. These guardians are waiting for the deceased, although they do not have gates to guard, but are spread out in the bends leading to the Lake of Fire. These guardians' names have their parallels in the Book of the Dead.[725]

CT Spell 1072/no. 43 and the Vignettes on the Left Side of the Two Ways

The left side of the Book shows vignettes and texts which comprise no. 43 on the plan. The texts and vignettes in this section mark an area preceding the two

---

718 Lesko, *JAOS* 91 (1971), 37.
719 Lesko, *JAOS* 91 (1971), 37.
720 Hermsen, *Die Zwei Wege des Jenseits*, 170.
721 Rößler-Köhler, *GM* 192 (2003), 83-97.
722 Backes, *Das altägyptische Zweiwegebuch*, 319-20.
723 Lesko, *The Book of the Two Ways*, 40
724 Lesko, *The Book of the Two Ways*, 75; Hermsen, *Die Zwei Wege des Jenseits*, 162; Müller, *BiOr* 20 (1963), 249; for a comparison between this section of the Book of the Two Ways and the Amduat, see below, 79-80.
725 See below, 74, n. 731.

ways from the left side. It begins with CT spell 1072/no. 43, and reads:

r3 n w3wt nt r3-st3w ḥr mw ḥr t3	A spell for the ways of Rosetau on water and on land.[726]
jw w3wt jptw mj nn m stnm	These two ways are like this, in winding.
wꜥt nbt jm ḫsft snnwt=s m stnm	Each one (way) is opposing its companion in winding.
jn rḫ=sn gmm w3wt=sn	Those who know them, are those who can find their ways.
jw=sn ḳ3j m jnbw nw dsw nt r3-st3w ḥr mw ḥr t3	They are high with walls of flint, of Rosetau on water and on land.[727]

The purpose of the spell as its title indicates is to show the deceased the ways he will have to navigate in Rosetau. These two ways are said to be over water and land, and they wind in their sections. The spell shows the deceased, who is already in the west, the ways of the Memphite necropolis Rosetau.[728] After being buried, the deceased will start his underworld journey, and he has to navigate on these two ways. The aim of the deceased's journey is to reach the Lake of Fire, which is both a dangerous and a right way for the deceased to cross over to reach his destination. These walls are described to be high and made of flint.

This section, in addition to CT spell 1072, includes also vignettes and texts of CT spell 1071/no.42. The spell names three keepers the deceased has to meet in his way on the land of Rosetau. The spell reads:

ḳ3j-ṯ3ww rn=f pw	High-of-Winds is his name.
r3 n sw3 ḥr=s nw ntj ḫr=s	A spell for passing it. This which is beneath it,
nb-3t rn=f pw	Lord-of-Striking-Power is his name.
nhsw N ꜥ3 ḫrw m 3ḫt	O watchmen,[729] N is loud of voice in the horizon,
wr=ṯn js ḥr ḥr=ṯn	(He is) your Great One. On your faces!
nhsw	Oh watchmen,
jrj w3t n nb=ṯn	Make way for your Lord.[730]

The spell enables the deceased to pass guardians whose names are High-of-Winds, Lord-of-the-Striking-Power, and the *Nhsw*. The deceased is also said to be loud of voice in the horizon and the orders are given to the watchmen to let him pass.[731]

CT Spell 1068/no. 39 and the Actual Beginning of the Lower Land Way

The next spell is 1068/no. 39, which occurs in section IV in Lesko's edition, within the plan drawn in the lower land way. It marks the actual starting point in the land way. As Assmann argues, this spell represents the first text to deal with the underworld journey of the sun god Re.[732] The spell reads:

jnḏ ḥr=k rꜥ	Hail to you Re.
sḥtp=k ḥr n wsjr N pn	May you propitiate the face of this Osiris N.
dw3 ṯw jmjw jmḥt	May those who are in the netherworld worship you.
s3ḫ ṯw jmjw dw3t	May those who are in the underworld glorify you.
dj=sn n=k j3w jj=k m ḥtp	May they give you adoration when you come in peace.
dj=k ḥtpt n wrw w3ḫj n šrrw	May you give offerings to the Great Ones, and abundance to the Little Ones.
dj=k n N pn ḥtpt	May you give to this N offering,
sbj N pn jm3ḫ mj rꜥ	that this N may pass the revered state like Re.[733]

The deceased greets the sun god Re when he enters into the West, which might also be an indication that he is already in the necropolis and will start his journey from the west from his burial place. The deceased wishes to take part in Re's journey through the underworld, which is made explicit from the use of *imḥt* and *dw3t*. Lesko argues that although the journey seems to take place on water, and in turn might refer to the upper waterway, the spell was inscribed on the lower black land way. *jmḥt* refers to the sky or part of the sky in which Osiris has his abode, and through which the sun god Re passes during the day. *dw3t* might represent the underworld through which Re passes at night, and in turn the spell refers to the water and land ways.[734] Lesko's conclusion is not convincing. Both *jmḥt* and *dw3t* can be considered as indications of the night journey of the sun god Re through the underworld. Those who live there greet the sun god Re when he enters their realm because he is

[726] As shown in de Buck's note in *CT* VII, 339 (spell 1072).

[727] *CT* VII, 339d-341b (spell 1072); Lesko, *The Book of the Two Ways*, 80.

[728] Rößler-Köhler, *GM* 192 (2003), 85.

[729] *nhs* is a designation of Seth: *Wb* II, 287. 14-17. Lesko translates it as watchman, which fits in the context of the spell: Lesko, *The Book of the Two Ways*, 77.

[730] *CT* VII, 334a-335b (spell 1071).

[731] The knowledge of the names of those who are standing at the gates is crucial for the successful passage through them. The same theme of this knowledge of the names is found in a decree issued to the Nome of the Silent Land, and published by Mark Smith, *RdE* 57 (2006), 219. This decree is one of six rituals preserved in P. MMA 39.9.21, and was inscribed for a man named Imuthes. The ritual preserved in this decree is about the deceased Osiris whom Isis and Nephthys mourn. At the end of the first episode of the ritual Osiris is transferred to a solar barque and in his way to the Underworld, Osiris is faced by the seven underworld gates. For the deceased Osiris to pass safely, he has to name each guardian of these gates as in our spells here: Smith, *RdÉ* 57 (2006), 217-32. For a comparison between the seven gatekEEpers in the Book of the Two Ways and in the Book of the Dead Chapter 144, see Waitkus, *GM* 62 (1983), 79-83. For the Seven gatekeepers in the Book of the Dead Chapter 144 as occurs on the walls of the Chapel of the Gods of Abydos in the temple of Ramesses II at Abydos, see Abdelrahiem, *SAK* 34 (2006), 1-16.

[732] Assmann, *Re und Amun*, 83-5.

[733] *CT* VII, 329a-331b (1068).

[734] Lesko, *The Book of the Two Ways*, 61-2.

the one who illuminates the darkness of the underworld. The sun god Re also enters the underworld to perform his night journey and to meet Osiris to be unified with him, which is a core theme in the Underworld Books found on the walls of the royal tombs in the Valley of the Kings. *jmḥt* and *dwꜣt* can also have the same meaning.[735] In the Book of the Dead Chapter 9, which has the title *rꜣ n wbꜣ jmḥt* 'a spell to open the underworld' the text reads 'may I open the doors of the underworld (*wbꜣ=j dwꜣt*)'.

The deceased who is identified with the sun god Re will start his journey on the lower land way which begins on the left side or the western side. This journey through the underworld is pictured as a journey on the lands of Rosetau and starts from the west.[736]

CT Spell 1067/no. 38

jnk sbj mdw nṯr n nṯr rꜥ	I am the one who conducts the sacred writing to the god Re.
jj.n=j sḏb=j wpt n nb=s	I have come that I may transmit the message to its lord.[737]

The deceased directs his speech to the guardians to let him pass. He is not the sun god Re himself, but he is close to him. He is the servant of his Lord, and the guardians will let him pass because of his position. The role of the deceased as the messenger of the sun god Re will not only allow him to enter to see Re, but also will give him the chance to proceed into the netherworld because of the mobility of his job of getting and delivering the messages from and to the sun god Re.[738] The same speech is directed by a deceased to guardians in Chapter 36 of the Book of the Dead, where he asks them to let him pass because he is Khnum who will deliver the message to his Lord (*iw=j smj wpwt n nb=s*).

CT Spell 1066/no. 37 reads:

ḥsf-ḥrj-ꜥnḫ-m-ꜣrwt (?) rn=f pw	The-One-with-Two-Opposing-Faces, He-who-lives-on *ꜣrwt* (?) is his name.
jrj n ḳꜣb š pw	He is the guardian (keeper) of this bend of the lake.
rꜣ n swꜣ ḥr=f pw	It is a spell for passing over him.[739]

The spell describes one of the guardians whom the deceased has to pass while proceeding in the netherworld from the Memphite necropolis. The keeper is said to guard a bend of a lake. The spell is inscribed exactly under the bend of the Lake of Fire, so there is no doubt that the spell is an address to one of the guardians of the Lake of Fire. The more the deceased proceeds into the lower land way, the more he faces the keepers of the Lake of Fire.

[735] Bickel, in: *Fs Hornung*, 55, no.44.
[736] Rößler-Köhler, *GM* 192 (2003), 89.
[737] *CT* VII, 328a-c (spell 1067).
[738] Backes, *Das altägyptische Zweiwegebuch*, 317.
[739] *CT* VII, 327a-c (spell 1066).

CT Spell 1065/no. 36 reads:

wn pt wn tꜣ	The sky opens; the earth opens;
wn ꜣḫt jꜣbtt wn ꜣḫt jmntt	The eastern horizon opens, and the western horizon opens;
wn jtrt šmꜥt wn jtrt mḥjt	The Shrine of Upper Egypt opens, and the Shrine of Lower Egypt opens;
wn snšw	The double doors open;
snš sbꜣw jꜣbtjw n rꜥ	The eastern doors open to Re,
prj=f m ꜣḫt	That he may go forth from the horizon.
wn n=f ꜥꜣwj sktt	The double doors of the night barque open for him.
snš n=f sbꜣw mnꜥḏt	The doors of the day barque open for him,
sn=f šw	That he may breath Shu,
ḳmꜣ=f tfnt	And may create Tefnut.
šms sw jmjw šmsw	Those who are in the suite shall follow him.
šms=sn wj mj rꜥ rꜥ-nb	They shall follow me like Re every day.[740]

This spell gives all the information concerning the cycle of the sun. The doors of the sky and of the earth, the eastern and western horizons, and the double doors are all open in a reference to the day and night cycles of the sun. A deceased who accompanies Re is performing this journey in order to reach his aim of going around the whole cosmos.[741]

CT Spell 1064/no.35

The vignettes on coffin B1C show a dog with long ears facing left on the top left side of the *šꜣsw* field.[742] Spell 1064/no. 35, deals with the passage of the deceased past the keeper whose name is Dog-Face and Great-of-Shapes. The spell is inscribed under the bend of the Lake of Fire, in an area separating the land way from the Lake of Fire.

ṯsm-ḥr ꜥꜣ-jrw rn=f pw	Dog-Face and Great-of-Shapes is his name.
rꜣ n swꜣ ḥr=s nw ntj ḥr š=sn	A spell for passing by it; those who are on their lake.[743]

CT Spell 1063/no.34

jwꜥ.n=j ꜣḫt nt rꜥ	I have inherited the horizon of Re,
jsṯ jnk js nb-tm	(And) I am indeed Lord of All.
jnk snj ḏdt n=f	I am the one who copies what has been said to him.
jnk jwꜥw ꜣḫt	I am the heir of the horizon,

[740] *CT* VII, 324a-326c (spell 1065).
[741] After this introduction in the later version of this spell, which is BD 130, the deceased says 'Osiris NN will not enter into the Lake of Fire' (*nn ꜥḳ wsjr NN m š n ḫbt*), Lapp, *The Papyrus of Nu*, pl.49, line 9.
[742] Backes, *Das altägyptische Zweiwegebuch*, 315.
[743] *CT* VII, 322c-323a (spell 1064).

jrj w3t n rʿ ẖnj=f	Who makes the way for Re, when he alights.
ʿwnt rḫ.n=j rn=ṯ	Oh Plunder, I know your name.[744]

The deceased directs his speech to a keeper whose name occurs at the end of the spell. The deceased says that he is the heir of the horizon and as result he has the right to pass safely. He inherited the horizon of Re and became the Lord of All. The spell occurs in the *š3sw*-field which is connected with the ascending of the deceased to the sky.[745] When the deceased says that he is the heir of Re, he refers to his ascent to the sky.[746] From this spell until we reach the Lake of Fire, the word *jwʿ* will be repeated in the next spells.

CT Spell 1062/no. 33

The vignettes on coffin B1C have a representation of a standing serpent with horns.

dbj-ḥr kh3-3t rn=f pw	Face-with-Horns and Striking-Power is his name.
š3sw=f pw	This is his marsh.
r3 n pḫr m ḥr	Spell for going around by day.
ḏr rḫ s r3 pn	If someone knows this spell,
pḥ=f š pn n mnj.n=f	He reaches this lake and he does not die.[747]

The spell gives the name of a guardian whose name is Face-with-Horns and Striking-Power, and guards the *š3sw*-field. This spell enables those who know it to reach the lake and not to die.

CT Spell 1061/no.31

This spells names another demon, which the deceased as a pilot of the solar barque will have to pass. The spell reads:

jnk rn wr	I am a Great Name.
jrj.n=ṯn w[j] ḥr w3t m3ʿt	You have steered me to the way of truth.
bwt=j pw ḫbtjw	Executioners are my abomination.
mkt=j pw mkt ḥr-smsw-rʿ	My protection is the protection of Horus, eldest son of Re.
jnk irj n jb=f	I am the one who acts according to his heart.
n nḏr rdwj=j	My legs will not be seized.
n ḫsf=j ḥr ʿrrwt pt	I will not be opposed on the gates of the sky
jnk ʿpr rwtj ḥḳt nṯrw ʿnḫw	I am the one who equips Ruty, Heket, the gods and the living
jmj=k ḫm wj	Do not destroy me.[748]

The deceased says that he follows the right way and executioners are his abomination. This might be an indication that he rejects to be executed by these keepers on his way to the Lake of Fire. To avoid execution, the deceased claims that his protection is the protection of the eldest son of Re and he follows his heart. In doing so, the deceased claims the authority of Re in his journey through the lower land way. This also might give an indication of the aim of the journey of Re who is on his way to see Osiris. With the mention of the eldest son of Re, the authority of Horus son of Re, as Lord of both day and night skies, is made explicit.

CT Spell 1059/no. 30

The keeper in this spell is an animal with four legs holding a dagger. It has a feather on a human head and its face is turned backwards. It is not a sphinx,[749] nor a quadruped.[750] It is a mythical beast.[751] The spell reads:

mktj-nṯrwj rn=f pw	His name is the Protector-of-the-Two-Gods.
jrj ḳ3b pw pw	This is the keeper of this bend.
swt s33 h33 jm=f	He is the guardian who goes down in it.[752]

The name of this god is the-Protector-of-the-Two-Gods, which might refer to the sun god Re and Osiris.

CT Spell 1058/no. 29

jnk dr ḫsft 3ṯw ḫpp r jtjt	I am the one who drives off the puishment[753] of the agressors,[754] who travels to seize.
jw=j ḥr swḥt rʿ sʿḥ=f mjn ḫʿ=f m nhpw	I am under the egg of Re, and his dignity of today, it appears in the morning.
s3 ṯw sʿḥ=f n pḥ=j sw	Beware of his dignity, because I have attained it.[755]
ḫʿ=f m3=j sw	When he appears, I see him.[756]
bwt=j pw jnn ḏr rḫ=j sw	Delay is my abomination, because I know him.
n ʿnḫ=f m 3ḫt	He shall not live in the horizon,
ḫmwt=f wj ḥnʿ nṯr nḫn	So that he would exclude me with the young god.[757]

[744] *CT* VII, 321a-322b (spell 1063).

[745] In *Pyr* 1763 *š3sw* fields represent one of the passages which the sun god Re has to pass before his ascent to the horizon: Backes, *Das altägyptische Zweiwegebuch*, 314.

[746] Backes, *Das altägyptische Zweiwegebuch*, 314.

[747] *CT* VII, 320a-d (spell 1062).

[748] *CT* VII, 317b-319c (spell 1061).

[749] Backes, *Das altägyptische Zweiwegebuch*, 74.

[750] Lesko, *The Book of the Two Ways*, 72.

[751] For the mythical beasts occurring on the plans of the Book of the Two Ways and their equivalents on Middle Kingdom tombs, see Robinson, in: *Mysterious Lands*, 149-52.

[752] *CT* VII, 312b-313b (spell 1059).

[753] B12C, B13C and B4L have *ḫsfwj* 'the two opponents', *CT* VII, 310a (spell 1058).

[754] This as we will see later is a name of one of the keepers. His name occurs in *CT* VII, 309a (spell 1056).

[755] B4L reads 'because I have not attained it'.

[756] B12 has a negation with *n* in front of *m3*.

[757] *CT* VII, 310a-312a (spell 1058).

The main concern of this spell is the sun god Re who is still in his egg and has not yet risen in the horizon. The deceased who might be at the prow of the boat of the Re wishes to be protected from this keeper, who guards the way of the sun god Re and threatens the deceased.[758] The deceased seeks the protection of the sun god Re by claiming a place on his boat. There is wordplay here with "*swḥt*" which can also mean inner coffin.[759] So the deceased who is here traveling in his coffin through the underworld looks like the sun god who is still in his egg. The reference to the egg of Re indicates that the sun god Re has not yet reached the place where his egg will be hatched. He also plays the role of a guardian of Re, since he is the one who protects his egg.[760]

The deceased here connects his fate with that of the egg, which has the power of birth, and through which the daily cycle of the sun Re begins and in which the deceased wishes to participate.[761] At the end the deceased says that he will be able to see Re when he appears in the horizon.

CT Spell 1057/no.28

The next spell is also a spell to pass one of the keepers who guards a bend. On coffin B1C this keeper is represented as a hound with long ears or as a hare holding a knife with both its hands.

mds jrj š	The Sharp-One is the keeper of the lake,
jrj ḳꜣb pw pw	This is the keeper of this bend.[762]

CT Spell 1056/ no.27

The keeper of this spell is represented as a Seth animal with a human head and a solar disk.

ꜥꜣ-ḥr-ḫsf-ꜣṯw	Great-of-Face-who-opposes-the-Aggressors,
jrj ḳꜣb pw pw	This is the keeper of this bend.[763]

The same warning of the keepers continues until we reach CT spell 1055, where the lower land way ends in the Lake of Fire.

CT Spell 1055/no 26

rꜣ n swꜣ ḥr=f nw nt ẖr š pn	A spell for passing over him who is beneath this lake.
dj swꜣ N pn m ḥtp	Let this N pass safely.[764]
jrj wꜣt n N pn sḳd=f wjꜣ	Make a way for this N that he may navigate the barque.
mkwt N mkwt=f	The protections of N are his protections.
ḫprtj.sj r=j	What will happen to me,
ḫpr mjtt r=f ḏr jrw=k	The like will happen to him, because of your actions.[765]

The spell as shown from its title enables the deceased to pass a keeper who is beneath a lake. By the end of this section of the lower land way, the deceased comes to the Lake of Fire, which separates the lower land way from the upper waterway.[766]

CT Spell 1054/no.25 and the Lake of Fire

š n sḏt ꜥꜣtyw rn=f	The Lake of Fire; its name is Aatiu.
n wnt s nb rḫ ꜥḳ m sḏt	There is no man who can enter in the fire;
šnꜥ.t(w)=f jm	And then he is repelled from (it).
šnꜥ=f im variant	And then escapes (?) from it (?)
jw=f iwꜥ[w]	He is succeeded (by his heir).
jwf jwꜥ=f variant	Flesh of his heir (?)
wꜣt pw r n š mꜣꜥ	This is the way: the entrance of the true lake.[767]

In Coffin Text spell 1166 on the short version the Lake of Fire is described as:

š nw n sḏt ꜥꜣtyw rn=f	This is the Lake of Firc; its name is Aatiu.
n wnt s nb ḫr m sḏt	There is no man fallen in the fire,
šnꜥ.t(w)=f jm=f	And can be repelled from it.
šnꜥ(t)=f sw (jm)=f variant	And can save himself (from) it.
nmtyw 4 iwꜥt pw rn=f š mꜣꜥ	Oh four opposers (enemies),[768] its name is inheritance, the true lake.[769]

In both spells the Lake of Fire is described as a place where there is no one who enters it who can be saved. As occurs in the former texts starting from the left western side of the lower land way of the Book of the Two Ways, the Lake of Fire is guarded by keepers. It might also be described as a place at the edge of cosmos which the deceased has to pass. It is a place

---

[758] Backes, *Das altägyptische Zweiwegebuch*, 73; Hermsen, *Die Zwei Wege des Jenseits*, 163.
[759] *Wb* IV, 74.4.
[760] Reference to the deceased as a protector of the egg of the sun god Re occurs also in the Book of the Dead Chapter 59 which reads: 'A spell for breathing air and for having power over water in the realm of the dead. To be recited by the justified N: Oh Atum may you give me the sweet air which is in your nostril. (For) I am the one who seeks every place that is located in Hermopolis. I am the one who protects the egg of the Great Cackler. When it is firm, I am firm, when it lives, I live and when it breathes I breathe': Lapp, *Papyrus of Nu*, pl. 33, lines 8-11.
[761] Hermsen, *Die Zwei Wege des Jenseits*, 163.
[762] *CT* VII, 309b (spell 1057).
[763] *CT* VII, 309a (spell 1056).

[764] *dj* is translated here as 'let' which is an usual form of imperative.
[765] *CT* VII, 307a-308b (spell 1055).
[766] Rößler-Köhler, *GM* 192 (2003), 90.
[767] (=The correct lake to sail on for passage), *CT* VII, 306d-g (spel 1054).
[768] *Wb* II, 271.20.
[769] *CT* VII, 508e-h (spell 1166).

where the sun god Re and the deceased renew themselves to be reborn in the next day.[770] It is also a place which witnesses the conflict between Re and the chaos powers which prevent him from being born every day. In Coffin Text spell 1054, the deceased says that he is on the right way and the Lake of Fire is the right way for passage. The deceased who says that he is the heir of the sun god Re can pass safely with the authority of his father.[771] In referring to the Lake of Fire as the right way, the deceased might refer to the upper waterway that will follow the Lake of Fire.[772] There is also strong stress here that the Lake of Fire also makes the passage of inheritance to the heir. After leaving the Lake of Fire, the deceased prepares himself to start a new journey as shown on the map. He will leave the lower land way and enter into an area that is divided between the upper waterway and the lower land way and forms the eastern borders of the Lake of Fire.

5.3. The Eastern Borders of the Lake of Fire: CT spell 1037/no.8

This area of passage comprises sections 8/7 and 5 on the map respectively. It is also the right entrance to the Lake of Fire. It is divided into upper and lower sections. The lower section is represented as a black half-disk and a square painted in red/no.8, which is described on B4L, B13C, and B1L coffins as the Gate of Darkness and the Gate of Fire. The two gates can also be the gates of the ways of Rosetau represented on the lower land way and the upper waterway (fig. 37). The text, which describes this section is CT spell 1037/8 and reads:

sḏt	Flame.
mꜣꜣ.n=j srwẖ(t).n=j m wsjr jm	I have seen what I have treated in Osiris there.
jmj ḳmꜣ m jwf=f	Do not mourn on his body.
ḥsf-ẖmjw rn=f pw	Opposer-and-Demolisher is his name.
ʿrrwt nt sḏt ʿrrwt nt kkw	Gate of Fire. Gate of Darkness.
rꜣ n š nby rn=f	A spell for the Lake of Fire is its name.[773]

The deceased says that he has treated Osiris, which means that he is in the place where Osiris is, or close to it. The image here is of Osiris lying on his bed in a place surrounded by fire, and guarded by a gatekeeper whose name is the Opposer-and-Demolisher. The deceased wishes to pass to see Osiris, and to take part in the treatment of his body. The next passage names the gate, which gives entrance to the place where the god is. The role of these guardians in the next spell is to resuscitate the deceased who is pictured as Re and Osiris.

As mentioned above, the spell is inscribed in the section that separates the two ways. In the upper section there is a label which reads flame and is painted in red,[774] which may refer to the *sḏt* occurring at the beginning of CT spell 1037.[775]

CT Spell 1036/no.7

The first keeper in this section is represented as a crocodile with a ram head holding a knife in his hand and guarding the Gate of Fire and the Gate of Darkness. Although this section of the Book of the Two Ways might represent another area or place of passage which the deceased has to cross, it still describes the fire circle. These keepers with knives in the Book of the Two Ways were described by Altenmüller as apotropaic gods (*apotropäische Götter)*, a group of gods in the shape of demons guarding the bends and passages in the Book of the Two Ways with their magical knives. They protect the sun god Re in his battle against the chaos powers and darkness.[776] The keeper is described on coffin B1C as *ḥsf-ẖmjw* (Punisher-of-Evil-Doer). Spell 1036/7 reads:

mk wj jj.kw m sʿḥ=j n šw	Behold! I have come in my dignity of Shu.
jw srwẖ.n=j wsjr	I have treated Osiris.
jrj n=j wꜣt swꜣ=j	Make a way for me that I may pass.
ḥwj ʿ=k ḥꜣt ḥḏw rʿ pw ntt m ʿ=j	Clap your hand, (for) it is the best of the maces of Re which is in my hand.
rwj ṯw	Pass away.
rꜣ n swꜣ ḥr=f	A spell for passing over him.[777]

In his study on Shu spells in the Coffin Texts, Willems argues that the deceased can be identified with Shu, and in this case he is traveling along the underworld to see his father Osiris and to take part in his mummification. Willems attributes all these actions of the son of Osiris to the vigil or the *Stundenwachen.*[778] In his way for the treatment of the body of his father Osiris, the deceased meets demons and gate-keepers who wish to stop him. The deceased in turn assumes the dignity of Shu to pass safely the place of passage. All these motifs are found in our spell, where the deceased comes in his dignity of Shu, who might also be considered as son of both Re and Osiris and his aim is to treat Osiris.

In CT spell 1036, the deceased is Shu son of Osiris who cares for the body of his father, and the one who

[770] Backes, *Das altägyptische Zweiwegebuch*, 322.
[771] Backes, *Das altägyptische Zweiwegebuch*, 322.
[772] Rößler-Köhler, *GM* 192 (2003), 91.
[773] *CT* VII, 286a-287c (spell 1037).

[774] *CT* VII, 287, n.1 (spell 1037).
[775] Lesko, *The Book of the Two Ways*, 42.
[776] Altenmüller, *LÄ* II, 635-40.
[777] *CT* VII, 284a-285c (spell 1036).
[778] Willems, in: Willems (ed.), *The World of the Coffin Texts*, 197-209; *Heqata*, 270-85.

holds the best of maces of Re in his hand. The deceased has now finished his night journey, in which he was identified with the sun god Re. He started his journey from the west and descended into the netherworld in the barque of Re. His aim was first to reach the Lake of Fire, the place where he will be reborn early in the morning, and with his capacity as son of Re he can pass the place of passage. After doing so, the deceased proceeds to another area which is divided between the two ways. Although this area belongs to another section, and does not belong to the lower land way, it has two gates of darkness and of fire. These two gates might also be considered as the two eastern entrances to the lower land way and to the upper waterway. As a place of passage this area is also a dangerous place, for which the deceased has to prove his identity to pass safely. The aim of the deceased's journey on the two ways is clear. First it is to accompany Re in his night journey through the lower land way. After doing so, the deceased will continue his journey through the separated area of passage which includes CT spells 1036 and 1037, where he changes the aim of his journey. The second aim of the deceased's journey on the upper waterway is to become the son who wishes to treat his father Osiris and to live with him. The Lake of Fire comes at the end of the night journey of the sun god Re and it is the starting point for the deceased's journey to see and treat his father Osiris.[779] It is a place at the edge of cosmos, which separates between life and death. It does not belong to any sphere, but it is a unique place that every deceased has to pass to escape the barriers of death and to reach life. Whether the deceased is Osiris or Re, his aim is the place of regeneration, the place from which he can get the power to continue his journey to resurrection.

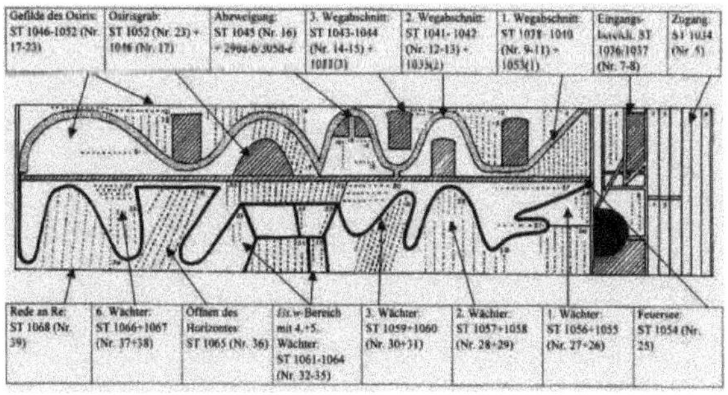

Fig. 37. A plan showing sections III and IV and the eastern borders of the Lake of Fire (CT spells 1034-1068)
(after Backes, *Das altägyptische Zweiwegebuch*, pl. 4)

5.4. The Topography of the Lower Land Way and the Fifth Hour of the Amduat

In the Book of the Two Ways, the Lake of Fire is described as a place where no one enters can be saved. This is as argued above refers to the Lake of Fire as a place of passage which is located on the ways of the Memphite necropolis. The deceased in the form of the sun god Re has to cross over it in his night journey. The same theme is also found in the Fifth Hour of the Book of the Amduat. The deceased as the sun god Re in his barque has to travel along the Kingdom of Sokar, which is also located in Rosetau. The Lake of Fire in the Amduat is depicted in the Fifth Hour and occupies the whole section below the lower register (fig. 38). It is half-filled with wavy lines to enable the insertion of a text. The water lines are painted red and blue.[780] The texts describe the Lake of Fire as a place for the sinners, and a place where the gods' boat cannot sail. Its water is described as the 'waves of water that cannot be controlled.' The text accompanying the Lake of Fire reads:

nwt j3kbjw nṯrw jmjw jmḥt	The water of mourning of the gods in Imhet (necropolis),
n ʿpj n wj3 ḥr=sn	No barque can traverse over them.
n sḫm.n dw3tjw m mw=sn	The ones who live in the underworld have no power over their water,
wnn m ḫrt-nṯr pn	Which is in this necropolis.
wnn mw=sn r ntjw jm=s m sḏt	Their water is fire for those who are in it.[781]

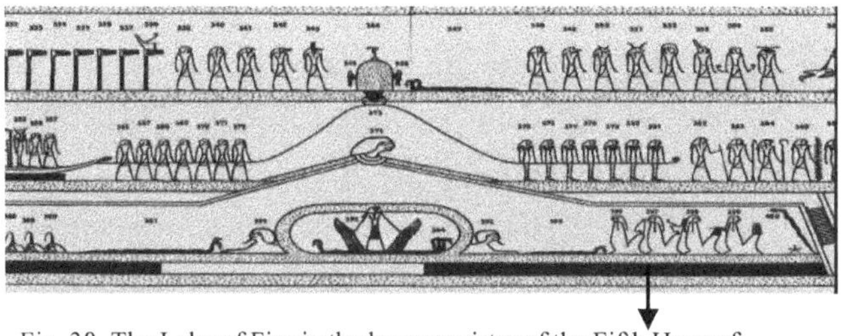

Fig. 38. The Lake of Fire in the lower register of the Fifth Hour of the Book of Amduat
(after Hornung, *The Egyptian Amduat*, 138 9).

The Lake of Fire is a place of punishment for sinners and a place of nourishment for the righteous. The lake is a fiery pain for the enemies of Re, and cool water for his followers.[782]

In the New Kingdom the Memphite necropolis Rosetau was chosen to be a model for the Underworld Books, which are depicted on the walls of the kings' tombs in the Valley of the Kings. Rosetau also became a term that designated the whole netherworld. The lord of the necropolis is Sokar, who is described in the Pyramid Texts as the lord of Rosetau, and was identified with Osiris. The lower land way in the Book of the Two Ways and the Fifth Hour of the Amduat were modeled after the ways of Rosetau, and they were designed for both Re and Osiris. This is not surprising as Re and Osiris can replace each other and can play the same

[779] On the Osiris-Re conjunction, see DuQuesne, in: *Totenbuch-Forschungen*, 23-33.

[780] Hornung, *The Egyptian Amduat*, 171.

[781] Hornung, *The Egyptian Amduat*, 171.

[782] The same theme also occurs in the Book of the Gates where the Lake of Fire is described as a place of nourishment for the righteous and a place of punishment for the sinners, see above, 31.

role. That is made explicit when the sun god Re travels through the underworld to see Osiris. In CT spell 1035 the ways of Rosetau are said to be at the borders of the sky. The spell reads:

sw3.n=j w3wt nt r3-st3w	I have passed the ways of Rosetau,
ḥrt t3 mw	Which are on water and on land.
w3wt nw nt wsjr	These are the ways of Osiris,
jw=sn m ḏr pt	And they are at the edge of the sky.[783]

We have seen above that CT spell 1072 tells that the ways of Rosetau are on water and land. CT spell 1068 marks the actual starting point in the journey of the sun god Re. Here CT spell 1035 also tells that these ways are for Osiris and they are at the edge of the sky. They might also be considered as the entrance points of the deceased into the cycle of both Re and Osiris. As these ways are passages to the deceased, they are located at the edge of cosmos. The underworld to the Ancient Egyptians belongs to the ordered cosmos, and it is also separated from this world. This may explain why the otherworld is seen on one side as day and night on top, and the necropolis and the tomb on the other side. This means that the underworld to the Ancient Egyptians has a part belonging to the sky, and the other part is represented in both the tomb and the necropolis. In CT spell 1035 the whole underworld is described, the day sky as the sphere of the sun god Re (here as the above underworld), and the underworld which is below as the sphere of Osiris, and the dead. The union of both Re and Osiris which is a core theme in the Underworld Books, appears here as the central theme in the Book of the Two Ways.

The Lake of Fire in the Book of the Two Ways can now be described as a place which the deceased will have to pass to reach the goal of his journey through the land of Rosetau. It is a place where the deceased will be reborn as the sun god Re, and it is also a place from which he will start his journey towards the abode of Osiris. To reach the Lake of Fire, the deceased has to prove his identity. He identifies himself with Re and sometimes as a messengers of Re. With this identification, the deceased has the right to pass over the Lake of Fire, a true place of passage.

---

[783] *CT* VII, 282a-c (spell 1035).

Chapter Six

The Rites of Passage

6.1. Van Gennep's and Turner's Studies on the Rites of Passage

In his study on the Rites of Passage, van Gennep describes them as 'rites which accompany every change of place, state, social position and age.'[784] Van Gennep classified all such rites as marked by three successive ritual stages:

1- Separation or the pre-liminal stage:
When a person or a group becomes isolated from an earlier fixed point in the social structure or from an earlier set of social conditions.
2- Marginal or the liminal stage:
This stage takes place when the state of a ritual subject is ambiguous and a person or a group is no longer in the old state and has not yet reached the new one.
3- Post-liminal stage:
The stage occurs when a ritual subject enters the new stable state with its own rights and obligation.[785]

The same theoretical approach was followed and developed by Victor Turner in his work on the Ndembu tribe rituals in Zambia. Turner concentrated in his study on the middle stage, categorized by van Gennep's term 'liminal' (derived from the *Latin* word *limen* or threshold).[786] Turner divided the Ndembu rites into rituals of life crises and rituals of affliction.[787] Life crisis rituals mark the transition of one phase in the development of a person to another. Such phases are important stages in the social and physical development of the ritual subjects. They include rituals of birth, puberty, and death, and are most easily observed in the context of initiation or illness, where they are marked by the three processual phases of van Gennep's classification. In the Ndembu Rituals, the first stage is that of separation from the previous state, place and time. The second is the marginal phase, when a ritual subject is separated from the everyday life and resides in a separated hut.[788] The third and final phase involves the celebration of the end of the ritual, when a ritual subject returns and reintegrates into society.[789] The Ndembu rituals are performed by cult associations gathered from the different Ndembu tribes regardless of their particular village or lineage membership, and in this way the system of the cults also helps to hold together the loosely organized Ndembu society.[790]

[784] Van Gennep, *The Rites of Passage*, 10.
[785] Turner, *The Forest of Symbols*, 94.
[786] Bowie, *The Anthropology of Religion*, 139.
[787] Turner, *The Forest of Symbols*, 7-15.
[788] This phase or stage can extend 'indefinitely', as for the monks who do not like to reintegrate with the society they have left. A clear example is the Christian monks in Egypt, who prefer to be separated from their society: Bowie, *The Anthropology of Religion*, 139.
[789] Turner, *The Forest of Symbols*, 14-5.
[790] Turner, *The Drums of Affliction*, 15.

Turner's study gained its importance from the fact that he was excited by the group life itself, and living within the Ndembu tribes he was able to get his information on ritual practice and its symbolic use from native informants and the experts of the Ndembu tribes. This informant base is what is missing from the Egyptian data. The most important point referred to in Turner's study is the use of symbols and metaphors in rituals. Turner defined ritual as 'prescribed formal behaviour for occasions not given over to technological routine, having reference to beliefs in mystical beings and powers.'[791] He also described the symbol as the smallest unit of the ritual, which has the same specific properties of the ritual.[792] The symbol can be an object, an action or words, gestures, events or even relationships.[793]

The performance of a ritual involves the handling of several symbols that each constitutes the smallest units of activity in a ritual, which means that symbols are carriers of individual units of meanings.[794] For instance, in the Ndembu life crisis rituals, Turner commented on the use of red, white and black symbolic objects. The relationship between the three colours is taken to refer to the three mystery rivers (the rivers of whiteness, redness and blackness), which flow from the power of the god Nzambi. The white symbols are associated with goodness, health, power, visibility, and life. Ritual whiteness refers to purity. Red symbols are associated with good and bad, where the red blood of the animal is shed by the hunters' blood, and bad blood is symbol of murder. Black symbols are associated with evil, diseases, witchcraft, and death.[795]

What concerns us here in Turner's study is the use of different sets of symbols and metaphors, and how the religious beliefs, symbols, rituals are all essentially related. In Turner's definition, the ritual performance involves manipulation of symbols, which make reference to religious beliefs.

6.2. The Construction of a Ritual

Applying the theoretical approach of Turner to Egyptian material is not without its problems. Ritual

[791] Turner, *The Forest of Symbols*, 19; *The Drums of Affliction*, 15.
[792] Turner, *The Forest of Symbols*, 48.
[793] Turner, *The Forest of Symbols*, 19.
[794] The question about the symbolism of a ritual can sometime be turned to be a question about the identity. In his interpretation of the rituals symbols among Umedas of Papua New Guniea, Alfred Gell says: 'among the Umeda informants I found none willing to discuss the meaning of their symbols -to discuss their symbols as symbols-'standing for' some other thing or idea, rather than as concrete things-in-themselves. In fact I found it impossible to even posit the question of meaning in Umeda, since I could not discover any corresponding Umeda word for the English 'mean', 'stand for', etc. Questions about symbols were taken by Umedas as Questions about the *identity*, rather than the *meaning* of a symbol: 'what is it?' not 'what does it mean?', (cited in Bowie, *The Anthropology of Religion*, 142).
[795] Turner, *The Forest of Symbols*, 59-92.

texts form a high proportion of the Egyptian writings, and they have a value that lies beyond the reconstruction of cosmology and mythological narrative.[796] The most crucial difficulty in approaching Egyptian ritual texts is their performative nature, but the impossibility of their observation. The first problem in applying the theoretical approach of Turner is that the Egyptian texts are inaccessible to a modern audience. Turner was able to apply an empirical approach on the Ndembu ritual because he had the chance to stay with the Ndembu tribes and to observe the performance of their rituals. He was also able to get his information from the experts and informants from the Ndembu tribes themselves. The second problem facing us with the Egyptian ritual texts is the absence of descriptive narrative texts that might help in understanding the Egyptian ritual texts.[797]

To have a better understanding of the performance of the Egyptian ritual texts, it is important to note that wording and content are not enough to have a clear picture of how the Egyptian ritual texts were performed. As Eyre argues, 'the essence of the ritual lies in the integration between words and actions performed in a highly charged context. Words without actions, like actions without words would fail to achieve an effective ritual.'[798] Both words and actions in ritual go together and no one has a primacy over the other, and they reflect and move forward the other.[799] It is hard to envisage a ritual performance without actions, since the rituals commonly involve participants in physical movement or action.[800] Uttering the word can also be described as an action, and that is made explicit from the fact that speaking and naming things are central themes in the mythical actions of the creator. For instance, Ptah is said to create the universe by the power of the word in the Memphite theology in which he plays the role of the creator.[801] Words can also be kept in writing, and in turn can be used in the cult of the deceased. For instance, in Assmann's words 'as artificial voice, writing was intended to extend cultic recitations beyond the time span of its ritual performance and to keep the deceased forever within the range of the priestly voice. In this function it served to realize permanent recitation'.[802] This role of the spoken word is made explicit in mortuary liturgies, which were texts, intended for recitation in the mortuary cult of the deceased. The recitation of these texts as a rite of passage mediates the passage of the deceased to his new state as an *3ḫ*.[803]

Egyptian ritual texts survive as a mixture of texts inscribed on pyramid walls, coffin sides, papyri and also as vignettes drawn on papyrus and temple and tomb walls.[804] The relation between the written texts, the drawn vignettes, and the ritual action is also highly complicated. For that reason the construction of a ritual can be described as 'imaginative exercise',[805] and the relation between the inscriptions and the representations should be considered.

It is true that the ritual performance is preserved in the mixture of vignettes and texts, which can give full record of the words and actions and thus can ease the construction of a ritual.[806] The ritual can be preserved in texts intended for recitation,[807] or in captions in the form of scenes, which can replace or play the same role of the written text. For instance, offering rituals are well preserved in the Pyramid Texts, and they are also depicted in captions on the private tomb walls of the Old Kingdom. Representations of ritual actions are mainly found as components of ritual scenes, and the other components of the ritual scene is its text.[808] Ritual texts belonging to ritual scenes may be termed liturgical. The representations of the laments of Isis and Nephthys may belong to this context, and their performance of the laments can refer to the actual performance of the ritual as it is recorded in the Coffin Texts, in the laments of Isis and Nephthys in P. Bremner-Rhind,[809] and P. Berlin 3008.[810]

Ritual texts intended for recitation are designated by the formulaic heading *ḏd mdw* (saying of words). The transcription of these spoken words as texts on papyrus, temple or tomb walls in the format that is equivalent to a service book, is not enough for assuming a performance of a ritual.[811] Ritual performance sometimes is indicated by the formula written on a Service-Book of the ritualist *ḫry-ḥbt*, whose name at the beginning of a text indicates that the

[796] Eyre, *Cannibal Hymn*, 25.
[797] Eyre, *Cannibal Hymn*, 26.
[798] Eyre, *Cannibal Hymn*, 25; speaking the words, as Eyre argues, can also have the power of action.
[799] The first spell in the *Ritual of Letting Seth and His Gang Fall* is to be recited over a figurine of Seth, and the actions taken are: spitting upon, trampling, spearing, and burning the figurine of Seth. These acts, as Egberts argues, 'may be said to visualise the contents of the spells': Egberts, in: Eyre (ed.), *Proceedings of the Seventh International Congress of Egyptologists*, 358.
[800] This is not only strict to the Egyptian ritual texts, but all the religious rituals can be defined as set of texts and actions that are well organized: Bell, *Ritual: Perspectives and Dimensions*, 136-61.
[801] On the role of the word in the creation of the universe see, Assmann, *Theologie und Weisheit im alten Ägypten*, 24-30; Eyre, *Cannibal Hymn*, 28.
[802] Assmann, *Death and Salvation*, 249. See also, *Totenliturgien* I, 53.
[803] Assmann, *Death and Salvation*, 238, 249; *Totenliturgien* I, 14-5; the same can also be said about the *Verklärungssprüchen*, the aim of which is to mediate the passage of the deceased to his new state of an *3ḫ*. Assmann, *Totenliturgien* III, 26-31.
[804] For the performative approach to the rituals in the Coffin Texts, see Willems, *Heqata*, 9-10.
[805] Eyre, *Cannibal Hymn*, 41.
[806] Eyre, *Cannibal Hymn*, 26.
[807] Assmann, *Totenliturgien* I, 15-7; *Totenliturgien* III, 26-31.
[808] Egberts, in: Eyre (ed.), *Proceedings of the Seventh International Congress of Egyptologists*, 359.
[809] Published by Faulkner, *JEA* 22 (1936), 121-40.
[810] Faulkner published also the lamentations of Isis and Nephthys in P. Berlin 3008, which is not very different from the lamentations of the two goddesses in P. Bremner-Rhind: Faulkner, *Mélange Maspero* I. 1, 337-48. For the lamentations of Isis and Nephthys in British Museum EA 10332, see Coenen and Kucharek, GM 193 (2003), 45-50.
[811] Eyre, *Cannibal Hymn*, 27.

text is for recitation. Several examples are found in the Old Kingdom private tombs at Saqqara. For instance, the deceased says: 'The ritualist (*ḫrj-ḥbt*) who will enact for me beneficial rituals...according to the craft of the ritualist.'[812]

The Service-Book used by the ritualist in the course of performing a ritual does not contain a coherent set of ritual, but discrete units of ritual wording rather than continuous ritual narratives. The Service-Book also contains fragments of material of a diverse nature, used for different occasions and purposes, which gives the ritual its flexibility to be extended or abbreviated or even varied for the individual performance.[813] It is not plausible to look for a great narrative and continuity in the Old Kingdom Pyramid Texts, any more than in the New Kingdom Book of the Dead. Lapp argues that it is even impossible to have continuous ritual narrative within a single spell in the Book of the Dead.[814]

Different theories have been proposed on the definition of ritual texts. Assmann distinguishes between two sets of texts, mortuary and funerary texts. Mortuary texts or liturgies, according to Assmann, are sets of ritual performed for the benefit of the deceased. In other words, mortuary liturgies are texts used in the context of the cult of the deceased, recited by the mortuary priest in the tomb, and the place where they were performed is the world of the living. Funerary liturgies (called mortuary literature by Assmann) serve as texts to be used in the Hereafter.[815] Mortuary liturgies, according to Assmann, were performed in the place of embalming and in the accessible cult chambers of the tomb; however they were recorded or placed in the inaccessible sarcophagus chamber.[816] The mortuary literature was recorded on the sarcophagus chamber walls (as the Pyramid Texts), on coffin sides (Coffin Texts), or on papyri (Book of the Dead). Mortuary liturgies were performed on the behalf of the deceased, while mortuary literature was intended to equip him magically.[817]

This classification by Assmann raises different issues. The most important ritual texts used in temple daily cult, were also used in funeral context. For instance, the New Kingdom Sun hymns were actually derived from a temple cult context, but they were inscribed on the private tomb walls in the New Kingdom to ensure their ongoing effect for the benefit of the deceased in the Hereafter.[818]

6.3. The Rites of Passage and the Lake of Knives

The Offering of the Headrest Ritual (CT Spell 823).

CT spell 823 occurs on the back of an outer coffin belonging to a Mentuhotep, son of a woman called Renefankh. Mentuhotep's tomb was located in the northern slopes of the Asasif necropolis.[819] The outer coffin with two other coffins belonging to Mentuhotep was then taken to the Berlin Museum. Unfortunately the outer coffin of Mentuhotep is now lost. The other objects originating from the tomb of Mentuhotep have been extensively studied by Steindorf and Vandier, who have argued that the statue of Mentuhotep can hardly be much earlier than the reign of Sesostris III.[820] Early drawings of the three coffins were done by Steindorf, and these are now held in the Griffith Institute archives. A typological study of the coffin has been done by Willems.[821] A recent study of the inner and outer decorations has also been done by Lapp.[822] The aim of the spell discussed here is to offer a headrest to the deceased as obvious from its title. It occurs only on this coffin.[823]

The spell is placed on the inside back of the outer coffin, directly behind the head of the deceased as he faces the offering list and the east. The object frieze contains an ornamental text, which reads 'An offering which the king and Osiris Lord of Abydos give, consisting of bread, beer....etc.' The first item in the object frieze is the headrest, placed directly behind the head,[824] so the object frieze agrees with the text, and the spell is in its right place (fig. 39).[825] Normally the

---

812 Eyre, *Cannibal Hymn*, 26.
813 Smith, *The Liturgy of Opening the Mouth for Breathing*, 6-18; Eyre, *Cannibal Hymn*, 26-7.
814 Lapp, *Papyrus of Nu*, 42-9; for the problem of the construction of a single ritual within a spell, see Lüscher, *Totenbuch Spruch 151*, 12-17, 74-77.
815 Assmann, *Totenlitrugien* I, 13; *Death and Salvation*, 238; *Studies Lichtheim* I, 2.
816 Assmann, *Totenliturgien* I, 13-14.
817 Assmann, *Death and Salvation*, 238.
818 The use of funerary literature by the living has been discussed by several Egyptology scholars. Among them is Junker who noted that many Pyramid Texts and chapters of the Book of the Dead (ch. 26, 69, 125, 148, 172, 178 and 180) were used in the *Stundenwachen*, which is well known and depicted on the temples of Dendara, Edfu, and Philae: Junker, *Die Stundenwachen*, 23, 110, 120. Walter Federn also noted the use of the so called Transformation spells in the Coffin Texts and their later extensions in the Book of the Dead in the initiation practices by the living: Federn, *JNES* 19 (1960), 241-257. For an expanded argument on this topic, see Gee, in: *Totenbuch-forschungen*, 73-6.
819 Willems, *Chests of Life*, 114.
820 Steindorf, *Grabfunde des Mitteleren Reiches* I, 10-24; Vandier, *Manuel d'archéologie égyptienne* III, pl. LXXIII, 3.
821 Willems, *Chests of Life*, 114-5.
822 Lapp, *Typologie der Särge und Sargkammernn*, 173-4.
823 For the text of the spell, see above, 36-7.
824 On the headrest and the object frieze, see Jéquier, *Les frises d'objects*, 235-8.
825 The headrest spell 532 is placed at the head end of the coffin of Mentuhotep, and reads:

r3 n rdjt tp n s n=f m ḫrt-nṯr	A spell for giving a man's head to him in the realm of the dead.
jm3ḫj N pn ḏd=f	The vindicated N says:
jw ṯsj n=j tp=j jn šw	My head is raised for me by Shu,
šmn n=j wsrt=j jn tfnt	And my neck is made firm for me by Tefnut,
ḥr pw n ṯsj tpw nṯrw r=sn	(In) that day when the heads of the gods are raised for them.
jw rdj n=j jrwt=j	My eyes have been given to me,
m33=j jm=sn	That I may see with them.
jw sšp.n=j jm3ḫ ḫr ptḥ-zkr	I have received my veneration before Ptah-Sokar.
jw rdj.n n=j mwt=j 3ḫ=s sšt3	My mother has given me her hidden power,

headrest is placed at the head end. However on some coffins it is placed at the back of the coffin as here.[826] In Middle Kingdom oblong coffins, the mummy was laid on its left side, head to the north and feet to the south.[827] The mummy then faces east, and for that reason the eastern side is called the front, and the western side the back of the coffin.[828]

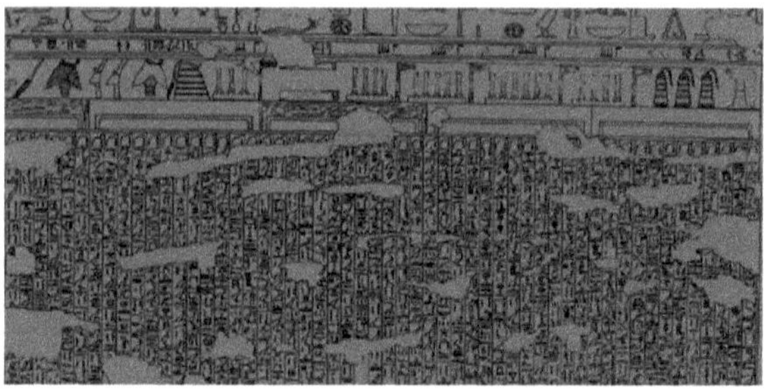

Fig. 39. The inner back of the coffin of Mentuhotep (after Lapp, *Typologie der Särge und Sargkammern*, pl. 38b).

The Ritual Context of CT Spell 823

CT Spell 823 on coffin T1Be does not stand by itself, but it fits into a sequence. The spell is followed by utterances 56-57 of the Pyramid Texts, which deal with the offering of seven unguents presented for the deceased during offering ritual. The offering of seven unguents in the Pyramid of Unas occurs in offering ritual contexts, and is placed in the burial chamber and the passage.[829] The object frieze at the head of a coffin usually depicts the items in PT spells 50-57, or the seven unguents vases, and two *wnḫ* clothes.[830] However, on the coffin of Mentuhotep the object frieze shows the items which are included in PT spells 56-57 on the back instead of placing them at the head end. The offering of these seven unguents began when the ritualist presented them in order to purify the offering room where the deceased can have his meal.[831]

The ritual of offering the seven unguents is among the most attested in ancient Egypt, and forms part of a liturgy in the Pyramid Texts.[832] The offerings of seven sacred unguents can concern either presentation of food offerings or items to be used in the Opening of the Mouth, and thus their use in the burial rites is clear.[833] Willems argues that the presentation of the sacred seven unguents stands in a close analogy to the glorification spells, which were recited during the offering ritual.[834] In the coffin of Mentuhotep, which concerns us here, the offering of seven unguents or PT spells 56-57 follows CT spell 823, but cannot give enough evidence to prove the ritual context of CT spell 823. The preceding spell at the foot end of the coffin of Mentuhotep is CT spell 822, which reads:

[r3 n tm rdjw] sj ẖwt m t3[835]	[A spell for not letting] corpses perish in earth.
jnk ipp sip.n dj jn gb ẖft mswt ḥk3//////// wr	I am one who has been counted; whom he-who-has-been appointed by Geb has counted at the time of the birth of the ruler..Great One.[836]
jnk jbḥ n spdw	I am the tooth of Sopd,
jnk ḥtjt nt nḥb-k3w	I am the throat of Nehebkau,
jnk šnw n wr nb/////	And I am the hair of the Great One, Lord of…
jnk ḥnn n b3bj	I am the phallus of Babi,
jnk m3s[837] *n k3 m ẖm*	I am the upper part of the leg of the Bull in Khem.
nn ḥw3 ẖ[t]=j m t3 wḏ3 [=j]/////	My b[ody] will not rot in earth, [I am] hale……
wsrt šw m ẖww nb	(My) neck is free from all decay.
jnk mndt nt ẖr///// wrt ḥk3w	I am the breast of her who is under [...?(of)] Weret-hekau.
*nn sj//////[p]r jdw ḥ*ˁ*w=j*	There is no decay…. efflux (?) of my flesh gone out.
jnk wr (?) 3ḫ rdj n=f msjt m ṯnnt	I am a Great One (?), a spirit, to whom *msjt* offering has been given in the *ṯnnt*-Shrine.
wḏt///////dj n=k m t3	A decree …has been given to you in earth.
//////jr.n=k sp sppj	…you have made time and again,
//////3t m wnt wn/////m=f n wrd-jb	…because of weariness of heart

---

dwn.n s3=j ˁ*wj=f ḥr=j*	And my son has extended his arms over me,
r ḏr nkn jrj. stš r sšt3	In order to put an end to the injury which Seth did in secret,
jrt.n=f r=j m rn=j pw	Which has done against me in that my name of N.
*jj ḥr št3w tpw jm3ḫ N m3*ˁ*-ḫrw*	Oh hidden faces, and venerated head, N is justified.

CT VI, 126a-l (spell 532). Willems argues that the presentation of a headrest to a deceased is designated by the idiom *ṯsj tp*, while the presentation of a mask is designated by the idiom *rdjt tp*: Willems, *Heqata*, 402, note. Aw, 69. The presentation of a headrest and the presentation of a mask occur in mummification ritual context: Willems, *Heqata*, 73.

826 Lesko, *Index*, 101. On the coffin Turin 15.774 (coffin of *jkr*) from Gebelen, the headrest is placed on the back of the coffin: Lesko, *Index*, 56.

827 Willems, *Chests of Life*, 122-4.

828 Willems, *Heqata*, 364.

829 Allen, *The Ancient Egyptian Pyramid Texts*, 23.

830 Willems, *Heqata*, 58.

831 Willems, *Heqata*, 58.

832 Lapp, *Die Opferformel des Alten Reiches*, 182-92. The seven unguents in the frieze objects of the Coffin Texts, as Willems argues, 'might at least be viewed as abstracted renderings of the ritual acts surrounding the presentation of the tomb inventory to the deceased, and not just drawings of the equipment itself': Willems, *Chests of Life*, 203.

833 For the construction of the ritual of the offering of the seven sacred unguents in the Old Kingdom, see Lapp, *Die Opferformel des Alten Reiches*, 182-92.

834 Willems, *Heqata*, 84.

835 The text is damaged and I follow de Buck's suggestion that the damaged part can be read *r3 n tm rdjw*, *CT* VII, 22, n. 6 (spell 822).

836 *Wb* I, 331, 14.

837 *Wb* II, 33,1.

jnk spjt ḫntj wḏ3t nw wsjr N	I am *spjt*[838](remnant) who is in front of the flourishing of Osiris N.[839]

Although the text is mostly damaged, the rest of the spell can give a clue to its content. The spell as its title indicates is a spell for not letting the corpses perish in earth. The deceased is already in the netherworld, which is made explicit when he says *m t3* 'in earth' and not *tp t3* 'on earth'. The deceased says that he has been counted by the one who has been appointed by Geb, which might refer to the deceased as being judged with the others in the netherworld. The counter is the one appointed by Geb, which might also refer to Osiris as the son of Geb and the one who counts and judges the spirits in the underworld. The deceased identifies the different parts of his body with deities. He says that he is the tooth of Sopd, the throat of Neheb-Kau, the hair of the Great One, the phallus of Babi, and the upper leg of the Bull in Khem. Because of this identification, his body will not perish in earth, he will be hale, and his neck will be devoid of decay. There is no efflux that will go out of his body, and he is a great spirit who will get his offerings in the *ṯnnt* shrine. The deceased gets all these benefits because of the decree that has been given to him in earth, and which will be repeated for him again and again. At the end the deceased says that he is a remnant of Osiris.

Altenmüller argues that this identification of the parts of the body of the deceased with deities -*Gliedervergöttung*- originates in the embalming ritual, where the deceased wishes to have the protection of these gods for each limb of his body, and that the motif was then developed to be used in the cult of the dead.[840] DuQuesne argues that these texts might be described as magical formulae recited for the protection of a deceased in the underworld, which appear from the Pyramid Texts on. He also notes that in CT spell 822 the deceased claims to be an *3ḫ* already, and he still seeks the protection of this spell when he wakes in the netherworld: the identification of the limbs with the gods will duplicate their functions.[841]

The most convincing opinion is that of Beinlich,[842] who argues that *Gliedervergöttung* is derived from the concept of Osiris Relics. The parts of the corpse of the deceased are identified with the gods, as the parts of the body of Osiris are identified with the nomes of Egypt. As the dismantled body of the deceased is reunited by his identification with the gods, the parts of the body of Osiris are also reunited when the flood comes and unites the whole body of Egypt in the image of Osiris' body. To give a clear picture of what is meant by Beinlich's argument, it is important to note that the word for body *ḫt* itself can refer to the body of the gods or men as a group.[843] So when the parts of the deceased's body are identified with the gods that simply means that the body of the god himself will be united and in turn the whole cosmos will be united.

When the parts of the body of the deceased are gathered for him in ritual at the hands of the priest, the corpse of the deceased is then collected and integrated as the deceased becomes complete.[844] Pyramid Text spell 213 in the Pyramid of Unas refers to the king as Osiris who passes alive, and every part of his body is identified as Atum. Eyre argues that *tm* means complete, and with this identification the ascent of the king is justified.[845] The deceased's bodily identification with the deities of Egypt can also give the deceased -as a spirit-the power to pass the place of passage, where he has been given a decree to proceed safely to the netherworld. If we combine the three theories about *Gliedervergöttung*, it can be concluded that this spell might refer to a resurrection ritual in which an offering of a headrest takes place.

The Reconstruction of the Headrest Offering Ritual

Most of the Egyptian liturgies performed for the deceased, according to Assmann, lie in two ritual contexts; mortuary offering cult and rituals performed for the deceased in the night before burial, which is better known as the *Stundenwachen*. The rites performed for the deceased at the end of the embalming include rituals concerned with offerings and mummification rituals.[846] CT spell 823 forms an episode of larger ritual in which a headrest is offered to the deceased. In this ritual, a priest, most probably a lector priest recites the spell, which is obvious from the title of the spell. In his study on Egyptian liturgies, Assmann argues that there are four types of address that ritual text can have. CT spell 823 fits precisely with the formal criteria determined by Assmann for the second category of genre of mortuary liturgies.[847] In our spell, an unidentified speaker is addressing an unspecified addressee about a specified third party. A priest is telling a story or a myth about Horus as standing at the head of the trappers. The speech is most probably directed to the deceased himself in the first part of the spell, while in the second part the address changes. The priest who is uttering the spell is speaking about the deceased, and describes how the

[838] *CDME*, 222.
[839] *CT* VII, 22p-23k (spell 822).
[840] Altenmüller, *LÄ* II, 624-5.
[841] DuQuesne, in: Koenig (ed.), *La magie en Egypte*, 240-1.
[842] Beinlich, *Osirisreliquien*, 308.

[843] *CDME*, 200.
[844] On the identification of the different parts of the body of the deceased with deities in funerary and magical texts see a list by Assmann, *Totenliturgien* I, 183-8.
[845] Eyre, *Cannibal Hymn*, 145, n. 35.
[846] Assmann, *Death and Salvation*, 250; *Totenliturgien* I, 5-8.
[847] Assmann identifies four types of forms; (A) an unidentified speaker (0) speaks to a specified addressee (2) about the later himself (0:2:2), (B) an unidentified speaker (0) speaks to an unspecified addressee (0) about a third party (0:0:3), (C) a specified speaker (1) speaks to unspecified addressee (0) about himself (1:0:1), (D) a specified speaker (1) speaks to a specified addressee (2) about himself (1) or about a third party (3) (1:2:1 or 1:2:3): Assmann, *Death and Salvation*, 241.

deceased is addressing the gods sailing over the Lake of Knives to save him on the day of chopping off the heads. Horus in this spell might represent the son of the deceased, which is indicated by the son's speech, when he says that his father will reward him by raising up his head. But what sort of action, if we can envisage that there was an action, was carried out when the spell was recited? And what is the relation between oral recitation and writing?

Most probably while a priest was uttering the spell, he was placing a headrest under the head of the deceased. A priest who is performing the headrest offering ritual is symbolically parallel to the divine world. In other words all the actions performed for the deceased were also performed in the divine world. By reciting this spell, a priest is warding off the powers of chaos in the Lake of Knives, which represents a place of passage for the deceased. The language plays the role of the actions, and all these actions were performed in the cult of the deceased and at the same time in the realm of the gods. Horus as the throw-stick catches the bad spirits or the enemies of his father and saves him. The priest is approaching the divine world not as a human, but as a member of the divine world itself. By reciting the spell, the communication between this world and the divine world takes place, where the priest is a member of the gods.[848]

Ritual and the Use of Symbols; Turner's Study and CT Spell 823

The meaning of the headrest as containing the specific properties of the ritual fits Tuner's definition as cited above. The headrest is a symbol of the sun rise.[849] It is also connected with the horizon, a place where the sun is born and dies every day, and it is also the means by which the head of the deceased is supported. It was painted yellow or red to enhance its horizon symbolism. Red symbolism of the headrest is connected with the blood that comes out from the enemies of the sun god Re, whom he defeats everyday at the horizon when he rises in the sky. The yellow colour of the headrest can also refer to the glow of the sun in its rising or setting in horizon. The symbols used in ritual can also include, as Turner argues, word or gesture, which also fits in this spell. The deceased is said to sail over the Lake of Knives, and he is frightened that his head will be chopped off by the gods in the Lake of Knives. The heads are chopped off by knives and the knives of the lake are the tool by which the gods will chop off the head of the deceased. The chopping off the heads (*ḥsḳ tpw*) and the living (*ʿnḫw*) are opposite, which gives strength to the meaning of the symbolism of the words used in ritual. On the other hand a pun is used to reinforce meanings between a headrest (*wrs*) and verb *wṯs* (to raise up a head), where both refer to the restoration of the deceased's head.

In the Ndembu life crisis ritual, the rituals are performed for a patient by members of his family or village. In CT spell 823, the son of the deceased is the one who performs the ritual for his father. The reintegration of the patient in the Ndembu life crisis rituals is characterized by his return to his family and society. As a result, a patient who has been initiated in these rituals will perform the same ritual for a member of the family or the society of the Ndembu tribes. In CT spell 823, the son of the deceased as a lector priest and a member of the family is the one who performs the ritual for father, and in turn his son will perform the same ritual for him when he dies. The family relationship of performance refers to the reintegration of the deceased with his family. The son here is envisaged as reincarnation/ replacement of his father. It is also important to note that the deceased for whom the ritual is performed will integrate with the gods in the place of passage over the Lake of the Knives and he will be one of them. This is made explicit in the son's speech at the end when he asks his father to raise up his head.

6.4. The Passage of the Barque of the Sun God Re over the Lake of Knives

The Journey of Re in Sun Hymns and Book of the Dead

The Lake of Knives occurs in a composite Sun Hymn from the New Kingdom, in which the journey of the barque of Re plays a prominent role.[850]

This hymn refers to the adoration of the sun god Re from the time of his rising to the time of his setting, and does not refer to his adoration in a specific hour of the day or night. Similarly, this hymn does not concentrate on the adoration of the sun god Re in one specific phase or shape, but it is designed for eternal adoration of Re at day and night.[851]

The hymn can be divided into three sections; the first section is an adoration of the sun god Re at his rising and setting. The sun god Re appears on the back of his mother Nut and there is no reference in which part of the sky the journey of the barque of the sun god Re might be located.[852] The sun god is greeted with *njnj* and embraced with Maat,[853] in an indication that the sun god Re is now united with his *Ka*, his living power.[854] The union of the god with his *Ka* and the embracement by Maat is attested in Amun ritual at

[848] Assmann, *Death and Salvation*, 244-6.
[849] For the symbolism of the headrest, see above, 37-40.

[850] For the text of this hymn, see above, 10.
[851] Assmann, *Liturgische Lieder*, 267.
[852] Assmann, *Liturgische Lieder*, 267-8
[853] Westendorf, in: *Fs Derchain*, 351-62.
[854] Assmann, *Liturgische Lieder*, 274.

Karnak and form an episode in the Opening of the Mouth Ritual.[855]

The second section describes the daily crossing of the sun god Re over the Lake of Knives. There is no hint of how and when exactly this crossing takes place or even what happens at the moment of crossing. The hymn refers only to the moment following the crossing, when the Lake of Knives becomes in peace (*ḫprw m ḥtpw*). The rest of this section shows the smooth journey of the sun god Re over the Lake of Knives, and how the enemy was destroyed and his spine was cut off. It is now safe for the barque to continue its journey as the dangers of the place of passage are over. [856]

It is important to note that the spine of the enemy is severed (*ḥsk*) with *dmt*-knife in the same way the god severed the head of the deceased in the Lake of Knives in CT spell 823. Zandee had argued that using the verb *ḥsk* indicates that the enemy's head is cut off, meaning that it would be the neck rather than the lower spine (fig. 40).[857] The common ritual parallel would be the snake whose back is cut by a knife. The *Msktt* Barque is not necessarily here the day or night barque, but as Assmann argues, *Msktt* might refer to the barque of Re in general. This is made explicit in the title of the hymn which is an adoration of the sun god Re from his rising to his setting.[858]

Fig. 40. A cat cutting a head of a snake
(after Malek, *The Cat in Ancient Egypt*, 85, fig. 52).

Assmann argues that the main function of the Sun Hymn was not only to praise the sun god Re; the sun god Re is not its focus point, but it tells about cosmic-natural and mythic over natural events. The two are, however, not necessarily exclusive. Assmann argues that here:

> Die Sonnenlieder preisen ja nicht den Sonnengott, nicht der Gott ist ihr Thema, sondern sie berichten ein gegenwärtiges, zugleich kosmisch-natürliches und mythisch-übernatürliches Geschehen.[859]

Most of the Sun Hymns inscribed on the private tomb walls of the New Kingdom are derived from temple liturgy, which means that they are rituals intended for recitations in a temple daily cult.[860] When this hymn is recited, the deceased and the sun god Re are both in an eternal adoration.

Recent Egyptologist tends to concentrate on what is called the cyclical aspect of mortuary texts, an aspect which needs to be taken in consideration when we attempt to understand the Sun Hymns and their ritual aspects. They might be regarded cyclical into different ways. First, when a hymn is recited everyday in a temple cult, both the sun god Re and the deceased will be in an eternal adoration.[861] They were also placed in the accessible parts of the tomb, and as a result they were available for the family and friends to read them aloud during different festival at the forecourt of the tomb.[862] There is no need for a professional priest to read or recite them, as happens in the rituals of the *Stundenwachen*, but a member of the family or relatives can play a role of a priest.[863] The cyclical performance of the Sun Hymns was required to set the cosmos in motion and the initial performance of the ritual repeats itself in an unending, continuous cycle, even without the direct participants of human actors.[864]

Assmann plausibly argues that Sun Hymns play the same role of the glorification spells, and both can equip the deceased magically.[865] By having such hymns inscribed for a deceased on the walls of his tomb, he will have the power to overcome the place of passage in the Lake of Knives. There is no performance of a ritual, but Sun Hymns are self-performed rituals. The language plays the role of actions, and these actions were performed for both the sun god Re and the deceased in their journey over the Lake of Knives.

In another Sun Hymn there is some detail on the description of the journey of the sun god Re over the Lake of Knives. Re is said to cross over the Sandbank of the Lake of Knives in his day barque.[866]

The journey of the sun god Re over the Sandbank of Apep is made explicit in other textual evidence. In the Seventh Hour in the middle register in the Book of the Amduat, the sun god Re crosses over the Sandbank of Apep in his barque encircled by Mehen serpent. The crew of the sun god Re are Isis, Sia, the Eldest Magician, Mehen, Flesh, Horus, Bull of Maat, the Vigilant One, Hu, and the Guide of the Barque. The text above the barque reads:

sḳdd nṯr pn ꜥꜣ m njwt tn	This Great god passes in this place,
m wꜣt nt ḳrrt wsjr	On the path of the cavern of Osiris,

[855] Assmann, *Liturgische Lieder*, 274-5.
[856] Assmann, *Liturgische Lieder*, 273.
[857] Zandee, *Death as an Enemy*, 149-50.
[858] Assmann, *Liturgische Lieder*, 274-5.
[859] Assmann, *Liturgische Lieder*, 363.

[860] Assmann, *Egyptian Solar Religion*, 16.
[861] Stewart, *JEA* 46 (1960), 83-90.
[862] Willems, *Heqata*, 241 and 383-4; Smith, *Papyrus Harkness*, 38.
[863] Assmann, *Totenliturgien* II, 17-8.
[864] The same can be applied on Chapter 15A III of the Book of the Dead mentioned above, 29.
[865] Assmann, *Liturgische Lieder*, 366-7.
[866] For this hymn, see above, 40.

ḥr sṯzw m ḥk3w3st ḥk3w smsw	On the supports of the magic of Isis and the Eldest Magician,
r sṯnm w3t r nḥ3-ḥr	To turn away from the Horrible of Face.[867]

The sun god Re passes over the Sandbank of Apep supported by Isis and the Eldest Magician, and turns away from Apep.

The next scene on the same register shows Apep as a huge serpent lying on his Sandbank facing the barque of Re and knives in his body. Selket is depicted at his head, and a god at his tail. The text which describes Apep and his Sandbank reads:

ṯs nḥ3-ḥr m dw3t	The Sandbank of the 'Horrible of Face' in the netherworld.
mḥ 440 pw m 3wt=f	It is 440 cubits in its length,
jw=f mḥ=f sw m ḳ3bw	And he fills it with his coils.
jrj.t(w) ᶜḏt=f r=f	His slaughter is made against him,
jwtj ᶜpp nṯr pn ᶜ3 ḥr=f	(And) this Great god does not pass by him.
sṯnm=f w3t r=f r ṯpḥt wsjr	He turns away from him to the Cavern of Osiris,
sḳdd nṯr pn m njwt tn	(And) this god passes in this place,
m sšmw n mḥn	In the image of Mehen-serpent.[868]

Here is a description of the passage of the sun god Re over the Sandbank of Apep. The Sandbank is 440 cubits in length and it is filled with the coils of Apep. The sun god Re did not pass over it because Apep swallowed the water, but instead he turns his way to the cavern of Osiris. A deceased in the shape of Re will lose his water if he passes over this Sandbank. This theme is made explicit in the name of Apep (Bringing of Water *sḏ3w mw*). The Mehen-serpent is envisaged here as a protective shield or a shell in which Re can traverse the place of passage.

The punishment of Apep is carried out by Selket who lassoes him, and He-who-is-above-his-Knives ties his feet. Here the image is of a bull being lassoed and his head is chopped off. The gods perform their punishment with knives, and that is made explicit in the text above Apep.[869]

This image is parallel to the image of the deceased who is frightened that his head will be chopped off with knives in the Lake of Knives which occurs in CT spell 823 mentioned above. It is also parallel to the image of the punishment of the sinners which occurs in CT spells 335 and 336.[870] After passing safely over the Sandbank of Apep and the Sandbank of the Lake of Knives, the sun god Re reaches the Beautiful West in peace as occurs in BD 15B.I mentioned above.[871]

Crossing the Lake of Knives takes the shape of a procession, and the day barque is in jubilation and the land is in festival. The gods greet the sun god Re after he has crossed the Lake of Knives. The appearance of the sun god Re in the west is connected with his crossing over the Lake of Knives. The barque of the sun god Re is said to be in *hnw*. It is a gesture that appeared in the Old Kingdom private tombs, where there are three lector priests depicted kneeling on the ground and beat their breasts with their hands. It is also described as corporeal music and rhythmic sound which accompanied the recitations.[872] The context here is different, where *hnw* does not express joy, but it expresses 'emotions at the presences of superhuman power'.[873] As Osiris is threatened by Seth in the place of embalming, the sun god Re is threatened by the Sandbank of Apep in the Lake of Knives. As Osiris managed to overcome death in the form of Seth by the help of liturgies, the sun god Re also managed to overcome the dangers of the place of passage by the power of the recited hymns.[874]

6.5. Having Food and Drink on the Two Banks of the Lake of Knives

BD Chapter 169 and the Erecting of the Bier

Book of the Dead chapter 169 belongs to what Assmann classifies as Liturgy B; a liturgy that was recited in the place of embalming and deals with the physical restoration of a deceased's body and his provisioning.[875] The context of this chapter is a wake in the place of embalming in the night before burial. The title of Book of the Dead Chapter 169 is *r3 n sᶜḥᶜ ḥnkjt* 'a Spell for Erecting the Bier'. The function of the spell is to guarantee the continuous performance of the mummification ritual for a deceased through the recitation of the spell in the night before burial in the place of embalming and in the sarcophagus chamber.[876] Its eternal performance is also guaranteed by inscribing it on the sides of the coffins,[877] or on the papyri included on the burial chamber of a deceased. Most of

[867] Hornung, *The Egyptian Amduat*, 228-9.
[868] Hornung, *The Egyptian Amduat*, 230-1.
[869] For the text, see above, 17-8.
[870] Further indications on the Sandbank of Apep and his punishment occur also in the Book of Overthrowing Apep. In this Book there is a detailed description of what has been done to the enemy of the sun god Re: Faulkner, *Papyrus Bremner-Rhind*, spell 29, lines 23-27, 45-6; *JEA* 24 (1938), 42-3. For the punishment of Apep with fire and knives see above, 13-6.
[871] See above page, 28-9.
[872] Dominicus, *Gesten und Gebärden*, 61-5.
[873] Assmann, *Liturgische Lieder*, 45; *Death and Salvation*, 243.
[874] On how the protection of Osiris and Re will keep the cosmos in motion, see Assmann, *Death and Salvation*, 70.
[875] Assmann, *Death and Salvation*, 292-298.
[876] Assmann, *Totenliturgien* I, 162.
[877] For the history of the transmission of the liturgy on Middle Kingdom coffin, see Assmann, *Totenliturgien* I, 57-8.

the rituals included in this chapter were adapted on Late Period coffins,[878] when the protective deities depicted on the sides of the coffins performed a wake around the bed of the deceased in the sarcophagus chamber.[879] As Assmann argues, despite the many references to the provisioning and offerings, the liturgy does not belong in the framework of either the daily or the festival offerings cult in the accessible areas of the tomb, but it belongs to the place of embalming.
It is not my aim to study the whole liturgy, but I will concentrate on the introductory passages of the wake, and then proceed to the passage where the Lake of Knives occurs. The introductory passage in the liturgy reads:

wṯs ṯw ḥr wnmj =k	Raise yourself on your right side!
wṯs ṯw ḥr jꜣbj =k	Raise yourself on your left side!
wn n=k gb jrwt=k špw	Geb opens for you your blind eyes,
dwn=f rdwj=kj ḳrfw	And he stretches your bent knees.
dj.tw n=k jb=k n mwt=k	You are given your *jb* heart of your mother,
ḥꜣtj=k n ḏt=k	And your *ḥꜣtj* heart of your body,
bꜣ=k r pt ẖt=k r ẖrt	Your *ba* (belongs) to the sky, and your body to the earth.
t n ẖt=k mw n ḫḫ=k	Bread for your body, water for your throat,
ṯꜣw nḏm n šrt=k	And sweet breathe for your nose.[880]

The liturgy starts with a call for the deceased to raise up his body, which has been collapsed at death. The deceased's body should be restored by means of the rituals performed for him.[881]

ḫfꜥ=k sm m ꜣbḏw	You shall grasp the whip in Abydos.
jw sšm.n=k šbw n wrw	You have guided the food offerings of the Great Ones,
mḥwt n ḥrjw	And the offerings bowls of those who are above,
smꜣw m ḥb n wsjr	And who join in the festival of Osiris,
dwꜣt nt wꜣg ḥr sštꜣw	In the morning of the Wag Festival and of the mysteries.
ẖkrw=k m nbw	You shall be adorned with gold.
wt=k smtrw m pꜣḳt	Your bandage is measured out (?) of fine linen,
ḥwj ḥꜥpj ḥr šnbt=k	And the inundation shall beat on your breast.
ꜣḫ n=k st r ḫtj ḥr ꜥb	It is more beneficial to you more than what is carved on an offering stone.
swr(=k) ḥr gswj mr nḫꜣwj	(You) shall drink on the two sides of the Lake of Knives,
ḥsj ṯw nṯrw ntjw jm	The gods who are there shall praise you.
prj=k r pt ḥnꜥ nṯrw	You shall ascend to the sky with the gods,
sꜥrjw mꜣꜥt n rꜥ	Who cause Maat to ascend to Re.
sṯꜣ.tw=k m-bꜣḥ psḏt	You shall be brought in the presence of the Ennead,
jrj.tw=k mj wꜥ jm=sn	And you shall be made as one of them.
ntk ḫꜣr jt n rꜣw	To you belongs the Syrian Goose the father of the Grey Geese.[882]
wdn=k sw n ptḥ rsj jnb=f	You shall offer it to Ptah to the south of his wall.[883]

The passage starts with a speech directed to the deceased. It is not known who is speaking, but most probably a priest playing the role of the god who stands watching over the corpse in the night of the vigil. The speech starts with a reference to the participation of the deceased in the Osirian secret rituals in Abydos. Both the Osirian and the Sokar festivals were incorporated in the rituals in the night before burial.[884] Assmann makes a comparison between the procession of the deceased to his tomb and the processions of Sokar and Osiris festivals. He argues that the night which precedes the processions of the deceased and the god was full of rituals performed for them before the procession takes place in the next morning. Assmann's argument seems convincing, where the deceased, who is equated with Osiris in the procession to his tomb, looks like a god in his festival procession. Assmann argues that here:

> Just as the Haker festival took place before the procession to Abydos and the *nṯrjt* divine festival occurred in the night before the *henu* procession, the wake was held on the night before the funeral procession.[885]

The deceased's bandage is said to be of fine linen, which indicates that the deceased is now in a mummification ritual.[886] Then the passage describes how the water of the flood will beat on the chest of the deceased. Here the motive of how the loss of water from the deceased's body is one of the factors that accompanies his death and its return is the cause for his resurrection. The deceased loses the water because of

---

[878] Assmann, *Totenliturgien* I, 159-60.
[879] Assmann, *Death and Salvation*, 297; for the gods' speeches on the Late Period coffins and how they were derived from the liturgy that occurs in BD 169, see Assmann, *Totenliturgien* I, 159-64.
[880] Naville, *TB*, Kapitel 169, pl. CXC, lines 1-4.
[881] Assmann, *Death and Salvation*, 292.

[882] This passage might allude to a deceased in the image of a bird crossing the place of passage.
[883] Naville, *TB*, Kapitel 169, pl. CXC, lines 23-7.
[884] Assmann, *Death and Salvation*, 267; in: *Essays te Velde*, 1-8.
[885] Assmann, *Death and Salvation*, 267.
[886] Assmann argues that fine linen might refer to an ornament worn by the dead in the procession of the Wag Festival to Abydos: Assmann, *Totenliturgien* I, 157, n. 191. The context might also refer to the bandage around the body of the deceased in the place of embalming.

his death, and it returns to him by pouring it on his body during the mummification ritual.[887]

The third section deals with drinking water on the two sides of the Lake of Knives. By drinking water on the two sides of the Lake of Knives, the deceased overcomes the dangers of the place of passage and ascends to the sky. He will be brought in the presence of the two Enneads as a sign of his successful passage over the Lake of Knives. Crossing the Lake of Knives comes at the end of the liturgy when the deceased has already been embalmed, received his offerings, and has ascended to the sky. So, crossing over the Lake of Knives can be envisaged here as the starting point of the deceased's journey across the sky. This journey might also be envisaged to take place in the next day when the deceased is ready to leave the place of embalming to start his journey to the tomb. Crossing the Lake of Knives, specifically in this text, might represent the funeral procession of the deceased from the embalming place to his tomb.

The deceased wishes also to have his meal on the two banks of the Lake of Knives, as on the New Kingdom stela of Chief of Guardians Thutmosis from Memphis, which reads: [888]

prj n=k wr mꜣꜣw ḥr jp	The *wr mꜣꜣw* priest comes out to you on the stairway,[889]
ḥr ʿnẖw nbw jšd	Carrying all bouquets[890] of the *jšd* tree,
m ꜣbd 1 prt ʿrḳy	In the first month of winter, the last day of the month,
ḥr mḥ wḏꜣt m jwnw	On the day of filling in the Eye of Horus in Heliopolis.
njs.tw=k wšb=k m rꜣ-stꜣw	You will be summoned, and you will answer in Rosetau,
m ꜣbd 3 prt sw 3	In the third month of winter, the third day.
ẖnty=k bꜣ=k r ꜣbḏw	You will travel southward (with) your *ba* to Abydos,
wsẖ n=f st m nšmt	Broad for him is a place[891] in Neshmet Barque,
šms=f nṯr r w-pḳr	When he follows the god to Poqer,
m ḥꜣb wꜣg <m> ḏḥwtj	In the Wag Festival and Thoth festival.
jw jrjj.n=f ẖkr n nb=f	He has performed the *Khaker* Festival for his Lord,
prt wpj-wꜣwt	And the Procession of Wepwawet.
dwꜣ.n=f rʿ ẖft wbn=f	He has worshipped Re at his rising.

dj.n=f psḏ=f r tꜣ 3 sbẖwt jmj ꜣbḏw	He has caused that he shines on these three portals, which are in Abydos,
ḥꜣpt nb=s ʿwj=s ḥr nb=s	And which hides its Lord, and whose arms are on its Lord.
wbn rʿ n mꜣꜣ=s	Re shines when he sees it.
jrj n=k nwj štꜣ	A secret return[892] will be made for you,
tp ḥḏ-ḥtpw m ẖrt ḥr	And the best products of the weaving god daily.
njs.tw=f ḥr wḏḥw m mr nẖꜣwj	He will be summoned on the offering table in the Lake of Knives,
ḥr mswt ꜣst	In the birthday of Isis.[893]
jw=f jm n ḥꜣb skr	He will come there for the Festival of Sokar,
ḥr rdjt ḥnw ḥr mfẖ	In the day when the *Henu* Barque is carried on shoulders.

The only difference between BD 169 and the texts on the stela of Thutmosis is that BD 169 was recited by a priest in the place of embalming in the night before burial, but the texts on the stela might be categorized as a biographical inscription. The wishes on the stela might be read aloud by tomb visitors and not by a professional priest.[894] They might also be considered as glorification spells, and their function is to transform the wishes into reality by the power of speech.[895] On both texts, the Lake of Knives features as a place where the deceased will have his food and drink. The same theme occurs in a tomb inscription and reads:

nmj=k njwt ḏꜣj=k ḥrt	May you cross the city[896] and traverse the sky.
swr=k mw ḥr gswj mr nẖꜣwj	May you drink water on the two sides of the Lake of Knives.
s[š]d=k r pt mj sbꜣ	May you shoot to the sky like a star.[897]

Here again the crossing of the Lake of Knives is connected with the crossing of the sky, and with the receiving of the deceased to his food and drink.

887 For the water as the discharge of Osiris, see above,4-8
888 Edwards, *BM Stelae* VIII, 47-9, pl. XXXIX, lines 9-17; Assmann, *Totenliturgien* II, 312-18.
889 Assmann translates *ʿb* 'pure stairway': Assmann, *Totenliturgien* II, 313; however it might be a miswriting of *jp* 'stairway', *Wb* I, 67, 3.
890 *Wb* I, 204- 3-5.
891 *wsẖ n=f*, 'He has a broad place': *CDME*, 69.

892 *CDME*, 127.
893 This might refer to the visit of the deceased to participate in the Epagomenal day in which Isis was born: Assmann, *Totenliturgien* II, 317. For the five Epagomenal days, see Spalinger, *JNES* 54 (1995), 33-47; For the five Epagomenal days in P. Leiden I 346, see Bommas, *Mythisierung der Zeit*, 15, 80-106.
894 Assmann, *Totenliturgien* II, 26.
895 Assmann, *Totenliturgien* II, 17-8.
896 The city may refer to the sky goddess Nut: Assmann, *Totenliturgien* II, 373. n. 132.
897 The text and the translation are after Assmann, *Totenliturgien* II, 373.

6.6. The Judgment of the Dead and the Lake of Fire

CT Spell 335 and the Rites of Passage

The Lake of Fire occurs in CT spell 335,[898] which is the most popular one among the Egyptian Coffin Texts.[899] It occurs on 33 coffins from different sites in Egypt.[900] The title of the spell defines its purpose to go out by day. This connects the passage of the deceased with that of the sun god Re, and thus both of them face the obstacles until they are reborn again the next day.[901] The spell occurs in most cases on the coffin lid, the preferred place for this spell, particularly on coffins from Meir and Saqqara.[902] Willems explains that arrangement of certain spells and ornaments in the coffin were not arbitrary. For instance, texts occurring on the feet usually deal with sandals, walking or treading on enemies.[903] On the head side, one finds texts dealing with offering of headrests.[904] The texts with cosmic background are usually found on the lid and bottom. CT spell 335, which deals with Re's (the deceased) arising and appearing in heaven is inscribed on the lid.[905] It is one of the most important lid texts, especially on the coffins from the 18th and 19th Dynasties.[906]

One of the most interesting features of CT spell 335 is the explanatory glosses, which interpret the texts. Silverman argues that simplifying was crucial to the editors and commentators of the Coffin Texts, since they were adapting royal texts of kings and queens to the use of the nobility.[907] The text was sometimes glossed to show the roles of those who were performing the ritual. In the New Kingdom, CT spell 335 became chapter 17 of the Book of the Dead.[908]

The spell starts with a speech by the deceased in which he is begging the sun god Re as the one who gives winds and illuminates the two lands. Then he mentions the egg of Re. The egg represents the different forms of life in their initial state, including the divine child and the human child. In Coffin Texts, such an egg is always the product of the sole creator god and forms the connection between the creator and the creation. References to the divine egg are common in later sources, and the egg of Hermopolis specifically[909] is connected with the primordial mound and the Lake of Knives in a New Kingdom magical context.[910] After this lengthy speech in the CT spell 335, the deceased asks Re to rescue him from the god whose shape is secret on the day of calculation of the difference.[911]

In the second section the god whose shape is secret puts a lasso on the evildoers on his slaughter-block. This passage alludes to a ritual that was widespread in ancient Egypt; the ritual of butchering an animal.[912] In this passage, the deceased is frightened that he might be butchered on a stone block. The god whose shape is secret is, according to the gloss, Horus Lord of Khem. He lassoes the evil-doers in his slaughterhouse and kills the *bas*. For instance, in the mastaba of Hetepherakhet from Saqqara, a man is shown lassoing a rope around the bull's horns to force down its head, and a second man is slipping a noose over its free front leg.[913] The men are doing so with the bull to force it down and to slaughter it on a block. The text under discussion has a relation with the scene discussed here. The deceased fears to be lassoed and to be slaughtered like a bull. The deceased also asks the sun god Re to save him from the wound inflictors of Osiris, the painful-fingered butchers. According to the gloss, these butchers of Osiris are his tribunal who inflicts punishment on his enemies, and take the sinners to their slaughterhouse.[914]

The deceased also says that he will not go down to the cauldrons as a reference to the cooked meat of the slaughtered enemy in the shape of a bull.[915] The deceased might be described as one of the butchers and not the victim. He also might be described as Osiris and the tribunal protects him against his enemies who might be described as followers of Seth.[916] The passage gives a full description of the slaughtering ritual as a symbol of overcoming death and presenting offering. First the bull (symbolising the deceased's enemies) is lassoed and his head is slaughtered on a block in the slaughter-house. Then the meat is taken to the cauldrons to be cooked. In this passage, the deceased

---

[898] For the text of the spell, see above, 15-6.
[899] Lapp, *Totenbuch Spruch 17*, XV.
[900] On the historical transmission of CT spell 335, see Jürgens, *SAK* 29 (2001), 111-138; *GM* 172 (1999), 29-46; Rößler-Köhler, *GM* 163 (1998), 71-93.
[901] Shalomi-Hen, *Classifying the Divine*, 13.
[902] Schenkel, in: *Göttinger Totenbuchstudien*, 40-1.
[903] Willems, *Chests of Life*, 233-5.
[904] Coffin Text Spell 823 (*CT* VII, 23L-24F).
[905] There are some exceptions where the spell does not occurs on top, for instance, on the coffin of *ḥr ḥḏ ḥtp*, the spell occurs at the bottom, on the head of the coffin of *ḏḥwty nḫt* and on the back of the coffin of *ḥr ḥtp*: Lesko, *Index*, 25 and 100.
[906] Assmann published the texts occurring on the lid of the coffin of Merenptah and reached the conclusion that the gods in the text columns must be seen in relation with certain funerary rituals. The long inscription is a speech by Neith, the divine embodiment of the coffin, to her son Merenptah who is pictured sailing within the body of his mother, the coffin. Actions in the place of embalmment are described, where rituals are performed for the king by Isis, Nephthys and the sons of Horus. Assmann associates the sequence of events with the night wake before the burial, the so called *Stundenwachen*: Assmann, *MDAIK* 28 (1972), 47-73, 115-138; Willems, *Chests of Life*, 141.
[907] Silverman, in: Allen et al., *Religion and Philosophy in Ancient Egypt*, 34.
[908] For the new edition of the Book of the Dead Chapter 17 from different sources, see Lapp, *Totenbuch Spruch 17*.

[909] Bickel, *Cosmogonie*, 238.
[910] Leitz, *Magical and Medical Papyri*, BM EA 10042, section K, VI, 10-VII, I mentioned above, 9-10.
[911] The first to translate *ḥsbt ꜥ3w* as the 'calculation of differences' was Clère, *BIFAO* 30 (1931), 425.
[912] For a recent discussion of this ritual, see Eyre, *Cannibal Hymn*.
[913] Eyre, *Cannibal Hymn*, 88-89.
[914] *CT* IV, 303a-304b (spell 335).
[915] For the theme of cooking the enemies in cauldrons (*wḥ3t*), see Verhoeven, *Grillen, Kochen, Backen*, 94, 103, and 107.
[916] Willems, *Heqata*, 94-5.

wishes to eat his meat offering and not to be eaten.[917] He might also wish to join the ranks of butchers and share in the slaughtering of the enemies of Osiris as one of his followers who share in his protection.[918]

The symbolic reference to cannibalism does not mean that the enemies are actually eaten, but it is crucially a context of destruction. Feeding is not meant here, but the destruction and the killing of the enemy is the main theme of this passage. The god and his followers do not feed on human beings, but the danger of being eaten by the supernatural was central to visions of hell.[919] The real threat to the body is expressed by the destruction of the soul, where the god whose shape is secret kills and most probably cut off the heads of the *bas*. It is widespread throughout ancient Egyptian history to see a king smashing or slaughtering his enemies with a mace or a sword,[920] although the context is different from being slaughtered on a block, but the fear of being dismembered is what meant in both.[921] The fear of the deceased to be slaughtered continues in CT spell 335 where he says:

nḥm=k wj m nw n jrjw sjpw	Save me from those who are in charge of examination,
rdj.n n=sn nb-r-ḏr ꜣḫ	To whom the Lord of All gave power,
r jrt sꜣwt r ḫftjw=f	To stand guard over his enemies,
ddw šꜥt m-ḫnw jꜣṯw	Who put slaughter inside the slaughterhouse,
jwtj prr m sꜣwt=sn	And who do not go away from their guarding.
nn ḫr=j n dsw=ṯn	I shall not fall to your knives,
nn ḥms=j m-ḫnw ṯmnw=ṯn	I shall not sit inside your cauldrons,
nn ꜥḳ=j jr jꜣṯw=ṯn	I shall not enter your slaughterhouse,
nn hꜣj=j r ḫnw ḥꜣdw=ṯn	And I shall not go down into your fish-traps.[922]

The deceased is frightened that his body and soul will be eaten by the eater of the dead, just as he feared the destruction of his body in his tomb, whether by fire, corruption or eaten by wild animals. As argued above, the deceased is frightened that his head to be cut off in the Lake of Knives in CT spell 823, and in CT spell 335 he is threatened to be slaughtered on a block as a bull with a knife.[923] The deceased is frightened to be taken to the slaughterhouse and to be slaughtered on the stone block like a bull. In ancient Egypt only slaughtered animals and birds were eaten. Dead or smashed animals were not eaten and as a result were not suitable to be presented as offerings to the gods. For that purpose, the king is usually represented offering enemies with heads chopped off to the god on the walls of the New Kingdom temples in Thebes. They were never represented with smashed heads or bodies, but captivate for slaughter, with arms tied behind their backs. Although these enemies were not meant to be eaten by the gods, since gods do not eat humans, the metaphor is that only fresh meat is suitable to be presented as offerings.

The deceased asks for rescue from these gods who protect Osiris, and says that their offerings will not be made from him.[924] The offering may represent the offerings presented while the judgment is taking place. As a symbol of overcoming death, a bull symbolising Seth is killed and its meat is distributed among the participants in ritual.[925] The passage ends with a speech by the deceased who says that he is in the train of the Ennead, which might refer to the Great Ennead of Heliopolis. As the title of CT spell 335 is going out by day, so the deceased assumes that he is following the Ennead and flies as a falcon, which might place the event before the sun rise.[926]

The second section opens with a speech by the deceased to Atum. He says that Atum is the Lord of the *nb ḥwt-ꜥꜣt* 'Great Mansion', as an indication to the role of Atum and the rest of the Ennead in the justification of Osiris against Seth, which took place in the Great Temple of Heliopolis.[927]

After this short speech, the deceased begs Atum to save him from the god who lives by slaughter, and whose face is of a dog and his skin human. He seizes the hearts and lives by the winding of the Lake of Fire. The god's name is swallower, as the gloss states.[928] In *CT* IV, 321b, the god in the gloss is said to be Seth. In coffin T1Cb, he is called 'this majesty of his'. The god is said to lick (*nsb*) putrefaction (*CT* IV, 320a). In an interesting parallel, which occurs in Papyrus Jumilhac XVI, 4-5, a licking of the body occurs in the course of mummification.[929] According to Vandier, the passage identifies a dog with Horus son of Isis, and, probably, with Anubis. The passage about this dog reads:

---

917 Eyre, *Cannibal Hymn*, 161.
918 Willems, *Heqata*, 94.
919 Eyre, *Cannibal Hymn*, 164.
920 This motif with the hunting scenes is dealt with by Davis as a core motif in Egyptian Art: Davis, *The Canonical Tradition in Ancient Egyptian Art*, 64-93.
921 Eyre, *Cannibal Hymn*, 164.
922 *CT* IV, 321e-23d (spell 335). The translation is after Eyre, *Cannibal Hymn*, 164.
923 The same theme occurs in CT spell 299 where the deceased says 'May you save me from the catchers of Osiris who cut off heads, who sever necks and take *bas* and spirits to their slaughterhouse, who eat fresh meat. May <my> head not be cut off, and may my neck not be severed: *CT* III, 295h-296a (spell 299). On the theme of destruction as a sign of the daily renewal of cosmos, see Goebs, *GM* 194 (2003), 29-51.
924 Eyre asserts that fear from being eaten by gods, is a manifestation of fear of the hostile supernatural: *Cannibal Hymn*, 162.
925 Willems, *Chests of Life*, 150.
926 Willems, *Heqata*, 289-291.
927 Assmann, *STG*, 46, n.g.
928 There are different representations of the god who catches the unworthy in the judgment of the dead, but none of them goes with the description in CT spell 335. These monsters were collected by Seeber on her work on the representations of the judgment of the dead in ancient Egypt: Seeber, *Untersuchungen zur Darstellung des Totengerichts im Alten Ägypten*, 163-84.
929 Vandier, *Papyrus Jumilhac*, 93.

> He has licked the body of his father Osiris in the place of embalming; he has bandaged him as far as his neck.[930]

As Willems argues, this dog refers to a man in the shape of a mythical dog rather than a real dog.[931] Although it is not known how this dog can be related to the god with a face of a dog and skin of human. Licking a body occurs also in the inscription of Merenptah published by Assmann.[932] The goddess who licks the body, in the case of Merenptah, is Neith who plays the role of a mother cow, and the king as her calf. The two contexts here are different. Most probably the god is represented with a face of a dog because the dog is a meat eating animal, which snatches human bodies and can drag the body out of its grave in the necropolis. Being eaten by a dog or thrown to a dog as a punishment means total destruction.[933] There is a passage in the Tale of the Two Brothers, which recounts how the elder brother threw the body of his wife to the dogs to eat as a sign of punishment. The passage reads:

> Then he went away to the Valley of the Pine, and his elder brother went to his home, his hands on his head and smeared with dirt. When he reached his house, he killed his wife, cast her to the dogs, and sat mourning for his young brother.[934]

The god is said to seize the hearts of the unworthy. The divine tribunal enacted in the Lake of Fire, not only consisted of killing of Osiris's enemies in the form of a bull, but Osiris is also justified in front of his enemies and assumed the *wrrt* crown in *nnjnsw* 'Herakleopolis',[935] as a sign of his victory over his enemies.[936]

Coffin Text Spell 336

The spell occurs on the back of the coffin of Gua BM 30840 from el-Bersha. The coffin was published in de Buck's edition of the Coffin Texts as B1L. The spell occurs on the front panel of the inside of the coffin, the one faced by the mummy lying on its left side. These sides of the coffin were used as places for spells dealing with travel across the netherworld. The object frieze on this side contains spells designed for food provision. The texts and representations of Gua's coffin are arranged in the same way. They start with a description of the Field of Offerings (CT spells 464-466), then the texts deal with well-known spells where the deceased refuses to eat dirty food 'faeces' and drink urine.[937] The deceased instead asks for divine offerings (CT spells 187-194).[938] CT spell 336 numbers three gates or portals that give entrance to further roads which the deceased should pass.[939] The spell reads:

sbẖt tpjt ḏd.t(w) r=f r=s	The first portal; one says about it,
jrt ꜣẖt n ns=s sḥrj ḥr=s	'The blue (?) of fire from its flame is raised above it.'
jw mḥ 50 ḥr gs=s m ẖt	50 cubits on its side consists of fire.
ḥꜣt nt tkꜣ=s ḏꜣ=s tꜣ m pt	The tip of its flame crosses the earth in the sky.
ḏd.n nṯrw r=s	The gods have said about it,
ḏrbt pw prj.n=s m ꜥwj sẖmt	'It is charcoal' and it has come from the hands of Sekhmet.'
ꜥḥꜥ.n=s ṯs.t(j) m rdjw	She has stood, erect in…among those who give.[940]
ḳmꜣ.n=s ḥꜥw=s	She had created her flesh.
jrj.n=s nṯrw m js-ḥꜣḳ	She has made the gods an easy prey,[941] ,
m-ẖt dwn=s rd=s r ḥꜣ	After she stretches her legs back.[942]
sšm db=s jmj st štꜣt rn=f	He-who-guides-her-horn, The-one-who-is-in-the secret-place is his name.[943]
wn n=j jrj n=j wꜣt	Open for me! Make a path for me!
mk wj jj.kw	See, I have come.
j itmw jmj ḥwt-ꜥꜣt iṯy nṯrw	Oh Atum who is in the Great Mansion, who seizes[944] the gods.[945]
nḥm=k wj m nṯr pw ꜥnẖ m ẖrjt	Save me from the hand of this god who lives by slaughter,
ntj ḥr=f m ṯsm inm=f m rmṯ	Whose face is of a dog and his skin human:
jrj ḳꜣb n š n sḏt	He is the guardian of the windings of the Lake

[930] The translation is that of Willems, *Heqata*, 276, n. 1591.
[931] Willems, *Heqata*, 276, n. 1591.
[932] Assmann, *MDAIK* 28 (1972), 47-73, 115-39.
[933] DuQuesne argues that 'eating the flesh signifies not merely annihilation but also the reintegration to which it is a necessary prelude': DuQuesne, in: *Totenbuch-Forschungen*, 29.
[934] The translation is that of Lichtheim, *AEL* II, 207.
[935] *CT* IV, 317a-b (spell 335).
[936] Willems, *Chests of Life*, 150; Roeder, *Mit dem Auge sehen*, 294-7; Goebs, *Crowns in Egyptian Funerary Literature*, 36-7.

[937] On eating dirty food and drinking urine, see Frandsen, in: Willems (ed.), *Social Aspects*, 141, 74. Eating faeces and drinking urine belong to the world of chaos, which the deceased wants not to live in: Bommas, *ZÄS* 131 (2004), 105.
[938] Borghouts, in: *Essays van Voss*, 12.
[939] Borghouts, in: *Essays van Voss*, 17.
[940] Borghouts supposes that *rdjw* as corruption of *rwḏw*, but his translation makes poor sense. He translated this passage as 'It has come to stand erect after it had been lashed together with tendons': Borghouts, in: *Essays van Voss*, 13.
[941] *Wb* I, 126. 6, which is an unfavorable role of Sekhmet.
[942] This may refer to Sekhmet.
[943] This translation is after Borghouts, who suggests that there was an omission before this sentence which is <there is a master of this portal > where this phrase occurs in 328e and 330r: Borghouts, in: *Essays van Voss* 19. n. 21.
[944] There seems to be a pun here between *ity* ' who seizes', which is written, and *iṯi* 'Sovereign' which might be expected
[945] From here until the second gate, *CT* IV, 311c-314e (spell 335) is repeated.

	of Fire.
ꜥm šwt ḫnp ḥꜣtyw	Who swallows shades and devours hearts,
wdd spḥw n mꜣ.n.tw=f	Who lassoes, but is not seen.[946]

The wording of the spell is not easy to understand. The first passage which concerns us here includes a description of the first portal. It is surrounded by blue fire above and 50 cubits around it consists of fire.[947] The tip of its flame reaches the sky from the earth. The gods describe it as charcoal, which comes from the hands of Sekhmet. The second section of the spell is a speech by the deceased to the guardian of the portal asking him/her to make a path for him. The rest of this section repeats the same passage from CT spell 335, where the deceased asks the god Atum to save him from the god who lives by the winding of the Lake of Fire.

CT spell 336 names three portals that house the body of Osiris, and the deceased makes his journey across them to resuscitate the divine body of the god, where the third portal is described as the portal of the members (*sbḫt ḥꜥw*). The guardians of these portals, in particular the third one, are seven in number, and might be compared with *Stundenwachen* gods in the vigil. The third portal is surrounded by a ring of four rivers of fire. Access to it is only possible with the intercession of Thoth, who brings the deceased into the presence of the tribunal also called the entourage (*šnwt*). The deceased wishes not to be suffered on the hands of these guardians.[948] The passage about the third portal reads:

ḏd.n=f r=s sbḫt ḥꜥw	He said about it: Portal of the limbs.
<n> tkn[949] *jm=s n mꜣꜣ srw tpw ꜥwj=s*	<No> one can approach it, the officials are not seen on the top of its arms,
hꜣj=s m pt wꜣḥ=s ḥzmn	It comes down from the sky, and it lays natron.
n tkn jm=s rsj	It is not approached at all.
jtrw 4 ḥꜣ=s m nbjw ḫt	Four rivers are around it consisting of flames of fire.
wꜥ m ḫt	(Number) one consists of fire,
2 m šmmwt	(Number) two consists of scorching heat,
3 nw m hh rꜣ n sḫmt	The third consists of the fiery blast of the mouth of Sekhmet,
4 nw m Nw n mꜣꜣ [ḏ]rw=f	And the fourth is Nu, and its limits cannot be seen.
n mꜣꜣ.n=sn ꜥḳ ḫnw=s	They cannot see how to enter within it.
jww sꜣrj=s n ḏḥwtj	The injustice of its needy man belongs to Thoth,
swt sꜥr sw n šnwt jmjt sbḫt tn	He is the one who leads him up to the court (entourages) who are inside the portal.
šw tfnt m ḫtm ḥr=s	Shu and Tefnut put the seal on it,
štt tw ḫrt ḏbꜥj	That *štt* (?) is the one under the signet.[950]
wr ḥrt=s r sbḫwt jptn	Great are its roads, toward these portals.
ḏꜣḏꜣwt jmjt wsḫt tn n ḏd jmj bsj m rn=f	The tribunals which are inside this hall be called by its name "Do not initiate",[951]
jrw///////rw	Who made (?)/////////*rw*
nrw-ḏswj=f	(The names of the seven tribunals) He-whose-sides-are-terrifying,[952]
gmḥ-ꜣm	He-Who-Seizes-Burning,[953]
jmj-tpḥt=f	He-Who-is-in-His-Cavern,
wṯsn-jrrw	He-Who-Deals-with-the-Evildoer,
jmj-nḳmt	He-Who-is-in-Affliction,
ḏw-hh	Evil-of-Hotness,
ḥsb[954] *ꜥrwtj*	And He-Who-Break-the-Two-Gates.[955]

The spell might be described as follows: first the deceased has to pass three portals which lead to a hall that houses the divine body of a god, most probably Osiris. The guardians in charge of these portals are seven, and although their names are different from those occurring in the *Stundenwachen*, the number seven may refer to the same gods of the vigil whose role is to protect the divine body of the god. The deceased has to pass these portals, and while doing so, he is obliged to pass a tribunal. They decide who is eligible to gain entrance to the portals. The deceased begs the gods not to fall a victim to the god whose face is of a dog and his skin human. The fate of the unworthy is the tearing of his body by the god who lives on slaughter by the winding of the Lake of Fire.

The group of seven guardians in CT spell 336 recalls the same situation in CT spell 335. The seven guardians in CT spell 335 mentioned above bear the same names as the guardians participating in the *Stundenwachen*.

[946] *CT* IV, 327a-327q (spell 336).
[947] On the measurements in the Netherworld, see Quirke, in: *Mysterious Lands*, 161-81.
[948] Willems, *Heqata*, 94-5.
[949] This amendment is done according to what follows in *CT* IV, 329g (spell 336).

[950] *tw* was added later and might be a corruption (*CT* IV, 329, n. 3), since the spell is recorded only on one coffin.
[951] *sbḫt* was omitted and replaced by *wsḫt* in this text, which might be translated 'broad hall or court': *Wb* I, 366. 3-4. *ḏd* would be passive participle, and *m* is imperative form of the verb *jmj*: Borghouts, in: *Essays van Voss*, 21, n. 54.
[952] The translation is that of Borghouts, in: *Essays van Voss*, 4.
[953] Can also be translated as 'He-who-looks-burning'.
[954] This reading is suggested by Faulkner: *Coffin Texts* I, 271.
[955] *CT* IV, 329c-330d (spell 336).

jw=j rḫ.kw rn n 3ḫw sfḫ	I know the name of these seven spirits,
jmjw šmsw nb sp3wt	Who are in the following of the Lord of Nomes,
jrj.n jnpw swt=sn	Whose seats Anubis made,
m ḥr pf mj r=k jm	On that day of the 'Come-thence'.
jr ḥr ḏ3ḏ3t tn	As for the chief of this tribunal;
n-3r-wr-rn=f	His name is the 'Great-One-is-not-driven-away',
dḥdḥ, 3ḳdḳd	(The names of the seven spirits are)[956] *'dḥdḥ'*,[957] *'3ḳdḳd'*,
k3-n-rdj=f-ḫnt-hwt-f	'The Bull-Who-was-not-put-in front-of his-Burning',
km-ḥr-jmj-wnt=f	'Black-Faced-who-is-in-His-Hour',
dšrty-ḫnt-ḥwt-jnsj	'Bloody-One-who-is-in front-of-the-Mansion-of-Red-Linen',
3sb-ḥr-prj-m-ḫtḫt	Radiant-Faced-Who-comes-out-after-Having-Turned-Back',
m33-m-grḥ-jnt-f-m-ḥr	And He-Who-sees-in-the-Night-what-he-brings-by-Day'.[958]

The image of a god who is in the place of embalming and protected by guardians occurs also in CT spell 49 and reads:

rs ḥr=ṯn jmjw wꜥbt	Be watchful , O you in the hall of purification,
s3w ṯn jmjw wrjt	Pay attention, O you in the hall of embalming.
mtn ḥꜥw nṯr snḏw n nbḏw	Behold, the flesh of the god is in fear of the enemies,
jrj.n ḫprw	(They) have made transformations.
sḥḏ.w tk3w jrw ꜥwt	Light the torches, O guardians of the members.
nṯrw imjw snkt	O gods who are in darkness,
dj s3=ṯn ḥr nb=ṯn	Put your protection around your lord,
psš wnwt ḥr nb ḥḏt	(And) divide the hours upon the Lord of the White Crown.[959]

In this spell a group of protectors also called the *šnwt* 'entourage' occurs, and they bear other names including *jrjw ꜥwt wsjr* 'Keepers of the members of Osiris'. These keepers appear in *wrjt* (the place of embalming),[960] guarding Osiris' body, lighting torches[961] and performing *Stundenwachen.*[962]

So, in CT spells 335 and 336 mentioned above there is a group of seven gods who participate in the protection of Osiris. They form a tribunal and decide who gains entrance to see and protect Osiris. The question to be asked now is how the judgment was enacted in the Lake of Fire.

The Enactment of the Judgment of the Dead in the Lake of Fire

There are some key words that give clue to the ritual context of the spells under discussion. The first one occurs in CT spell 335, and it is called *ḥsb ꜥ3w* 'the calculation of difference'. Different interpretations have been given to the meaning and context of the term. *ḥsb ꜥ3w* designates a tribunal that the deceased has to pass in his way to the netherworld. In his study on Middle Kingdom coffins, Willems analysed the decorations of the texts columns and reached the conclusion that the gods who are shown at the corner-columns of the coffin must be seen in relation with the protection of the deceased. They protect the deceased and pronounce a judgment.[963] Assmann similarly published the outer coffin of Merenptah and reached the conclusion that the gods at the corners of the coffin play the role of coffin protectors, and one of their roles is to pronounce a judgment for the deceased. Willems' interpretation to the term *ḥsb ꜥ3w* is based on two theories; the first is that the calculation of difference is a term designating a tribunal that the deceased has to pass in his way to Sais, which means that the burial rites included a ceremonial passage of divine tribunal.[964] There are two points concerning the judgment of the dead and the divine tribunal; the first is that it is sometimes represented as a court where the gods determine whether the deceased was guilty of sin or not. The deceased's heart was weighed on a balance against a feather of truth, and he had to pronounce his innocence before Osiris and his forty two gods. References to this judgment in the Coffin Texts were collected by Grieshammer in his work on the judgment of the dead in Coffin Texts.[965] The other model of the judgment of the dead was patterned after the mythical tribunal of Horus and Seth. According to the myth, Seth murdered his brother Osiris and took over his kingship. Horus summoned the court in Heliopolis and that court was on his side. Osiris was crowned as king of the netherworld, while Horus was appointed as King of Egypt. The deceased, who was identified with Osiris, is then also one of the actors in the myth. He can win the trial against Seth and be justified in the netherworld as Osiris.[966]

As Willems argues, this complex of thoughts is referred to in the texts and representations of the journey to Sais.[967] According to the inscriptions of

[956] The words in brackets are not there in the original text.
[957] There are different variations and corruptions in the texts, and the names differ from one coffin to another.
[958] *CT* IV, 263b-270c (spell 335).
[959] *CT* I, 216b-217a (spell 49).
[960] Willems, *Chests of Life*, 146; *Heqata*, 308; Assmann, *Totenliturgien* I, 271.
[961] For the lighting of torches in the *Stundenwachen*, see Assmann, *Totenliturgien* I, 272.
[962] The term is mentioned in CT spell 49 as the gods dividing the hours as a sign for the night protection.

[963] Willems, *Chests of Life*, 141-159.
[964] Willems, *Chests of Life*, 150-5.
[965] Grieshammer, *Jenseitsgericht*.
[966] Grieshammer, *Jenseitsgericht*, 111-5.
[967] Willems, *Chests of Life*, 148-9.

Merenptah, after the mummification process finished Osiris was justified and crowned as king in the presence of the Enneads and the Two State Chapels. When Osiris reached Sais, his enemies were destroyed. The text columns' gods are mentioned individually, stating their positions to the left and right, head and feet of the deceased. The Ennead features as a court of justice, and they are depicted at the corners of the coffin to protect the deceased. Most probably the role of the gods in the court of justice was played by priests attending the mummy of the deceased. Thus the journey to Sais seems to incorporate Osiris' victory over his enemies and his coronation as a king in the netherworld.[968]

In Middle Kingdom Coffin Texts, there is a liturgy described by Assmann as performed in the *Stundenwachen*.[969] It is his Coffin Texts liturgy I, which includes CT spells 1-29, and starts with a call upon the deceased to raise himself up:

wsjr N pn	O Osiris N!
ṯsj ṯw ḥr jꜣbj=k	Raise yourself on your left side,
dj ṯw ḥr wnmj=k	And put yourself on your right side.[970]

After the deceased Osiris gains his physical power, he goes to a trial, where he is justified against his enemies. In Coffin Text spell 15, the judgment is said to be pronounced by the goddess Neith, which, according to Willems, is evidence that the trial takes place near Sais, where Neith appears against the evil word (*ḫꜥj Njt r mdw pf ḏw*) (*CT* I, 45d, 46d).[971] Neith in this Text appears as embodiment of the coffin and the protector of the deceased.[972] In the same context in CT spell 15 (*CT* I, 45c), a god named *bn-kꜣ* is ordered to pull the bonds of a bull (*j bn-kꜣ jtḥ nṯtw kꜣ*), which might refer to a slaughter ritual of a bull representing Seth. The Bull as a personification of Seth was killed and his meat was distributed among the participants in the ritual.[973] The victory of Osiris over Seth was completed by the placing of the *wrrt*-crown on Osiris.[974] This is the first viewpoint concerning the occurrence of the *ḥsbt ꜥꜣw* in the context of a judgment, which features in the journey to Sais.

Assmann considers the judgment of the dead as an early form of the *Stundenwachen*.[975] The navigation to Sais was incorporated in the *Stundenwachen*; the two might be envisaged as one and cannot be separated. First, in Coffin Text spell 335 mentioned above, the names of the members of the divine tribunal are identical with the gods participating in the *Stundenwachen*. For instance, the name of the seventh guardian in CT spell 335 is 'Black-One-Who-is-in-His-Hour',[976] which refers to the hour-service of this god and occurs also in the *Stundenwachen* at Edfu.[977]

In CT spells 335 and 336 mentioned above, the entourage called *šnwt* was responsible for the protection of Osiris and the punishment of his enemies. After his victory over his enemies, Osiris gained the *wrrt* crown. So, all the themes mentioned in the journey to Sais occur also in CT spells 335 and 336. This might also give evidence that the entourage in the two spells protect Osiris and punish his enemies, and they play the same role of the text columns gods and a tribunal that decide who will pass the place of passage over the Lake of Fire.

If the journey to Sais might represent an early parallel to the *Stundenwachen*, how might the ritual be performed in the place of embalming? The journey to Sais, where the *ḥsbt ꜥꜣw* is reached, was in the form of processions, and the *Stundenwachen* was a wake in the place of embalming, which adds more confusion to envisage the journey to Sais as being performed symbolically in the place of embalming. The procession to Sais should have included a procession by boats, which cannot be performed in the place of embalming unless they are in the form of models, or merely referred to in the recitation.[978] In CT spell 237, which deals with protection of the deceased's mummy during the *Stundenwachen*, the processions to Sais and to Abydos are said to be performed in the place of embalming. In CT spell 237, as in CT spell 335, the deceased reached the *ḥsbt ꜥꜣw* in his way to Sais. CT spell 237 reads:

jnḏ ḥr=ṯ ḥꜣjt wsjr	Greetings to you, O (lady) who is behind Osiris,
rmnwtt kꜣ n ndjt	Companion of the Bull of Nedit,
snfjt wtw ḥbst bꜣgj	Who makes the ones who are enwrapped breath, and who wraps the limpness,
rdjt.n wsjr sꜣ=f r=s	To whom Osiris turned his back,
ḥrjt-ꜥ wt jnpw	And assistant of the embalmer Anubis,
m srwḫ ḥꜥw wrḏ-jb	During the treatment of the body of the One-Whose-Heart-is-Inert,
sꜣḫ wj	Glorify me,
wp=ṯ n=j rꜣ=j	Open my mouth for me,
sšm bꜣ=j r wꜣwt dwꜣt	Guide my *ba* towards the roads of the netherworld,
dj=ṯ n=j ḥtpwt m-m wrw	And give me offerings among the Great Ones,
ḥr ḫꜣwwt nt nbw rnw	On the altars of the Possessors of Names.

[968] Willems, *Chests of Life*. 150.
[969] Assmann, *Totenliturgien* I, 52-60 and 69-103.
[970] *CT* I, 6b-c (spell 1).
[971] Willems, *Chests of Life*, 149.
[972] Assmann, *Totenliturgien* I, 112.
[973] Willems, *Chests of Life*, 149.
[974] Wearing the *wrrt* crown is a sign for the justification of the deceased against his enemies: Assmann, *Totenliturgien* I, 101; Goebs, *Crowns in Egyptian Funerary Literature*, 36.
[975] For the *ḫbs-tꜣ* liturgy as referring to the judgment of the dead, see Assmann, *Totenliturgien* I, 69-103.
[976] *CT* IV, 268d (spell 335).
[977] Willems, *Chests of Life*, 156.
[978] Willems, *Heqata*, 154-5.

jnk wsjr jw=j r ꜣbḏw	(For) I am Osiris and I go to Abydos.
šsp=j ꜣwwt ḥr ḥtp ꜥꜣ	I receive offerings from the great offering table,
ḥr rdjt snmw ḥtpwt n rnw ꜥšꜣw	On the day of giving food supplies and offerings to numerous names.
dmj.n=j sbḫt ḳꜣt šnwt	I have reached the High Portal of the entourage,
ḥr ḥsbt ꜥꜣw	On the day of the calculation of the difference.
ꜥḳ=j r ẖm wr ḥnꜥ wrw	May I enter to the Great Shrine together with the Great Ones,
m-m šmsw ꜥꜣ n wsjr	And among the Great Followers of Osiris.
jj.n=j ḥꜣp=j bꜣgj n wrḏ-jb	I have come that I might cover the limpness of the Weary One,
ḥbs.n=j gmt.n=j tšj	And I have covered up what I have found missing.
wpj n=j wꜣt	Open a path for me!
jnk nb spꜣ	(For) I am the Lord of Sepa.[979]

In this spell, there is a description of the activities of the deceased in the workshop of Anubis. The second section of the text is a speech by the deceased to the goddess who is behind Osiris, and who participates in the treatment of his body. The text also situates the arrival of the deceased at the 'High Portal of the Entourage' on the day of the calculation of the difference.[980] Here all the acts in the place of embalming parallel these associated with the journey to Sais and the tribunal that the deceased has to pass in his way, and with the journey to Abydos. So can we envisage that there were processions to Sais and Abydos in the *Stundenwachen*?

CT spell 237 mentions a ritualized tribunal session among elements of the Osiris Festival at Abydos, and pays particular attentions to the activities of the deceased in the treatment of Osiris and to the offering rites performed in this connection. Willems argues that:

> There is little room for doubt that the 'Great Ones' mentioned in our texts are none other than the *wrw nw ꜣbḏw*, 'Great Ones of Abydos', who play such prominent part in the Osiris mysteries. On the other hand, we can hardly go amiss in identifying them with the 'Great Ones who are in the Portal' together with whom the deceased eats offering bread on the day of calculation of difference i.e. in connection with a session of the divine tribunal.[981]

It seems that the judgment of the dead, in the form of a divine tribunal, features in the Osiris secret rituals and also in the procession to Sais, and the three appear in the context of the *Stundenwachen*. The nautical element was reduced to allusion in the spells or glorifications recited and the libation offerings.[982] This means that the deceased might symbolically be present on his bier in the place of embalming and all the acts are performed around the bier. Of course the procession should be performed with boats, and in this case the boat might be represented with a bier, and the water over which the boat sails might be reduced to the form of water poured around the bier. A representation of boats on the bier can also solve this problem. There are some pictorial representations on the New Kingdom temples, where the god on the mummification bed is said to be in his boat.[983] In a similar scene from the Temple of Hibis, one of the gods attending Osiris' bier is called 'Anubis who is in his barque'.[984]

In all rites of passage cited above, the Lake of Knives and the Lake of Fire are two metaphorical places that do not exist in rituals. They do not have fixed physical locations, but they exist in myth. Crossing over the two lakes is dangerous, but is also necessary for a deceased to continue his journey and to enter into a different status, status of being an *ꜣḫ*. The aim of the deceased's journey over the two lakes differs from one context to another. It is also explicit that there is no single specific explanation for the rites of passage over the two lakes, and they draw on different metaphors.

[979] *CT* III, 311h-315d (spell 237).
[980] Willems, *Heqata*, 132-3.
[981] Willems, *Heqata*, 133.
[982] Willems, *Chests of Life*, 158; *Heqata*, 133.
[983] Willems, *Chests of Life*, 158.
[984] Willems, *Chests of Life*, 158.

Chapter Seven

Conclusion

The passage of the deceased from this life to the next can be described as taking place in a boat crossing the borders of the realm of death to the realm of *3ḫw*. Crossing the lake is a ritual enacted for the deceased at the day of his funeral. Pictorial and textual evidence from different periods show that the crossing of the deceased's boat over the lake was accompanied by recitations of *s3ḫw*. This recitation runs at the same time with the crossing over the lake. The crossing was a symbolic one, and can be abbreviated in a libation offering ritual in which the water offered to the deceased was envisaged as the lake over which his boat sails. Crossing the lake as a rite of passage was parallel to the crossing of the sun god Re over the waters of the sky, and also to the crossing of the *wrrt* boat of Osiris. Recitation accompanying the crossing is a rite of passage, the aim of which is to mediate the passage of the deceased over dangerous places of passage.

The Lake of Knives and the Lake of Fire are places of passage over water. They represent two paths which the deceased follows in his journey to the netherworld. As passages over water, they have the creative powers of the primeval ocean Nun. In Egyptian myth, water was the first element from which life came into being. In water lies the power of creation. This creative image of water was envisaged in the annual Nile flood which covered the whole land bringing all life substances to the land of Egypt. Nun was a place where the dead reappear to a new life. In ritual, water was the elixir of life, which is poured to the deceased during ritual so he can be refreshed by means of it. Water offered to the deceased comes from the body of Osiris, and it returns to his body during libation offering. Water was also the means by which the deceased mediates his passage and becomes an *3ḫ*. As water was the power of life, it also caused violent death. The negative aspects of water are made clear in many texts dating to different periods. The High Nile can cause damage to the whole land. This is made explicit in a hieratic inscription in the hypostyle hall of Luxor Temple, which dates to third year of the reign of King Osorkon III, and in which the high flood is said to cause great damage to the temples of the gods, and the whole land drowned in water.[985]

The Lake of Knives, as a part from the primeval ocean Nun, was also a place of creation. In the Hermopolitan creation myth, the sun god Re is said to come into existence over the Lake of Knives in the Island of Fire. It is also a dangerous place where the deceased's head can be chopped off by the gods who sail over it. The Lake of Fire is also a place of creation. The deceased travels on the ways of Rosetau in the Book of the Two Ways to be reborn in the morning with Re in the Lake of Fire. In the Book of the Amduat, it is a dangerous place of passage, which the deceased has to pass while sailing over the Kingdom of Sokar. In the Book of the Gates the Lake of Fire is a place of cool water for the righteous and burning fire for the sinners.

As indicated from their names, fire and knives are the tools of destruction in the two lakes. Fire and knives were used into daily and funerary rituals. They were used to ward off the harm of the enemy of the god and the deceased. In nightmares demons are driven off by the aid of fire and knives. The guardians of the places of passages are also equipped with fire and knives; serpents spit their flames against the damned, chop off the heads of the unprepared dead, and shoot their knives against the passers. The names of the places of passage are also connected with fire and knives, so we find mountains guarded by serpents equipped with fire and knives, and even there are places of passages named after them; the Island of Fire, the Lake of Fire and the Lake of Knives.

The location of the Lake of Knives and the Lake of Fire changes from one context to another depending on the ritual performed and the orientation of the ritualist. As places of passage, they appear in the east where the sun god Re, and the deceased identified with him, are born in the morning. They can also be located in the west as transitional areas that take the deceased to an advanced stage in the netherworld.

Depending on textual evidence, the Lake of Knives can be best described as a stretch of water winding through the sky. By constructing the journey of the sun god Re and the deceased over the Lake of Knives, it is evident that the lake extends from the east to the west of the sky, and has two banks. It is also a place which divides the sky into the southern and northern skies. The deceased's wish to cross from the southern side of the sky to its northern side over the Lake of Knives might refer to his wish to travel from the Field of Reeds to the Field of Offerings where he can consume his food and drink his water on the two banks of the Lake of Knives.

The Lake of Fire in the Book of the Two Ways is a place over which the deceased sails through the land of Rosetau. It is a place where he will be reborn with the sun god Re, and it is also a place from which he will start his journey towards the abode of Osiris. On the floors of el-Bersha coffin the Lake of Fire is depicted as a red band. It has two gates called the Gate of Darkness and the Gate of Fire. To reach the Lake of Fire, the deceased has to prove his identity. He identifies himself with Re, or sometimes as a messenger of Re. With this identification, the deceased has the right to pass over the Lake of Fire, the true place of passage.

In the vignettes of the Book of the Dead Chapter 126, the Lake of Fire is represented as a stretch of water with four *nsrt* signs on the four corners. Four baboons sit on the four sides of the lake and act as judges in the

[985] See above, 13.

barque of Re. The same depiction of the Lake of Fire occurs also in the New Kingdom Mythological Papyri, with the exception that the deceased is depicted pouring water on the two sides of the lake. It can also be represented as a lake where the sinners are burnt by its fire, as evident from the vignettes of the Papyrus of *b3k-n-mwt* Louvre No. 3279. In the Book of the Amduat, the Lake of Fire is depicted as an oblong, half-filled with wavy lines, and its water is painted in red. In the Sixth Hour of the Book of the Gates, the Lake of Fire is depicted at the end of the lower register. It is represented as a cavity full of fire. It appears also on the 21st Dynasty coffins from Thebes. Its depiction is not very different from those occurring on the New Kingdom Mythological Papyri. The role of the Lake of Fire as a place of passage on these coffins is not different from their antecedents in the Middle Kingdom. On these papyri and coffins, which include vignettes from the Book of the Dead and scenes from the Underworld Books, the rituals are kept in images. Four baboons and fire signs are represented on the four corners of the lake, as occurs in the vignettes of the Book of the Dead Chapter 126.

The rites of passage concerning the crossing over the Lake of Knives and the Lake of Fire show that the two lakes are metaphorical places that do not exist in rituals. They do not have fixed physical locations, but they exist in myth. Crossing over the two lakes is dangerous, but is also necessary for the deceased to continue his journey and to enter into a different status, the status of being an *3ḫ*. It is also explicit that there is no single specific explanation for the rites of passage over the two lakes, and they draw on different metaphors. In ritual, the two lakes can be replaced by libations basins, and the crossing can be interpreted as an offering of libation.

The rites of passage over the two lakes are not coherent rituals, but represent sets of different rituals, in which the crossing represents an episode of a bigger ritual. For instance, the headrest offering ritual in the Lake of Knives represents an episode of a resurrection ritual in which a headrest is placed under the head of the deceased. The raising of the discharge of Osiris in the Lake of Fire is an episode of the libation offering ritual, in which water is presented for the deceased in the Lake of Fire. The performance of these rites involves the handling of symbols, which constitute the smallest unit of the ritual. These symbols are embedded in the ritual performance, and they give indications of the religious beliefs and practices of the ancient Egyptians.

As places of passage over water, the Winding Waterway and the Island of Fire share the ritual aspects of the Lake of Knives and the Lake of Fire. They represent transitional areas for the barque of Re and the deceased to the hereafter. The journey of the deceased over the Winding Waterway can be interpreted on two levels, mythical and ritual. On the mythical level the deceased is featured as the sun god crossing the Winding Waterway. On the ritual level, the deceased is featured as Osiris in the place of embalming while the acts of the participants in the vigil are interpreted as ritual acts. The bier, on which the body of Osiris was placed, was envisaged as the boat of the sun god Re crossing the sky.

The Island of Fire as a place of passage is not connected with death or the rituals taking place immediately after death, but with what happens when the deceased enters the netherworld. As a primordial place, the Island of Fire represents a place where the world came into existence. As a place in the netherworld, it represents a passage that the deceased wishes to pass in his journey to the hereafter. It is a marginal place that is separated from the world of the living and from the world of the dead. It is also one of the places where the deceased can see Osiris in the final judgment. The deceased sails over the Island of Fire to reach the place of Osiris, where he can participate in the treatment of the body of the god. The ritual aspects of the Island of Fire and the Winding Waterway are not very different from the ritual aspects of the Lake of Knives and the Lake of Fire. In all these places of passage, seeing Osiris and participating in the treatment of his body is the main aim of the deceased's journey. It is also evident that these four places of passage are places where food and drink are available for the deceased, who will be able to secure his food and pass safely over them. He will have his water on the two banks of the Lake of Knives, and raise the discharge of Osiris in the Lake of Fire as a sign for having water. He will be able to visit the Field of Offerings which is located on the banks of the Winding Waterway, and fills his body with *ḥk3w* when he visits the Island Of Fire.

Studying the Lake of Knives and the Lake of Fire, and the rites of passage concerning the crossing over them, does not in fact give us a clear indication of any major dramatic changes in the conceptions regarding the hereafter. In any event, such changes are not made explicit in the texts regarding the crossing over the two lakes. Both lakes served as places of passage, and their ritual aspects are not very different from each other, nor from the Winding Waterway and the Island of Fire.

Bibliography

Abdelrahiem, M., 'Chapter 144 of the Book of the Dead from the Temple of Ramesses II at Abydos', *SAK* 34 (2006), 1-16.

Alexanian, N., 'Ritualrelikte an Mastabagräbern des Alten Reiches', in: *Fs Stadelmann*, 3-22.

Allen, J. P., *The Inflection of the Verb in the Pyramid Texts*, BAe 2, Malibu, 1984.

——, *Genesis in Egypt: The Philosophy of Ancient Egyptian Creation Accounts*, YES 2, New Haven, 1988.

Allen, J. P., J. Assmann, A. B. Lloyd, R. K. Ritner and D. P. Silverman, *Religion and Philosophy in Ancient Egypt*, YES 3, New Haven, 1989.

——, 'Reading a Pyramid', in: *Hommages Leclant* I, 1-25.

——, 'The Egyptian Concept of the World', in: *Mysterious Lands*, 23-30.

——, *The Ancient Egyptian Pyramid Texts*, WAW 23, Atlanta, 2005.

Allen, T. G., 'Some Egyptian Solar Hymns', *JNES* 8 (1949), 349-356.

——, *Occurrences of the Pyramid Texts with Cross Indexes of These and Other Egyptian Mortuary Texts*, SAOC 27, Chicago, 1950.

——, *The Book of the Dead or Going Forth by Day*, SAOC 37, Chicago, 1974.

Altenmüller, B., *Synkretismus in den Sargtexten*, GOF IV/7, Wiesbaden, 1975.

Altenmüller, H., 'Messersee, gewundener Wasserlauf und Flammensee. Eine Untersuchung zur Gleichsetzung und Lesung der drei Bereiche', *ZÄS* 92 (1966), 86-95.

——, 'Zur Lesung und Deutung des Dramatischen Ramessumpapyrus', *JEOL* 19 (1967), 421-442.

——, *Die Texte zum Begräbnisritual in den Pyramiden des Alten Reiches,* Wiesbaden, AÄ 24, 1972.

——, 'Apotropäische Gottheiten', *LÄ* II, 1975, 635-640.

——, 'Dramatischer Ramessumpapyrus', *LÄ* I, 1975, 1132-1140.

——, 'Gliedervergottung', *LÄ* II, 1975, 624-627.

——, 'Messersee', *LÄ* IV, 1975, 113-114.

——, *Die Wanddarstellungen im Grab des Mehu in Saqqara,* AV 42, Mainz am Rhein, 1998.

——, 'Der Konvoi der Sonnenschiffe in den Pyramidentexten', *SAK* 32 (2004), 11-33.

Assmann, J., *Liturgische Lieder an den Sonnengott. Untersuchungen zur ägyptischen Hymnik* I, MÄS 19, Berlin, 1969.

——, *Der König als Sonnenpriester. Eine kosmographischer Begleittext zur kultischen Sonnenhymnik in thebanischen Tempeln und Gräbern*, ADAIK 7, Glückstadt, 1970.

——, 'Die Inschrift auf dem äuβeren Sarkophagdeckel des Merenptah', *MDAIK* 28 (1972), 47-73.

——, 'Neith spricht als Mutter und Sarg. Interpretation und metrisch Analyse der Sargdecklinschrift des Merenptah', *MDAIK* 28 (1972), 115-139.

——, 'Die Verborgenheit des Mythos in Ägypten', *GM* 25 (1977), 7-43.

——, 'Harfnerlied und Horussöhne', *JEA* 56 (1979), 54-77.

——, 'Horizont', *LÄ* III, 1980, 3-7.

——, *Sonnenhymnen in thebanischen Gräbern*, Theben 1, Mainz am Rhein, 1983.

——, *Re und Amun: die Krise des polytheistischen Weltbilds im Ägypten der 18-20. Dynastie*, OBO 51, Freiburg and Göttingen, 1983.

——, 'Death and Initiation in the Funerary Religion of Ancient Egypt', in: Allen et al., *Religion and Philosophy in Ancient Egypt*, 135-59.

——, *Ma'at. Gerechtigkeit und Unsterblichkeit im Alten Ägypten*, Munich, 1990.

——, 'Egyptian Mortuary Liturgies', in: *Studies Lichtheim* I, 1-45.

——, *Das Grab des Amenemope (TT 41)*, 2 vols, Theben 3, Mainz am Rhein, 1991.

——, 'When Justice fails: Jurisdiction and Imprecation in Ancient Egypt and the Near East', *JEA* 78 (1992), 149-162.

——, 'Maat und die gespaltene Welt oder: Ägyptertum und Pessimismus', *GM* 140 (1994), 93-100.

——, 'Solar Discourse. Ancient Egyptian Ways of Worldreading', in: Assmann, A., *Stimme, Figur: Kritik und Restitution in der Literaturwissenschaft*, Deutsche Vierteljahrsschrift für Literaturwissenschaft und Geistesgeschichte 68, Sonderheft, Stuttgart and Weimar, 1994, 107-123.

——, 'Spruch 23 der Pyramidentexte und die Ächtung der Feinde Pharaos', in: *Hommages Leclant* I, 45-59.

——, *Egyptian Solar Religion in the New Kingdom. Re, Amun and the Crisis of Polytheism*, London and New York, 1995.

——, 'Spruch 62 der Sargtexte und die ägyptischen Totenliturgien', in: Willems (ed.), *The World of the Coffin Texts*, 17-30.

——, 'Verkünden und Verklären. Grundformen hymnischer Rede im Alten Ägypten', in: Loprieno (ed.), *Ancient Egyptian Literature: History and Forms*, PdÄ 10, Leiden, 1996, 313-334.

——, 'Ein Wiener Kanopentexte und die Stundenwachen in der Balsamierungshalle', in: *Essays te Velde*, 1-8.

——, 'Der Ort des Toten. Bemerkungen zu einen verbreiteten Totenspruch', in: *Fs Stadelmann*, 235-245.

——, *Ägyptische Hymnen und Gebete*, Zurich und Munich; revised 2nd edition, OBO, Freiburg und Göttingen, 1999.

Assmann, J., M. Bommas, *Altägyptische Totenliturgien*, vol. I, *Totenliturgien in den Sargtexten des Mitteleren Reiches*, Supplemente zu den Schriften der Heidelberger Akademie der Wissenschaften, Philosophisch-historische Klasse 14, Heidelberg, 2002.

Assmann, J., 'Das Leichensekret des Osiris: Zur kultischen Bedeutung des Wassers im alten Ägypten', in: *Hommages Fayza Haikal*, 5-16.

——, *Theologie und Weisheit im Alten Ägypten*, Munich, 2004.

——, *Death and Salvation in Ancient Egypt*, translated from German by D. Lorton, Ithaca and London, 2005.

Assmann, J., M. Bommas and A. Kucharek, *Altägyptische Totenliturgien,* vol. II, *Totenliturgien und Totensprüche in Grabinschriften des Neuen Reiches*, Supplemente zu den Schriften der Heidelberger Akademie der Wissenschaften, Philosophisch-historische Klasse 17, Heidelberg, 2005.
——, *Altägyptische Totenliturgien,* vol. III, *Osirisliturgien in Papyri der Spätzeit*, Supplemente zu den Schriften der Heidelberger Akademie der Wissenschaften, Philosophisch-historische Klasse 20, Heidelberg, 2008.
Backes, B., *Das altägyptische >>Zweiwegebuch<<: Studien zu den Sargtext-Sprüchen 1029-1130*, ÄA 69, Wiesbaden, 2005.
Badawy, A., 'On Both Sides in Egyptian', *ZÄS* 103 (1976), 1-4.
Baines, J., 'Interpreting the Story of the Shipwrecked Sailor', *JEA* 76 (1990), 55-72.
——, 'Egyptian Myth and Discourse: Myth, Gods, and the Early Written Iconographical Record', *JNES* 50 (1991), 81-105.
——, 'Modeling Sources, Processes, and Location of the Early Mortuary Texts', in: S. Bickel, M. Bernard (eds), *Textes des Pyramides & Textes des Sarcophages*, BdÉ 139, Cairo, 2004, 15-43.
Barguet, P., *Les textes des sarcophages égyptiens du Moyen Empire*, Paris, 1986.
Barta, W., *Die altägyptische Opferliste von der Frühzeit bis zur griechisch-römischen Epoche,* MÄS 3, Berlin, 1963.
——, *Das Gespräch eines Mannes mit seinem Ba*, MÄS 18, Berlin, 1969.
——, *Die Bedeutung der Pyramidentexte für den verstorbenen König*, MÄS 39, Munich, 1981.
——, *Die Bedeutung der Jenseitsbücher für den verstorbenen König,* MÄS 42, Munich, 1985.
——, 'Zur Überlieferung des Opferrituals der Pyramidentexte auf Privatsärgen des Mittleren Reiches', *GM* 12 (1991), 7-13.
Barthelmess, P., *Der Übergang ins Jenseits in den thebanischen Beamtengräbern der Ramessidenzeit*, SAGA 2, Heidelberg, 1992.
Beinlich, H., 'Zur Bedeutung der sogenannten Osirisreliquien', *GM* 54 (1982), 17-29.
——, *Die "Osirisreliquien". Zum Motive der Körperzergliederung in der altägyptischen Religion*, ÄA 42, Wiesbaden, 1984.
——, 'Der Moeris-See nach Herodot', *GM* 100 (1987), 15-18.
——, *Das Buch vom Fayum: Zum religiösen Eigenverständnis einer ägyptischen Landschaft*, 2 vols, ÄA 51, Wiesbaden, 1991.
——, 'Ein Fragment des Buches von Fayum (W/P) in Berlin', *ZÄS* 123 (1996), 10-8.
——, *Das Buch vom Ba*, SAT 4, Wiesbaden, 2000.
——, 'Zwischen Tod und Grab: Tutanchamun und das Begräbnisritual', *SAK* 34 (2006), 17-31.
Bell, C., *Ritual: Perspectives and Dimensions*, New York, 1997.
Beylage, P., *Aufbau der königlichen Stelentexte von Beginn der 18.Dynastie bis zur Amarnazeit*, 2 vols, ÄAT 54, Wiesbaden, 2002.
Bickel, S., 'Die Jenseitsfahrt des Re nach Zeugen der Sargtexte', in: *Fs Hornung*, 41-56.
——, *La cosmogonie égyptienne avant le Nouvel Empire*, OBO 134, Freiburg and Göttingen, 1994.
——, 'Un hymne à la vie: Essai d'analyse du Chapitre 80 des Textes des Sarcophages', in: *Hommages Leclant* I, 81-97.
——, 'D'un monde á I'autre: le theme du Passeur et de sa barque dans lapensèe funèraire', in: S. Bickel, M. Bernard (eds), *Textes des Pyramides & Textes des Sarcophages*, BdÉ 139, Cairo, 2004, 91-117.
——, 'Creative and Destructive Waters', in: *L'acqua nell'antico Egitto*, 191-200.
Bidoli, D., *Die Sprüche der Fangnetze in den altägyptischen Sargtexten*, ADAIK 9, Glückstadt, 1976.
Billing, N., 'The Secret One: An analysis of a core motif in the Books of the Netherworld', *SAK* 34 (2006), 51-71.
Blackman, A. M., 'The Significance of Incense and Libation in Funerary and Temple Ritual', *ZÄS* 50 (1912), 69-75.
——, 'Ancient Egyptian Practices of Washing the Dead.' *JEA* 5 (1918), 117-24.
Bleiberg, E., 'East is East and West is West: A Note on Coffin Decoration at Asyut', in *Studies Redford*, 113-120.
Bochi, P. A., 'Death by Drama: The Ritual of *Damnatio Memoriae* in Ancient Egypt', *GM* 171 (1999), 73-86.
Bolshakov, A. O., 'The Old Kingdom Representations of Funeral Procession', *GM* 121 (1991), 31-54.
——, *Studies on Old Kingdom Reliefs and Sculpture in the Hermitage*, ÄA 67, Wiesbaden, 2005.
Bommas, M., Die Mythisierung der Zeit, GOF IV/37, Wiesbaden, 1999.
——, 'Zwei magische Sprüche in einem spätägyptischen Ritualhandbuch (pBM EA 10081): Ein weiterer Fall für die „Verborgenheit des Mythos", *ZÄS* 131 (2004), 95-113.
——, 'Situlae and the Offering of Water in the Divine Funerary Cult: A new Approach to the Ritual of Djeme', in: *L'acqua nell'antico Egitto,* 257-272.
——, 'Das Motiv der Sonnenstrahlen auf der Brust des Toten. Zur Frage der Stundenwachen im Alten Reich', *SAK* 36 (2007), 15-22.
Borchardt, L., *Das Grabdenkmal des Königs Sa3ḥu-Reʿ*, 2 vols, Lepizig, 1910-1913.
Borghouts, J. F., *The Magical Texts of P. Leiden I 348*, Leiden, 1971.
——, *Ancient Egyptian Magical Texts*, Nisaba 9, Leiden, 1978.
——, 'An Early Book of the Gates: Coffin Text Spell 336', in: *Essays van Voss*, 12-21.
——, 'Book of the Dead Chapter 39: Some Preliminary Remarks', in: *Totenbuch-Forschungen*, 11-22.
——, *Book of the Dead [39]: from Shouting to Structure*, SAT 10, Wiesbaden, 2007.
Bowie, F., *The Anthropology of Religion: An Introduction*, revised 2nd edition, Oxford, 2006.
Brunner, H., 'Vom Sinn der Unterweltsbücher', *SAK* 8 (1980), 79-85.

Buchberger, H., *Transformation und Transformat*, Sargtextstudien 1, ÄA 54, Wiesbaden, 1993.
De Buck, A., *The Ancient Egyptian Coffin Texts*, 7 vols, Chicago, (1935-1961).
Burkard, G., *Überlegungen zur Form der Ägyptischen Literatur. Die Geschichte des Schiffbrüchigen als Literarisches Kunstwerk*, ÄAT 22, Wiesbaden, 1993.
Cabrol, A., *Les voies proceesionnelles de Thèbes*, OLA 97, Leuven, 2001.
Carter, H., *The Tomb of Tutankhamun* III, London, 1933.
Clère, J. J., 'Un Passage de le stèle du général Antef (Glyptothèque Ny Carlsberg, Copenhague)', *BIFAO* 30 (1931), 425-447.
Coenen, M., and A. Kucharek, 'New Findings on the Lamentations of Isis and Nephthys', *GM* 193 (2003), 45-50.
Colin, M., 'Presenting Water to the Deities within the Barque Sanctuaries of Graeco-Roman Times', in: *L'acqua nell'antico Egitto,* 283-291.
Cruz-Uribe, E., *Hibis Temple Project* I, San Antonio, 1988.
——, 'Opening of the Mouth as Temple Ritual', in: *Studies Wente*, 69-73.
Daressy, E., 'Inscriptions de la Chapelle d'Ameniritis à Médient-Habou', *Rec Trav* 23 (1901), 4-18.
Darnell, J. C., *The Enigmatic Netherworld Books of the Solar Osirian Unity. Cryptographic Compositions in the Tombs of Tutankhamun, Ramesses VI, and Ramesses IX*, OBO 198, Freiburg, 2004.
Davis, W. M., 'The Ascension Myth in the Pyramid Texts', *JNES* 36 (1977), 161-79.
——, *The Canonical Tradition in Ancient Egyptian Art*, London, 1989.
Davies, N. de Garis, *The Tomb of Rekh-mi-rē at Thebes*, 2 vols, PMMA 11, New York, 1943.
——, *The Temple of Hibis in el-Khargheh Oasis,* Part III: *The Decoration*, PMMA 17, New York, 1953.
Deflem, M., 'Ritual, Anti-Structure, and Religion: A Discussion of Victor Turner's Processual Symbolic Analysis', *Journal for the Scientific Study of Religion* 30 (1991), 1-25.
De Jong, A., 'Coffin Text Spell 38: The Case of the Father and the Son', *SAK* 21 (1994), 141-159.
Delia, D., 'The Refreshing Water of Osiris', *JARCE* 29 (1992), 181-190.
Depuydt, L., 'Der Fall des Hintersichschauers', *GM* 126 (1992), 33-38.
Derchain, P., 'L'intrusion inattendue de l'Histoire dans les inscriptions d'Edfou', *GM* 220 (2009), 29-32.
Dominicus, B., *Gesten und Gebärden in Darstellungen des Alten und Mittleren Reiches,* SAGA 10, Heidelberg, 1994.
Duell, P. et al., *The Mastaba of Mereruka*, 2 vols, Chicago, 1938.
DuQuesne, T., 'La déification des parties du corps: correspondances magiques et identification avec les dieux dans l'Égypte ancienne', in: Koenig, Y. (ed.), *La magie en Egypte: à la recherche d'une définition: actes du colloque organisé par le musée du Louvre les 29 et 30 septembre 2000*, Paris, 2002, 240-272.
——, 'The Osiris-Re Conjunction with Particular Reference to the Book of the Dead', in: *Totenbuch-Forschungen*, 23-33.
Edwards, I. E. S., *Hieroglyphic Texts from Egyptian Stelae, etc., in the British Museum*, vol. VIII, London, 1983.
Egberts, A., 'Action, Speech, and Interpretation: Some Reflections on the Classification of Ancient Egyptian Liturgical Texts', in: Eyre (ed.), *Proceedings of the Seventh International Congress of Egyptologists*, 357-363.
El-Weshahy, M., 'Studying the Representations of the <<Flame Lake>> in the Egyptian Underworld', in: J.-C. Goyon and C. Cardin, *Proceedings of the Ninth International Congress of Egyptologists*, 2 vols, OLA 150, Leuven and Paris, 2007, vol. I, 641-652.
Englund, G., 'The Border and the Yonder Side', in: *Studies Wente*, 101-9.
Eschweiler, P., *Bildzauber im alten Ägypten: Die Verwendung von Bildern und Gegenständen im magischen Handlungen nach Texten des Mittleren und Neuen Reiches*, OBO 137, Switzerland, 1994.
Eyre, C. J., 'The Water Regime for Orchards and Plantations in Pharaonic Egypt', *JEA* 80 (1994), 57-80.
—— (ed.), *Proceedings of the Seventh International Congress of Egyptologists*, OLA 82, Leuven, 1998.
——, *The Cannibal Hymn: A Cultural and Literary Study*, Liverpool, 2002.
Faulkner, R.O., The *Papyrus Bremner-Rhind*, BAe 3, Brussels, 1933.
——, 'The Lamentations of Isis and Nephthys', in: *Mélanges Maspero* I, MIFAO 66, Cairo, 1935-1938, 337-348.
——, 'The Papyrus Bremner-Rhind-I', *JEA* 22 (1936), 121-40.
——, 'The Papyrus Bremner-Rhind-II', *JEA* 23 (1937), 10-16.
——, 'The Papyrus Bremner-Rhind-III', *JEA* 23 (1937), 166-85.
——, 'The Papyrus Bremner-Rhind-IV', *JEA* 24 (1938), 41-53.
——, 'Spells 38-40 of the Coffin Texts', *JEA* 48 (1962), 36-44.
——, *The Ancient Egyptian Pyramid Texts. Translated into English*, Oxford, 1969.
——, *The Ancient Egyptian Pyramid Texts. Supplement of Hieroglyphic Texts,* Oxford, 1969.
——, *The Ancient Egyptian Coffin Texts*, 3 vols, Warminster, 1973-78.
——, *The Ancient Egyptian Book of the Dead*, London, 1985.
Federn, W., 'The "Transformation" in the Coffin Texts: A New Approach', *JNES* 19 (1960), 241-57.
Fischer, H., *The Orientation of Hieroglyphs*, New York, 1977.
Frandsen, P. J., 'On the Avoidance of Certain Forms of Loud Voices and Access to the Sacred', in: *Studies Quaegebeur* II, 975-1000.
——, 'On the Origin of the Notion of Evil in Ancient Egypt', *GM* 179 (2000), 9-34.

Franke, D., 'Arme und Geringe im Alten Reich Altägyptens: „Ich gab Speise dem Hungernden, Kleider dem Nackten…"', *ZÄS* 133 (2006), 104-120.
Gardiner, A. H., *Hieratic Papyri in the British Museum, Third Series, Chester Beatty Gift*, 2 vols, London, 1935.
Gardiner Sir Alan, *Egyptian Grammar, being an Introduction to the Study of Hieroglyphs*, 3rd edition, Oxford, 1957.
Gasse, A., *Les stèles d'Horus sur les crocodiles*, Paris, 2004.
Gauthier, H., *Le Temple d'Amada*, vol. I, Les Temples Immergés de la Nubie, Cairo, 1913.
Gee, J., 'The Use of Daily Temple Liturgy in the Book of the Dead', in: *Totenbuch-Forschungen*, 73-86.
Gestermann, L., *Die Überlieferung ausgewählter Texte altägyptischer („Sargtexte") in spätzeitlichen Grabanlagen*, 2 vols, ÄA 65, Wiesbaden, 2005.
Geßler-Löhr, B., *Die heiligen Seen ägyptischer Tempel: Ein Beitrag zur Deutung sakraler Baukunst im alten Ägypten*, HÄB 21, Hildesheim, 1983.
——, 'Die Totenfeier im Garten', in: Assmann et al., *Das Grab des Amenemope TT41*, 162-183.
Gillam, R., *Performance and Drama in Ancient Egypt*, London, 2005.
Goebs, K., 'Zerstörung als Erneuerung in der Totenliteratur: Eine kosmische Interpretation des Kannibalenspruchs', *GM* 194 (2003), 29-49.
——, *Crowns in Egyptian Funerary Literature: Royalty, Rebirth, and Destruction*, Oxford, 2008.
Goedicke, H., *Königliche Dockumente aus dem Alten Reich*, Wiesbaden, 1967.
Goyon, J.-C., *Rituels funéraires de l'ancienne Egypte*, Paris, 1972.
——, 'Momification et Recomposition du Corps Divin: Anubis et les canopes', in *Essays van Voss*, 34-44.
——, *Le Papyrus d'Imouthès Fils de Psintaês: Au Metropolitan Museum of Art de New-York (Papyrus MMA 35.9.21)*, New York, 1999.
Grapow, H., 'Zweiwegebuch und Totenbuch', *ZÄS* 46 (1909), 77-81.
Griffiths, J. G., *Plutarch's De Iside et Osiride*, Cardiff, 1970.
——, *The Origin of Osiris and his Cult*, Studies in the History of Religions (Supplement to Numen) XL, Leiden, 1980.
——, 'The Phrase *ḥr mw.f* in the Memphite Theology', *ZÄS* 123 (1996), 111-115.
Grieshammer, R., *Das Jenseitsgericht in den Sargtexten*, ÄA 20, Wiesbaden, 1970.
Grimm, A., 'Der Tod im Wasser: Rituelle Feindvernichtung und Hinrichtung durch Ertränken', *SAK* 16 (1989), 111-119.
Gülden, S. A. and I. Munro, *Bibliographie zum Altägyptischen Totenbuch*, SAT 1, Wiesbaden, 1998.
Hägg, H. F., *Clement of Alexandria and the Beginnings of Christian Apophaticism*, Oxford, 2006.
Haikal, F., *Two Hieratic Funerary Papyri of Nesmin*, 2 vols, BAe XIV-XV, Brussels, 1970-1972.
Harpur, Y. and P. Scremin, *The Chapel of Ptahhotep: Scenes Details*, Egypt in Miniature 2, Oxford, 2008.
Hassan, S., edited by Z. Alexander, *Excavations at Saqqara 1937-1938*. Volume I. *The Mastaba of Neb-Kaw-Her*. Volume II. *The Mastabas of Ny-ʿankh-Pepy and Others*. Volume III. *The Mastabas of Princess Hemet-Ra and Others*, Cairo, 1957.
Hays, H. M., 'The Worshipper and the Worshipped in the Pyramid Texts', *SAK* 30 (2002), 153-167.
Hawass, Z., 'An Inscribed Lintel in the Tomb of the Vizier Mehu at Saqqara', *Ling Aeg* 10 (2002), 219-224.
Hermsen, E., 'Die Bedeutung des Flammensees im Zweiwegebuch', in: *Studies Stricker*, 73-86.
——, *Die Zwei Wege des Jenseits: das altägyptische Zweiwegebuch und seine Topographie*, OBO 126, Freiburg and Göttingen, 1991.
Hellinckx, B. R., 'The Symbolic Assimilation of Head and Sun as expressed by Headrests', *SAK* 29 (2001), 61-95.
Hoffmann, N., 'Reading the Amduat', *ZÄS* 123 (1996), 26-40.
Hoffmeier, J. K., 'Are There Regionally-Based Theological Differences in the Coffin Texts?', in: Willems (ed.), *The World of the Coffin Texts*, 45-54.
Hölzl, R., *Ägyptische Opfertafeln und Klutbecken. Eine Form-und Funktionsanalyse für das Alte, Mittlere und Neue Reich*, HÄB 45, Hildesheim, 2002.
——, 'Libation Basins from the Old to the New Kingdom: Practical Use and Religious Significance', in: *L'acqua nell'antico Egitto*, 309-317.
Hornung, E., *Altägyptische Höllenvorstellungen*, ASAW 59/3, Berlin, 1968.
——, *Ägyptische Unterweltsbücher*, Zurich and Munich, 1972.
——, 'Flammensee', *LÄ* II, 1975, 259-260.
——, *Das Totenbuch der Ägypter*, Zurich and Munich, 1979.
——, *Das Buch von den Pforten des Jenseits*, 2 vols, Aegyptiaca Helvetica 7 and 8, Basel and Geneva, 1979/1980.
——, *Der Mythos von der Himmelskuh: Eine ätiologie des Unvollkommen*, OBO 46, Freiburg and Göttingen, 1982.
——, *Conceptions of God in ancient Egypt: The One and the Many*, translated from German by J. Baines, London, 1982.
——, *Texte zum Amduat*, 3 vols, Aegyptiaca Helvetica 3, 14, and 15, Geneva, 1987-1992 and 1994.
——, *The Ancient Egyptian Books of the Afterlife*, translated from German by D. Lorton, Ithaca, 1999.
Hornung, E., and T. Abt (eds), *The Ancient Egyptian Amduat: The Book of the Hidden Chamber*, Zurich, 2007.
Hugonot, C. J., *Le jardin dans l'Égypte ancienne*, Frankfurt am Main, 1989.
Isler, M., 'An Ancient Method of Finding and Extending Direction', *JARCE* 26 (1989), 191-206.
Jansen-Winkeln, K., 'Horizont und Verklärtheit: Zur Bedeutung der Wurzel *ꜣḫ*', *SAK* 23 (1996), 201-215.
——, *Inschriften der Spätzeit*, Teil II: *Die 22.-24. Dynastie*, Wiesbaden, 2007.
Jequier, G., *Les frises d'objets des sarcophages du Moyen Empire*, Cairo, 1921.

Junker, H., *Die Stundenwachen in den Osirismysterien nach den Inschriften von Dendera, Edfu, und Philae*, DAWW 54, Vienna, 1910.
Jürgens, P.,'Textkritische und überlieferungsgeschichtliche Untersuchungen zu den Sargtexten', *GM* 105 (1988), 27-40.
——, *Grundlinien einer Überlieferungsgeschichte der altägyptischen Sargtexte. Stemmata und Archetypen der Spruchgruppen 30-32+33-37, 75-83, 162+164, 225+226 und 343+345*, GOF IV/31, Wiesbaden, 1995.
——, 'Anmerkungen zu Sargtextspruch 335 und seiner Tradierung', *GM* 172 (1999), 29-46.
——, 'Zum überlieferungsgeschichtlichen Zusammenhang der Sargtextsprüche 335 und 397', *SAK* 29 (2001), 111-38.
Kadish, G. E., 'Seasonality and the Name of the Nile', *JARCE* 25 (1988), 185-194.
Kamrin, J., *The Cosmos of Khnumhotep II at Beni Hasan*, London, 1999.
Kanawati, N. and M. Abdel-Raziq, *The Teti Cemetry at Saqqara* III. *The Tombs of Neferseshemere and Seankhuiptah*, ACE Reports 11, Warminster, 1998.
Kees, H., 'Die Feuerinsel in den Sargtexten und im Totenbuch', *ZÄS* 78 (1942), 41-53.
——, *Totenglauben und Jenseitsvorstellungen der alten Ägypter*, Berlin, 1956.
Kessler, D., 'Zur Bedeutung der Szenen des täglichen Lebens in den Privatgräbern (I): Die Szenen vom Schiffsbaues und der Schiffahrt', *ZÄS* 114 (1987), 58-88.
Kettel, J., 'Canopes, *rḏw.w* d'Osiris et Osiris-Canope', in: *Hommages Leclant* III, 315-330.
Kloth, N., *Die (auto-)biographischen Inschriften des ägyptischen Alten Reiches: Untersuchungen zu Phraseologie und Entwicklung*, SAK Beihefte 8, Hamburg, 2002.
Klotz, D., *Adoration of the Ram: Five Hymns to Amun-Re from Hibis Temple*, YES 6, New Haven, 2006.
Klug, A., *Königliche Stelen in der Zeit von Ahmose bis Amenophis III*, Monumenta Aegyptiaca VIII, Brussels, 2002.
Konrad, K., 'Bes zwischen Himmel und Erde: Zur Deutung eines Kopfstützen-Amuletts', *ZÄS* 134 (2007), 134-137.
Krauss, R., *Astronomische Konzepte und Jenseitsvorstellungen in den Pyramidentexten*, ÄA 59, Wiesbaden, 1997.
Lapp, G., *Die Opferformel des Alten Reiches*, DAIK Sonderschrift 21, Mainz am Rhein, 1986.
——, 'Die Papyrusvorlagen der Sargtexte', *SAK* 16 (1989), 171-202.
——, *Typologie der Särge und Sargkammern von der 6. bis 13 Dynastie*, SAGA 7, Heidelberg, 1993.
——, *The Papyrus of Nu*, Catalogue of the Books of the Dead in the British Museum I, London, 1997.
——, *Totenbuch Spruch 17*, TbT 1, Basel, 2006.
Leahy, A., 'Death by Fire in Ancient Egypt', *JESHO* 27 (1984), 199-206.
Leclant, J., 'Les textes des pyramides', in *Textes et Langages de l'Égypte pharaonique,* 3 vols, BdÉ 64, Cairo, 1972, II, 37-52.
Leclant, J. (ed.), *Les Textes de Pyramide de Pepy I*[er], 2 vols, MIFAO 118/1-2, Cairo, 2001.
Lefebvre, G., *Le Tombeau de Pétosiris*, 3 vols, Cairo, 1923-4.
Leitz, C., 'Die obere und untere Dat', *ZÄS* 116 (1989), 41-57.
——, 'Die Schlangensprüche in den Pyramidentexten', *Orientalia* 65 (1996), 381-427.
——(ed.), *Lexikon der ägyptischen Götter und Götterbezeichnungen*, 8 vols, OLA 110-116 and 129, Leuven, 2002-2003.
——, *Magical and Medical Papyri of the New Kingdom*, Hieratic Papyri in the British Museum 7, London, 1999.
Lepsius, C. R., *Denkmäler aus Ägypten und Äthiopien*. Abtheilung 1-6 in 12 Bands, Berlin, 1849-1859.
Lesko, L. H., 'Some Observations on the Composition of the Book of the Two Ways', *JAOS* 91 (1971), 30-41.
——, *The Ancient Egyptian Book of the Two Ways*, Berkeley, 1972.
——, *Index of the Spells on Egyptian Middle Kingdom Coffins and Related Documents*, Berkeley, 1979.
Lichtheim, M., *Ancient Egyptian Literature*, 3 vols, Berkeley and Los Angeles, 1973-1980.
Loprieno, A. (ed.), *Ancient Egyptian Literature: History and Forms*, PdÄ 10, Leiden, 1996.
Lorton, D., 'The Invocation Hymn at the Temple of Hibis', *SAK* 21(1994), 159-219.
Lucarelli, R., 'Demons in the Book of the Dead', in: *Totenbuch-Forschungen*, 203-12.
——, *The Book of the Dead of Gatseshen: Ancient Egyptian Funerary Religion in the 10*[th] *Century BC*, EU XXI, Leiden, 2006.
Lüscher, B., *Untersuchungen zu Totenbuch Spruch 151*, SAT 2, Wiesbaden, 1998.
——, *Die Verwandlungssprüche (Tb 76-88)*, TbT 2, Basel, 2006.
Magdolen, D., 'On the Orientation of Old Kingdom Royal Tombs', in: M. Bárta and J. Krejčí (eds), *Abusir and Saqqara in the Year 2000*, Archiv Orientální Supplementa 9, Prague, 2000, 491-498.
Malek, J., *The Cat in Ancient Egypt*, London, 1993.
Mariette, A., *Dendérah: description générale du grand temple de cette ville*, Cairo, 1875.
——, *Mastaba de l'Ancien Empire*, Paris, 1889; reprint, Hildesheim, Zurich, New York, 2006.
Menu, B., 'Le tombeau de Pétosiris (1). Nouvel examen', *BIFAO* 94 (1994), 311-327.
——, 'Le tombeau de Pétosiris (2). Maât, Thoth et le droit', *BIFAO* 95 (1995), 281-295.
——, *Recherches sur l'historie juridique, économique et sociale de l'ancienne Égypte* II, BdÉ 122, Cairo, 1998.
Mohr, T. H., *The Mastaba of Hetep-Her-Akhti: Study on an Egyptian Tomb Chapel in the Museum of Antiquities Leiden,* Mededeelingen en Verhandelingen 5, Leiden, 1943.
Morenz, L. D., 'Apophis: On the Origin, Name, and Nature of an Ancient Egyptian Anti-god', *JNES* 63 (2004), 201-205.
Morgan, J. de, *Fouilles à Dahchour en 1894-1895*, Vienna, 1903.

Mostafa, M.M.F, *Untersuchungen zu Opfertafeln im Alten Reich*, HÄB 17, Hildesheim, 1982.
Moussa, A. M. and H. Altenmüller, *Das Grab des Nianchchnum und Chnumhotep*, AV 21, Mainz am Rhein, 1977.
Müller, D., 'Rezension zu CT VII', *BiOr* 20 (1963), 246-250.
Murray, M. A., Saqqara Mastabas, vol.1, London, 1905.
Moussa, A. M. and H. Altenmüller, *Das Grab des Nianchchnum und Chnumhotep*, AV 21, Mainz am Rhein, 1977.
Münster, M., *Untersuchungen zur Göttin Isis*, MÄS 11, Berlin, 1968.
Naville, E., *Das Aegyptische Todtenbuch der XVIII. bis XX. Dynastie aus verschiedenen Urkunden*, Berlin, 1886.
Nelson, H., 'Certain Reliefs at Karnak and Medinet Habu and the Ritual of Amenophis I', *JNES* 8 (1949), 201-232, 310-345.
Newberry, P. E., *Beni Hasan* I, ASE Memoir I, London, 1893.
Niwinski, A., 'The 21st Dynasty Religious Iconography Project Exemplified by the Scene with Three Deities Standing on a Serpent', in: Schoske, S., H. Altenmüller, D. Wildung (eds), *Linguistik, Philologie, Religion. Akten des Vierten Internationalen Ägyptologen-Kongresses München 1985*, SAK Beihefte 1-4, Hamburg, 1988-1991, III, 305-314.
——, 'The Book of the Dead on the Coffins of the 21st Dynasty', in: *Totenbuch-Forschungen*, 245-264.
——, 'Iconography of the 21st Dynasty: Its Main Features, Levels of Attestation, the Media and their Diffusion', in: Uehlinger, C. (ed.), *Images as Media: Sources for the Cultural History of the Near East and the Eastern Mediterranean (1st millennium BCE)*, OBO 175, Freiburg, 2000, 21-43.
——, *21st Dynasty Coffins from Thebes, Chronological and Typological Studies*, Theben 5, Mainz am Rhein, 1988.
——, *Catalogue General of Egyptian Antiquities of the Cairo Museum Numbers 6069-6082, The Second Find of Deir El-Bahri (Coffins)*, 2nd vol.1st Fascicle, Cairo, 1999.
O'Connor, D., 'The Interpretation of the Old Kingdom Pyramid Complex', in: *Fs Stadelmann*, 135-144.
Ogdon, J., 'A New Dramatic Argument in the Coffin Texts (Spells 30-37)', in: *L'Egyptologie en 1979: axes prioritaires de recherché*, 2 vols, Colloques Internationaux du Centre National de la Recherche Scientifique 595, Paris, 1982, II, 37-43.
Oldfather, C. H., *Diodorus of Sicily* I, London and Cambridge MA, 1946.
Op de Beeck, L., 'Relating Middle Kingdom Pottery Vessels to Funerary Rituals', *ZÄS* 134 (2007), 157-165.
Otto, E, *Das ägyptische Mundöffungsritual*, AÄ 3, Wiesbaden, 1960.
Pamminger, P., 'Das Trinken von Überschwemmungs-wasser: Eine Form der jährlichen Regeneration des Verstorbenen', *GM* 122 (1991), 71-75.
Parkinson, R. B., *Voices from Ancient Egypt: An Anthology of Middle Kingdom Writings*, London, 1991.
——, *Poetry and Culture in Middle Kingdom Egypt: A Dark Side to Perfection*, London and New York, 2002.
Pasquali, S., 'Les fouilles de S. Hassan à Gîza en 1938 et le temple d'Osiris de Ro-Sétaou au Nouvel Empire', *GM* 216 (2008), 75-78.
Perraud, M., 'Untersuchungen zu Totenbuch Spruch 166: Vorbemerkungen', in: *Totenbuch-Forschungen*, 283-293.
Piankoff, A., 'Le livre de Quererets', *BIFAO* 41 (1942), 1-11; 42 (1944), 1-62, 43 (1945), 1-50; 45 (1947), 1-42.
——, *The Tomb of Ramesses VI*, 2 vols, Egyptian Religious Texts and Representations 1, New York, 1954.
——, *Mythological Papyri*, 2 vols, Egyptian Religious Texts and Representations 3, New York, 1957.
——, *Pyramid of Unas*, Egyptian Religious Texts and Representations 5, Princeton, 1968.
Pinch, G., 'Red Things: the Symbolism of Colour in Magic', in: Davies, W. V. (ed.), *Colour and Painting in Ancient Egypt*, London, 2001, 182-185.
Quack, J., 'Zur Lesung und Deutung des Dramatischen Ramesseumspapyrus', *ZÄS* 133 (2006), 72-89.
——, 'Apopis, Nabelschnur des Re', *SAK* 34 (2006), 377-379.
Quirke, S., 'Measuring the Underworld', in: *Mysterious Lands*, 161-181.
Raven, M., J., 'Egyptian Concepts of the Orientation of the Human Body', *JEA* 91 (2005), 37-53.
Reeves, N., *The Complete Tutankhamun: the King, the Tomb, the Royal Treasure*, London, 1990.
Ritner, R. K., 'Horus on the Crocodiles: A Juncture of Religion and Magic in Late Dynastic Egypt, in: Allen et al., *Religion and Philosophy in Ancient Egypt*, 103-16.
——, 'O. Gardiner 363. A Spell against Night Terrors', *JARCE* 27 (1990), 25-41.
——, *The Mechanics of Ancient Egyptian Magical Practice*, SAOC 54, Chicago, 1993.
——, ' "And Each Staff Transformed into a Snake": The Serpent Wand in Ancient Egypt', in: Szpakowska (ed.), *Through a Glass Darkly*, 205-226.
Robinson, P., 'Crossing the Night: the Depiction of Mythological Landscapes in the Amduat of the New Kingdom Royal Necropolis', in Ives, R., D. Lines, C. Naunton, and N. Wahlberg (eds), *Current Research in Egyptology* III, BAR 1192, 2003, 51-61.
——, 'As for them who know them, they shall find their paths: Speculations on the Ritual Landscapes in the Book of the Two Ways', in: *Mysterious Lands*, 139-159.
Roeder, G., 'Zwei Hieroglyphische Inschriften aus Hermopolis (Ober-Ägypten)', *ASAE* 52 (1952), 315-442.
——, *Hermopolis 1929-1939: Ausgrabungen der Deutschen Hermopolis Expedition in Hermopolis, Ober-Ägypten*, Hildesheim, 1959.
Roeder, H., 'Themen und Motive in den Pyramidentexten', *Ling Aeg* 3 (1993), 81-119.
——, *Mit dem Auge sehen: Studien zur Semantik der Herrschaft in den Toten- und Kulttexten*, SAGA 16, Heidelberg, 1996.

——, 'Das >> Erzählen der Ba-u<< Der *Ba-u*-Diskurs und das altägyptische Erzählen zwischen Ritual und Literatur im Mittleren Reich', in: B. Dücker and H. Roeder (eds), *Text und Ritual: Kulturwissenschaftliche Essays und Analysen von Sesostris bis Dada*, Hermeia 8, Heidelberg, 2005, 187-242.

Rößler-Köhler, U., 'Sargtextspruch 335 und seine Tradierung', *GM* 163 (1998), 71-94.

——, 'Königliche Vorstellungen zu Grab und Jenseits im Mittleren Reich, Teil I: Ein 'Gottesbegräbnis' des Mittleren Reiches in königlichem Kontext: Amduat, 4. und 5. Stunde', in Gundlach, R. and W. Seipel (eds), *Das frühe ägyptische Königtum. Akten des 2. Symposiums zur ägyptischen Königsideologie in Wien 24.-26. 9. 1997*, ÄAT 36/2, Wiesbaden, 1999, 73-96.

——, 'Das eigentliche Zweiwegebuch', *GM* 192 (2003), 83-98.

Roth, A. M., 'The *psš-kf* and the 'Opening of the Mouth' Ceremony: A Ritual of Birth and Rebirth', *JEA* 78 (1992), 113-147.

——, 'Fingers, Stars, and the 'Opening of the Mouth': The Nature and Function of the *nṯrwj*-Blades', *JEA* 79 (1993), 57-79.

Rotsch, H., 'The Primeval Ocean Nun and the Terminology of Water in Ancient Egypt', in: *L'acqua nell'antico Egitto,* 229-240.

Roulin, G., 'The Book of the Night: A Royal Composition Documenting the Conceptions of the Hereafter at the Beginning of the Nineteenth Dynasty', in: Eyre (ed.), *Proceedings of the Seventh International Congress of Egyptologists*, 1005-1013.

——, *Le livre de la Nuit: une composition égyptienne de l'au-delà*, 2 vols, OBO 147, Friburg and Göttingen, 1996.

Rusch, A., 'Doppelversionen in der Überlieferung des Osirismythus in den Pyramidentexten', *ZÄS* 67 (1930), 88-92.

Saleh, M., *Das Totenbuch in den thebanischen Beamtengräbern des Neuen Reiches: Texte und Vignetten*, AV 46, Mainz am Rhein, 1984.

Sauneron, S., *Le Rituel de l'Embaumement. Pap. Boulaq III. Pap. Louvre 5.158*, Cairo, 1952.

Schack-Schakenberg, H., *Das Buch von den Zwei Wegen des seligen Toten*, Leipzig, 1903.

Schott, S., 'Das Löschen von Fackeln in Milch', *ZÄS* 73 (1937), 1-25.

——, *Die Reinigung Pharaos in einem memphitischen Tempel*, NAWG 3, Göttingen, 1957.

Seeber, C., *Untersuchungen zur Darstellung des Totengerichts im Alten Ägypten*, MÄS 35, Munich, 1976.

Schenkel, W., 'Redaktion und Überlieferungsgeschichte des Spruchs 335a der Sargtexte', in *Göttinger Totenbuchstudien*, 37-79.

——, *Die Bewässerungsrevolution im alten Ägypten*, Mainz am Rhein, 1978.

Shalomi-Hen, R., *Classifying the Divine: Determinatives and Categorisations in CT 335 and BD 17*, GOF IV/38, Wiesbaden, 2000.

Sethe, K., *Die altägyptischen Pyramidentexte*, 3 vols, Lepizig, 1908-22.

——, *Übersetzung und Kommentar zu den altägyptischen Pyramidentexe*, 6 vols, Glückstadt, n.d.

Settgast, J., *Untersuchungen zu altägyptischen Bestattungdarstellungen*, ADAIK 3, Glückstadt, 1963.

Silverman, D., 'Textual Criticism in the Coffin Texts', in: Allen et al., *Religion and Philosophy in Ancient Egypt*, 29-53.

——, 'Coffin Texts from Bersheh, Kom el Hisn, and Mendes', in: Willems (ed.), *The World of the Coffin* Texts, 129-53.

Smith, M., *The Liturgy of Opening the Mouth for Breathing*, Oxford, 1993.

——, *On the Primeval Ocean*, The Carlsberg Papyri 5, CNI 26, Copenhagen, 2002.

——, *Papyrus Harkness (MMA 31.9.7)*, Oxford, 2005.

——, 'Osiris NN or Osiris of NN', in: *Totenbuch-Forschungen*, 325-337.

——, 'The Great Decree Issued to the Nome of the Silent Land', *RdÉ* 57 (2006), 217-232.

——, *Traversing Eternity: Texts for the Afterlife from Ptolemaic and Roman Egypt*, Oxford, 2009.

Sourdive, C., *La main dans l'Égypte pharaonique: Recherches de morphologie structurale sur les objets égyptiens comportant une main*, Bern, 1984.

Spalinger, A., 'Some Remarks on the Epagomenal Days in Ancient Egypt', *JNES* 54 (1995), 33-47.

Spiegelberg, W., 'Ein Bruchstück des Bestattungsrituals der Apisstiere: (Demot. Pap. Wien Nr. 27)', *ZÄS* 56 (1920), 1-33.

Spencer, P., *The Egyptian Temple: A Lexicographical Study*, London, 1984.

Spieser, C., 'L'eau et la régénération des morts d'après les représentations des tombes thébaines du Nouvel Empire', *CdÉ* 72 (1997), 211-228.

Stadelmann, R., 'Die sogenannten Luftkanäle der Cheopspyramide: Modellkorridore für den Aufstieg des Königs zum Himmel', *MDAIK* 50 (1994), 285-294.

Stadler, M. A., 'War eine Dramatische Aufführung eines Totengerichts Teil der ägyptischen Totenriten?', *SAK* 29 (2001), 331-348.

Steindorf, G., *Grabfunde des Mittleren Reiches in den Königlichen Museen zu Berlin,* MÄSB 8-9, Berlin, 1896-1901.

Stewart, H. M., 'Some Pre-Amarna Sun Hymns', *JEA* 46 (1960), 83-90.

Strudwick, N., *Texts from the Pyramid Age*, WAW 16, Atlanta, 2005.

Szpakowska, K., 'Playing with Fire: Initial Observations on the Religious Uses of Clay Cobras from Amarna', *JARCE* 40 (2003), 113-122.

——, *Behind Closed Eyes: Dreams and Nightmares in Ancient Egypt*, Swansea, 2003.

—— (ed.), *Through a Glass Darkly. Magic, Dreams and Prophecy in Ancient Egypt*, Swansea, 2006.

Turner, V. W., *The Forest of Symbols: Aspects of the Ndembu Ritual*, Ithaca, 1967.

——, *The Ritual Process: Structure and Anti-Structure*, Chicago, 1969.

——, *The Drums of Affliction: A Study of Religious Processes among the Ndembu of Zambia*, Oxford, 1986.

Vandier, J., *Papyrus Jumilhac,* Paris, n.d.
——, *Manuel d'archéologie égyptienne,* vol. III, Paris, 1958.
Van Gennep, A., *The Rites of Passage*, translated from French by M. B. Vizedom and G. L. Caffee, Chicago, 1975.
Van Walsem, R., *The Coffin of Djedmonthuiufankh in the National Museum of Antiquites at Leiden: Technical and Iconographical/Iconological Aspects*, 2 vols, EU 10, Leiden, 1997.
Verhoeven, U., *Grillen, Kochen, Backen im Alltag und im Ritual Altägyptens: Ein Lexikographischer Beitrag*, Rites Égyptiens IV, Brussels, 1984.
Vernus, P., 'La Notion de Mythe dans la Civilisation Pharaonique', *Cadernos de Filosofi* 10 (2001), 11-31.
Versiljević, V., 'Embracing his Double: Niankhkhnum and Khnumhotep', *SAK* 37 (2008), 363-372.
Vischak, D., 'Common Ground between Pyramid Texts and Old Kingdom Tomb Design: The Case of Ankhmahor', *JARCE* 40 (2003), 133-157.
Von Bissing, W., 'Stele des Nechtmin aus der El Amarnazeit', *ZÄS* 64, 112-117.
Von Der Way, T., 'Überlegungen zur Jenseitsvorstellung in der Amarnazeit', *ZÄS* 123 (1996), 157-64.
Von Falck, M., 'Text-und Bildprogramm ägyptischer Särge und Sarkophage der 18. Dynastie: Genese und Weiterleben', *SAK* 34 (2006), 125-140.
Von Lieven, A., 'Im Schatten des Goldhauses. Berufsgeheimnis und Handwerkerinitiation im Alten Ägypten', *SAK* 36 (2007), 147-155.
Vos, R. L., *The Apis Embalming Ritual. P. Vindob. 3873*, OLA 50, Leuven, 1993.
Voβ, S., 'Ein liturgisch-Kosmographischer Zyklus im Re-Bezirk des Totentempels Ramses' III. in Medinet Habu', *SAK* 23 (1996), 377-396.
Waitkus, W., 'Anmerkungen zu der Verteilung der Dämonennamen aus TB 144/147 im Zweiwegebuch', *GM* 62 (1983), 79-83.
Wells, R. A., 'The Mythology of Nut and the Birth of Re', *SAK* 19 (1992), 305-21.
Westendorf, D., 'Uräus und Sonnenscheibe', *SAK* 6 (1978), 201-227.
——, 'Die Nini-Begrüßung', in: *Fs Derchain*, 351-362.
Westendorf, W., 'Der Sonnenzyklus im Weltgebäude: Zusatzbemerkungen zu einer oranmentalen Inschrift Amenophis' II.', *GM* 219 (2008), 95-97.
Wilkinson, A., 'Landscapes for Funeral Rituals in Dynastic Times', in: *Fs Shore*, 391-401.
Wilkinson, R., *Reading Egyptian Art: A Hieroglyphic Guide to Ancient Egyptian Painting and Sculpture*, London, 1992.
——, *Symbol and Magic in Egyptian Art*, London, 1994.
——, 'Symbolic Orientation and Alignment in New Kingdom Royal Tombs', in: *Valley of the Sun Kings*, 74-80.
Willems, H., *Chests of Life*, Leiden, 1988.
——, 'Crime, Cult, and Capital Punishment (Moʿalla Inscription 8)', *JEA* 76 (1990), 27-54.
——, 'The Shu-Spells in Practice', in: Willems (ed.), *The World of the Coffin Texts*, 197-209.
——, *The Coffin of Heqata (Cairo JDE 36418): A Case Study of Egyptian Funerary Culture of Early Middle Kingdom,* OLA 70, Leuven, 1996.
—— (ed.), *The World of the Coffin Texts. Proceedings of the Symposium held on the Occasion of the 100th Birthday of Adriaan de Buck. Leiden, December 17-19, 1992*, EU 9, Leiden, 1996.
——, 'The Embalmer Embalmed. Remarks on the Meaning of the Decoration of Some Middle Kingdom Coffins, in: *Essays te Velde*, 343-372.
—— (ed.), *Social Aspects of Funerary Culture in the Egyptian Old and Middle Kingdoms. Proceedings of the International Symposium held at Leiden University 6-7 June 1996*, OLA 103, Leuven, 2001.
——, 'The Social and Ritual Context of a Mortuary Liturgy of the Middle Kingdom (CT Spells 30-41)', in: Willems (ed.), *Social Aspects*, 253-272.
——, 'Gärten in thebanischen Grabanlagen' in: *Fs Assmann*, 421-439.
Willems, H., Lies O. D. B, Troy L. S., Stefanie V., and René V. W., *Dayr al-Barsha:* vol. I, *The Rock Tombs of Djehutiankht (No. 17K74/1), Khnumnakht (No. 17K74/2), and Iha (No. 17K74/3) With an Essay on the History and Nature of Nomarchal Rule in the Early Middle Kingdom*, OLA 155, Leuven, 2007.
—— (ed.), *Les Textes des Sarcophages et la Démocratie: Éléments d'une Historie culturelle du Moyen Empire Égyptien*, Paris, 2008.
Wilson, J, A., 'Funeral Services of the Egyptian Old Kingdom', *JNES* 3 (1944), 201-218.
Winkler, A., 'The Efflux that Issued from Osiris: A Study on *rḏw* in the Pyramid Texts', *GM* 211 (2006), 125-39.
Žabkar, L.V., 'Six Hymns to Isis in the Sanctuary of her Temple at Philae and their Theological Significance. Part I', *JEA* 69 (1983), 115-37.
Zandee, J., 'Sargtexte, Spruch 75 (Coffin Texts I 314-348 a)', *ZÄS* 97 (1971), 155-62.
——, 'Sartexte, Spruch 75 (Coffin Texts I 348 b-372 c)', *ZÄS* 98 (1972), 149-55.
——, 'Sargtexte, Spruch 75. Schluβ: (Coffin Texts I 372d-405c)', *ZÄS* 99 (1973), 48-63.
——, *Death as an Enemy According to Ancient Egyptian Conceptions*, Leiden, 1960.
——, 'Sargtexte um über Wasser zu verfügen (Coffin Texts V 8-22; Sprüche 356-362)', *JEOL* 24 (1976), 1-47.
——, *Der Amunhymnus des Papyrus Leiden I 344, Verso*, 3 vols, Collections of the National Museum of Antiquities at Leiden, Leiden, 1992.
Zeidler, J., *Pfortenbuchstudien*, 2 vols, GOF IV/36, Wiesbaden, 1999.

www.ingramcontent.com/pod-product-compliance
Lightning Source LLC
Chambersburg PA
CBHW042059120726
47911CB00030B/755